# Cultures of the North Pacific Coast

Chandler Publications in

ANTHROPOLOGY AND SOCIOLOGY

Leonard Broom, *Editor*

PHILIP DRUCKER

# Cultures of the
# North Pacific Coast

With an Introduction by

HARRY B. HAWTHORN

UNIVERSITY OF BRITISH COLUMBIA

**CHANDLER PUBLISHING COMPANY**
An Intext Publisher  •  Scranton, Pennsylvania 18515

# ILLUSTRATION CREDITS

*Color photographs* 1–4, 11, 15, 20, 33, 34 courtesy of Royal Ontario Museum.

*Color photographs* 5–10, 12–14, 16–19, 21–32, 35–39 courtesy Robert H. Lowie Museum of Anthropology, University of California, Berkeley. The photographs were taken by Eugene Prince.

The illustrations that appear on the following pages are the work of Zenon Pohorecky: 12, 14, 16, 18, 26, 28, 32, 33, 40, 44, 78, 133.

The illustrations that appear on pages 126 and 198 are from *The Story of Metlakahtla* by Sir Henry S. Wellcome. London & New York: Saxon & Co., 1887.

The illustrations that appear on pages 39, 146, and 147 are the work of John Webber. Courtesy of Peabody Museum, Harvard University.

The illustrations that appear on pages 130 and 206 are from the personal collection of Professor Robert F. Heizer, Department of Anthropology, University of California, Berkeley.

The maps that appear on pages 2 and 104 are the work of Elinor Rhodes.

# Contents

**Chapter 4. RELIGION AND RITUAL (continued)**

**Chapter 5. POPULATION AND CULTURE SUBDIVISIONS .** . 103

**Chapter 6. THE OPULENT TSIMSHIAN** . . . . . 114

**Chapter 7. THE NOOTKAN WHALERS** . . . . . 132

# Illustrations

**PHOTOGRAPHS IN FULL COLOR** (following page 108)

Bella Coola mask
Kwakiutl mask (Alert Bay)
Kwakiutl mask (Quatsino Inlet)
Bella Bella mask
Skokomish basket
Quinault basket
Haida basket
Haida rainhat
Chief's hat
Hat (*probably* Nootka)
Tlingit figure
Yurok carved paddles
Totem pole
Kwakiutl house post
Gitksan medicine man's kit
Shaman's box (*probably* Tlingit)
Kwakiutl feast bowl, 5-foot "wingspan"
Kwakiutl feast bowl, 77-inch "wingspan"
Bella Bella frog bag
Kwakiutl shaman's wand
Dentalium money string
Yurok spoon
Yurok carved mauls
Hupa elkhorn purse
Scalp mosaic headdress
Haida box
Wooden carved bowl

**MAPS**

# Introduction

CERTAIN REGIONS OF THE tribal world have become important to scholars in almost the same sense as certain periods in the history of nations or certain phases of the work of great laboratories. The Northwest Coast is one of these regions, and the anthropologists who reported on the life of the peoples in this region and those who reflected on the anthropologists' reports have made major gains for the social sciences.

The leading figure among the first scholars to study the culture of the Northwest Coast was Franz Boas, whose own observations were followed by the pioneering large-scale research of the Jesup North Pacific Expedition. Boas's greatest legacies to science grew from the special nature of his observations of the coast peoples whose arts and social life flowered in their rich habitat. The rich complexity of these tribal societies as well as his own scholarly acumen led him to stress the importance of firsthand description and to insist on the need for detail in anthropological evidence. His perception that culture was a unity, that everything mattered in the patterning of the whole, followed from his herculean attempts to make order out of the bewildering variety of impressions that assailed him. Boas saw the many techniques of fishing and hunting, the making and storing of goods, the gatherings of people at which the goods were distributed, and heard songs and speeches in ceremonies that succeeded one another throughout the winter and mixed the sacred and profane in the context of startling dramas of the supernatural and spectacular contests for everyday social position. He searched for reasons and antecedents and his efforts laid a foundation for much of the later development of theory in anthropology. But it must be admitted that his first great work, *The Social Organization and the Secret Societies of the Kwakiutl Indians,* was one of the less readable works in anthropology.

The long roster of names of subsequent workers on Northwest Coast materials includes Edward Sapir and Ruth Benedict; the theoretical contributions and topics range through many considerations of method, the function and interpretation of mythology, the growth of language, ethical relativity, culture and personality, primitive economics, evolution, and the programming of social change. Even though not many of the results of the work of the earlier scholars are now accepted in full, in their time they played important parts in the continuing dialogue of science.

In this book Philip Drucker is not directly concerned with the history of anthropology but with presenting anew the rich variety of networks, structures and roles, arts and techniques that inspired these theories and interpretations. He is unusually well equipped to do this and his own concern with the Northwest now extends over thirty years. As a student, he spent parts of several years in the region, making a penetrating study of the Northern and Central Nootkan tribes, systematically compiling culture-element lists as the basis for studies of distribution and development of cultural institutions, and preparing the ground for his later works: a survey of archeological sites over a large part of the coastline, a study of the Native Brotherhood, the contemporary organization founded by the Indians and related to their commercial fishing interests, and an excellent summary of the cultures of the region, a forerunner of the present book.

Except for the last chapter Drucker is writing of the past, of a period before the major changes that followed the goods of trade, the materials and ideas, the jobs, the schools, the officials and the regula-

tions that came with Canadian and American settlement and nation-
hood. Accordingly some of the culture that is described has not been
witnessed by anthropologists, but has been told to them by Indians
who recalled it. Nevertheless, most of the life of the Indians set out
here has been seen by outside observers over the past two hundred
years, and the operations of kinship and social class, the winter dances,
and the potlatch continue at a variable level of intensity and completeness even today.

Prior to Drucker's earlier summary, a barrier to the use of the
materials by anyone not a specialist in the region had been the lack of
a comprehensive study. Such a treatment of the over-all norms and
the range of behavior, ideas, and institutions was needed before the
significance of the many variant cultural forms, creative and adaptive,
could be realized. For instance, how ought one to view the gross
similarities in many of the institutions of the tribes of the region from
Alaska to northern California? What interaction with different tech-
nologies and with the potentials of an unusual habitat maintained these
institutions? Again, the elaborate texture of life showed many variations in detail, even in closely adjacent localities; what patterns of invention, adjustment, and integration account for this? The answers
that are now forthcoming to some of these queries are supplying elements of a theory of social change, which is one of the most important
goals of contemporary anthropology and sociology, but many other
questions posed by these cultures still remain unanswered and require,
first of all, the best possible treatment of the complicated area considered as a unit.

This treatment is what Drucker has attempted and with remarkable
success. It could only be essayed by someone who knew the full range
of ethnographic fact and the scholarly uses made of it. In this work
he describes a culture area, its boundaries and salient features. This
culture area is not a local group or community and it should be remembered that the people who lived in its constituent groups had no name
for the whole region; until the extension of Canadian and American
sovereignty few traveled far from home, and they had no reason for
conceiving of ethnographic unities embracing more than one or two
adjacent groups of their communities. Thus the culture area is something artificially created by the anthropologist.

This artificial creation has a proper use and this book demonstrates it.

There are obvious virtues in treating the facts in this way; in many respects the culture area is a better representation than can be achieved by describing the partly divergent, partly similar small communities that were recognized as separate and so named by the people in them. The wider view perceives that the peoples of the area in spite of different languages possessed some common identity. This identity is here made the foundation for a fuller report of many key institutions, such as kinship and the use of wealth, the significance of the winter societies, the techniques and the arts, than would be afforded by a close description of their manifestations confined to any one locality; occasionally Drucker offers conclusions on the interaction of the varieties of ritual, art, technology, and social organization that existed each in different regions, their spread from one place to another and their transformation.

There is of course a cost to this mode of treating ethnographic fact. Each institution has qualities related to scale and the complex interweaving of events in their local occurrence is also part of the scientific story. Drucker retrieves part of the cost by describing four local cultures and two of the more dramatic enterprises of the region in greater detail, which puts back into the culture area some of life as it is experienced by the Indian and as the anthropologist sees or hears about it.

No book is the final work on a germinal topic like the peoples of the Northwest Coast where factual knowledge still accumulates and theoretical developments and revisions are continuous. Drucker has written this excellent work with the major established findings and interpretations as his guide. These findings are not static, and scholars are working today on new interpretations of the potlatch, kinship, the changes of language, and prehistory. In the next decade the contributions of Duff, Borden, Elmendorf, Suttles, and others will have borne additional fruit. This book will stand as the definitive statement until that time. It would then be most fitting for Philip Drucker to undertake another over-all review of the culture of the Northwest Coast and its significance.

H. B. HAWTHORN

Cultures of the North Pacific Coast

# CHAPTER 1

# The Habitat

THE ENTIRE COASTLINE FROM southwest Alaska, well south into California, is steep and abrupt. From the Gulf of Alaska to the vicinity of Puget Sound the mainland is rimmed by a chain of rugged mountains that rise to peaks and crests 3,000 to 4,000 and more feet high at the very edge of salt water, and by a maze of mountainous islands and islets. In the Puget Sound region the coast ranges merge with the Cascades, inland, to be replaced along the shoreline by steep but lower and more rounded coast hills. In the north, the islands off the Alaskan panhandle and along most of the British Columbia coast are structurally part of the coast range. Subsidence of the coast in past geologic eras transformed lower drainage systems into sounds and channels of the sea, so that peaks and plateaus became islands. Narrow steep-walled valleys of the resulting mainland became the scenically spectacular fiords of the northern coast. Farther offshore a mountain chain, now partially submerged, forms the Queen Charlotte Islands, disappears beneath the sea in the Queen Charlotte Sound area to reappear as the

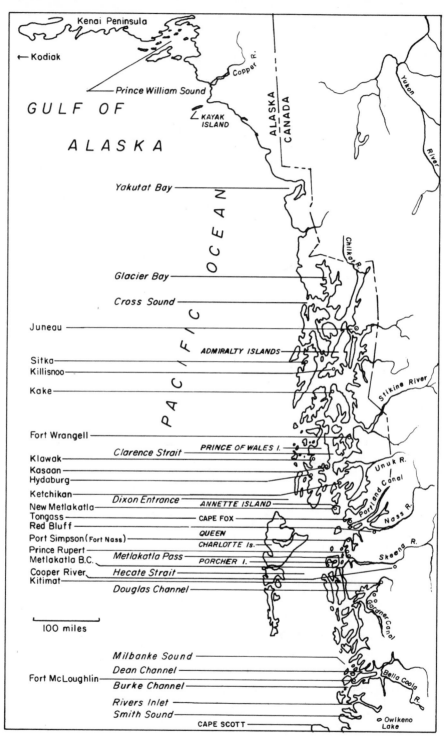

The North Pacific Coast—Northern Localities

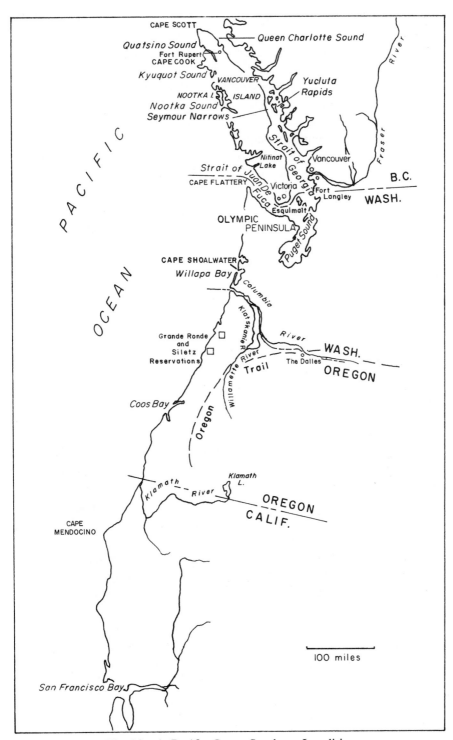

The North Pacific Coast—Southern Localities

backbone of Vancouver Island, and terminates in the majestic Olympic Peninsula of Washington state.

Along these northern coasts there are few gentle beaches and low level areas convenient for habitation by man. From this point of view the hill region to the south likewise seems at first glance unfavorable for human occupation. Although the hills are lower and more rounded, they tend to drop steeply to the water's edge and to form long straight beaches exposed to the pounding of the heavy seas that roll in from across the Pacific. Mouths of rivers and a few localities such as the Shoalwater (Willapa) Bay area of southwestern Washington are the only exceptions. Yet the whole area, mountainous as well as hilly, was densely populated in aboriginal times.

The long narrow strip of coast forms a climatic unit whose distictive characteristics of even temperatures and heavy rainfall are produced by the Japanese Current. This mighty river of warm tropical water has its source somewhere between western Micronesia and the Philippines, flows in a northerly direction along the coasts of Asia, is forced eastward by the Aleutian chain and the shallows of Bering Sea, and then assumes a southerly course along the shore of North America. As it flows, the Current releases its warmth in the form of banks of warm vapor, which the prevailing winds drive shorewards. The shoreline is warmed, then drenched as the warm vapor is forced upward against the coast mountains until its moisture content is precipitated. In the southern portion of the coast, the hills produce a similar effect with the aid of the Cascade and Sierra Nevada ranges a short distance inland. Thus it drizzles in San Francisco, rains in Seattle, and pours in Juneau. The British Columbia coast rainfall averages well over a hundred inches a year.

The effect of the Japanese Current on the coast is to produce moderate temperatures with but minor seasonal variation, and heavy precipitation. There are occasional chill days in Juneau, particularly when abnormal pressure conditions force cold, dry continental air over the mountain crests and down through the passes; but such days are few even though Juneau lies near 60 degrees north latitude. Winters are colder in Washington, D.C., on the Atlantic coast twenty degrees of latitude farther south. In contrast, just a few miles inland, east of the Pacific Coast Ranges, which shut out the Current's warmth, subarctic conditions prevail. In this interior the ground freezes deep, and snow lies from early fall until late in the spring.

The mild, even temperatures and the heavy rainfall, plus a general pattern of thin acid soils, combine to produce a very specialized coastal vegetation pattern. The dominant plant cover consists of conifers, chiefly firs and spruces, replaced in the southernmost portion by coast redwood, along with hemlock, two species of cedar, and yew. These forests grow in dense stands from the water's edge to timberline in the mountains, where altitude and cold continental air inhibit luxuriant plant growth. Individual trees attain great size. The forest floor is carpeted with small shade- and moisture-loving plants such as ferns and mosses. Deciduous bushes and shrubs and a few small trees grow along the margins of water courses and around the edges of swamps, where the conifers do not shade them out. In the southern portion of the coast are small groves of oaks.

The fauna of the area is also distinctive and was plentiful in prehistoric times. Aquatic forms were noteworthy, both for variety of species and for sheer abundance. Five species of Pacific salmon—Chinook (also popularly known as king, tyee, and spring salmon), coho or silver salmon, sockeye, pink, and chum—appeared by the millions each year in inshore waters to ascend the numerous coastal streams and rivers to spawn. Three species of small fish—herring, smelt, and olachen (candlefish)—also appeared in immense schools annually to spawn, herring and smelt along the sea beaches, olachen in certain major rivers. A fourth species, the pilchard, passed offshore in the course of its annual migration between arctic and tropical waters, but did not come close inshore. Halibut and several species popularly called cod were year-round residents of coastal waters. Lower forms of marine life likewise occurred in profusion on coastal beaches. Molluscs, such as clams of numerous kinds, mussels, and various univalves abounded on the beaches. Other orders were represented: sea urchins and various crustaceans. The coastal waters were teeming with life. Fresh waters—rivers, streams, and lakes—had permanent populations of trout. Other species of trout and steelhead spent part of their lives in salt water and part in fresh.

In addition to and because of the wealth of fish and lower forms, there was an abundant sea-mammal fauna. Several species of whales frequented the coast; hair seals, sea lions, and porpoises were common. A form that had especial historical importance because of its highly prized lustrous pelt was the sea otter. The main herds of fur seal passed too far offshore in their annual migration to southern waters to be counted part of the areal fauna, although a few stragglers occasionally came into Dixon Entrance between the Queen Charlotte Islands and the Alexander Archipelago, and traveled southward between the Queen Charlottes and the mainland.

Land game was abundant too, although not in quantities comparable to the aquatic species. Deer were common; because of their ability to subsist on buds, shoots, and leaves where grass was scarce, they prospered even in the dense forests. Bands of elk ranged the woods everywhere from Vancouver Island and the Puget Sound region southward. On the mainland, from the Strait of Georgia northward, the mountain goat shared the rocky crags above timberline with ptarmigan and the silky-furred marmot. Both mountain goat and ptarmigan descended the slopes to near the edge of salt water occasionally, when especially severe storms lashed the mountain crests. Black and grizzly bear, and in the north the formidable brown bear were common. These beasts were assiduous salmon fishers during the runs, and the grizzly and brown bear were dangerous competitors of the native Indian fishermen. Other large carnivores were the mountain lion from Vancouver Island southward, and the wolf, found everywhere along the coast. Fur bearers included beaver, mink, land otter, fisher, and pine marten. Squirrels, wood rats and mice, and weasels were among the minor forms. Enormous flights of waterfowl—ducks, brant, geese, and swans —followed the Pacific flyway in their seasonal migrations to and from their artic and subartic nesting grounds. Sea gulls were the most abundant of the permanent avifauna. Hawks, eagles, ravens, and crows were also numerous. Grouse were nowhere abundant along the coast, but a few could be found almost everywhere. In addition, there was a host of small birds of many different species.

A rapid survey of large animal forms absent from the coast but found in the adjacent interior serves to point up the difference between coastal and interior environments. Caribou were not found, except for a few small bands that entered the Chilkat Valley at the northern extreme of the Alaska panhandle, and an isolated species formerly occurring on the Queen Charlotte Islands. Neither moose nor mountain sheep occurred on the coast, nor did wolverine and lynx. Bobcat, coyote, fox, skunk, and jackrabbit were likewise lacking, except sporadically in the southern portion of the coast, and even there examples of these forms were strays from the interior rather than part of the resident coastal fauna. Snakes, aside from a few harmless species popularly called gartersnakes, were also absent.

It is apparent that the North Pacific Coast was a complex environment for primitive man. The coast environment was highly favorable in quantities of food resources, but unfavorable in regard to their availability. Land game was abundant, but land hunting was very difficult because of the ruggedness of the terrain and density of the vegetation. Fishing and sea hunting were more profitable in terms of yield, but required much more equipment and knowledge. Travel on land for any purpose was slow and painful, while travel by water was easier and more efficient if the primitive navigator possessed the skills necessary to cope with swift, treacherous river currents, surf-pounded reefs and beaches, and dangerous riptides. One might expect the aboriginal inhabitants of the North Pacific Coast to have a very simple, rude culture that permitted them to eke out a marginal existence in the midst of inaccessible plenty. However, they achieved an elaborate culture with a well-developed technology and a high degree of specialized crafts for exploiting the area's resources. North Pacific culture was distinct from other Indian civilizations of North America in its high technology and its efficient environmental adaptation.

The development of Indian culture in this region argues strongly against a theory of environmental determinism. The limits of North Pacific Coast culture can be defined with considerable precision. On the northwest, Yakutat Bay represented the last outpost of the culture pattern. Beyond this point, the coast was inhabited by Indians whose way of life was of the much ruder interior pattern; still farther west along the shores of the Gulf of Alaska were the Pacific Eskimo and the Aleut. Yet in terms of physical environment there is no abrupt change in landscape, climate, flora, or fauna west of Yakutat Bay. Similarly, at the southern extreme, Cape Mendocino on the California coast can be marked as the border of the culture area, although the general environmental pattern extends with little variation to the San Francisco Bay region or a little farther south. Nonetheless, the Indians inhabiting the coast south of Cape Mendocino had a basically Californian culture, not a North Pacific Coast one. These different cultures, thus occurring in the one environment, cannot plausibly be deemed environmentally determined. This natural environment, as does any natural environment, offered certain resources to its human occupants. But how these resources came to be used, or even whether they were used, depends on historical and other factors, not on simple automatic responses to geographical surroundings.

# CHAPTER 2

# Economy and Technology

UNTIL SEVERAL GENERATIONS AFTER the first white contacts, the Indians of the North Pacific Coast shared basic cultural patterns that marked them off as a distinctive unit in the American cultural scene. They shared these patterns although they differed in language (a dozen linguistic stocks were represented) and in physical type, and therefore must be presumed to have differed in origin. The neighbors who ringed the area landwards either lacked the basic patterns of North Pacific Coast culture or had only pallid imitations of them. The several coastal groups and these interior neighbors had numerous contacts, especially trade contacts, but the culture elements they shared were minor.

It has already been mentioned that the areal culture was both elaborate and highly adapted to its environment. Exploitation of the fisheries was the foundation of native economy. This fact was reflected in more than just the daily food-quest routine and diet. It gave the areal culture an orientation toward sea and river that regulated settlement

9

patterns and was reflected in social organization and religion. Techno-
logical development of carpentry and carving was the expression of
another basic pattern, representing the exploitation of the forests and
forest products. These fundamentals of areal culture persist in modern
adaptations to the area's two major resources. The two chief industries
of the region are still fishing and logging.

To demonstrate the essential unity of North Pacific Coast culture,
and to bring out the way in which the fundamental themes just mentioned permeated its every phase, I shall discuss the areal patterns in
the fields of economy, technology, society, religion, and ritual before
turning to a consideration of local variation and local specializations.

## ECONOMY

### Fishing

Exploitation of the fisheries, particularly of salmon—the most abundant fish—was the crux of North Pacific Coast economy. Salmon
fishing, both the aboriginal and the modern industrialized variety,
depends on behavior of the fish at spawning time. As is well known,
salmon live in salt water but spawn in freshwater rivers and streams
(one species in lakes). On hatching, the young fish live in fresh water
a relatively short time, working their way downstream to the sea,
where they develop to maturity. Two, three, or four years after
spawning, depending on the species, the mature salmon appear in
schools in the bays and inlets near the mouths of the spawning streams.
After a period in the inshore waters, during which tentative entries
into fresh water are made, the fish begin to ascend the streams to the
grounds where they themselves hatched, to spawn and die. While there
are local differences—in general the "runs" begin earlier in the year
in the southern portion of the coast—in each locality the same species
appears and runs at the same season each year. The period of the run,
when the fish were limited in movement by the dimensions of the
stream's bed and were doggedly fighting their way upstream, afforded
primitive man his best opportunity to take salmon in quantity.[1]

[1] Laws regulating modern fishing of salmon, in both British Columbia and
Alaska, prohibit commercial fishing in fresh water in order to permit escapement
of species-conserving numbers of salmon to the spawning grounds. Under abo-

In their salmon fishery, the Indians used several kinds of harpoons, nets, and traps. Variants of each of the devices were made in different parts of the coast. Some of the variation depended on cultural preference, some on adaptations to local conditions, such as depth of water, speed of current, rocky or sandy bottom. Weirs, that is, openwork fences, were built to permit flow of the water but to divert the fish so that they could be more easily harpooned, netted, or trapped. To construct an effective weir in a small stream is no great feat, but the Indians of the North Pacific Coast built these devices in large as well as small streams and even in good-sized rivers, where both engineering skill and organization of labor were necessary. Some weirs were large enough to permit the construction of catwalks from which fishing could be done.

To take fish as large as salmon, any form of harpoon is superior to a spearing device with a fixed point; the fish is almost sure to tear free from a fixed point in its violent struggles to escape, whereas a detachable point or blade has a shock-absorber effect that lets the quarry thrash about without coming free. The most common salmon harpoon was made with a long wooden shaft to which two diverging foreshafts were fixed. The harpoon points consisted of two barbs of bone or horn fitted together to form a socket at their base and usually to hold a cutting tip or blade. These points were mounted on the foreshafts and secured to the shaft by short lines. Modifications of this basic type included harpoons with a single point and foreshaft, with three points, with a buffer to prevent shattering the points against rocks, and a shorter-hafted lightweight form intended primarily for throwing rather than thrusting. A different type of harpoon consisted of a one-piece barbed blade, mounted in a socket of the shaft.

Salmon were netted with various kinds of equipment. Dipnets, bags of webbing affixed to V-shaped or Y-shaped frames, or a frame like that of a modern fisherman's landing net, but larger, were manipulated from scaffoldings erected over streams, from the catwalks of large weirs, from canoes, or from the bank. Large squares of netting were gathered into baglike forms and manipulated somewhat like a

---

riginal conditions, however, the fishing was less intensive, and the requirements of the Indians were much smaller, so that depletion of the salmon population by man was not a problem.

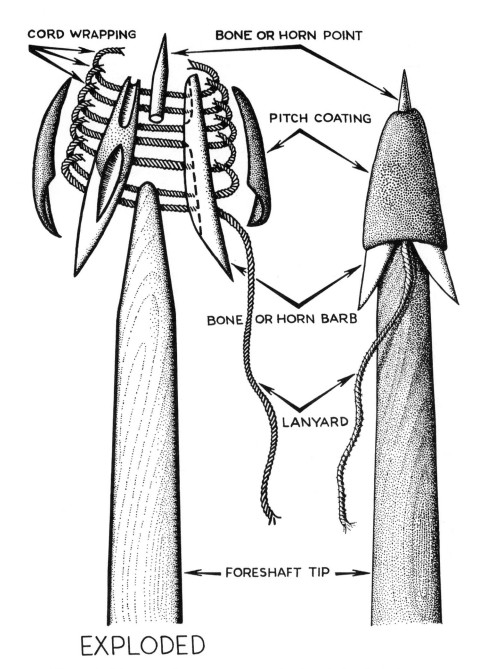

CORD WRAPPING

BONE OR HORN POINT

PITCH COATING

BONE OR HORN BARB

LANYARD

FORESHAFT TIP

# EXPLODED

The basic Northern three-part harpoon head and foreshaft for salmon fishing.

modern trawl. Long nets of the seine and gill-net type were of limited distribution.

A number of efficient, simple traps were made for salmon. They were ingeniously placed where current and formation of the bottom, assisted by leads or a weir, would direct the salmon into them. Near-cylindrical and boxlike forms were made of lattices of poles and withes, with funnel-like entry ways. Another variety of trap was a tray or grid so placed in swift current that the fish in attempting to pass over an obstacle were swept back by the current and stranded high and dry on the raised part of the grid. A similar trap—a large trough-shaped receptacle of latticework—caught the fish as they jumped waterfalls in their upstream migration. The trap was set below a falls so as to interfere slightly with the jump, and fish that failed to clear the falls fell back into the trap.

Another type of trap utilized the great tidal differences typical of the coast. At a place that was bare at low tide and frequented by schools of salmon at high tide, a large enclosure was built of sections of lattice and beach boulders. The salmon could swim freely over the trap when the tide was at flood, but some would be stranded at low tide.

Even today, when the demands of modern commercial fishing have depleted the salmon population along the coast, a salmon run at its peak is an impressive spectacle. In former times it must have been awe inspiring. Day after day the fish thronged the waters so thick, as old-timers on the coast say, "You could walk across on their backs." This wealth of foodstuff permitted a dense aboriginal population in an inhospitable rugged terrain. It also permitted the elaboration of North Pacific Coast Indian culture to a point where it ranked among the higher native civilizations of the New World.

In addition to its abundance, another advantage of the salmon was the ease with which it could be preserved. The flesh, flensed thin, could be smoke-dried to last for a considerable time, despite the humid climate. In a comparatively few days, including the time it took him to ready his harpoons, nets, and traps, to repair the smokehouse, and to do his share in building the weir, a man could catch and his wife could prepare enough salmon to feed his family for several months, thus providing him with leisure.

Studies in culture history the world over have shown that only

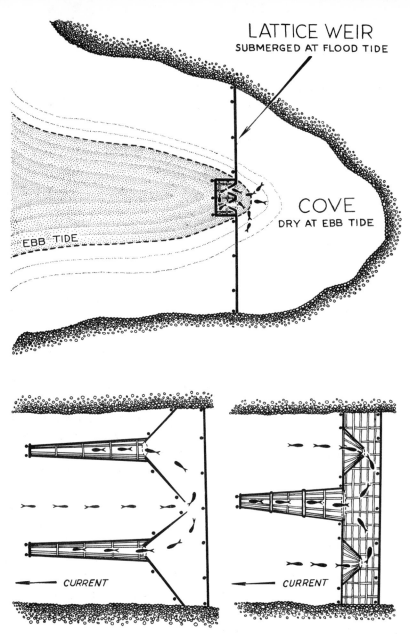

LATTICE WEIR
SUBMERGED AT FLOOD TIDE

COVE
DRY AT EBB TIDE

EBB TIDE

CURRENT

CURRENT

Salmon traps. *Top:* A tidal trap. At flood tide the salmon swim over the lattice weir into the cove. As the tide ebbs, the weir is exposed, forcing the salmon into the trap. *Bottom:* Varieties of stream traps. Weirs are stretched from one bank of the stream to the other (*right side of each diagram*), and from the banks to the funnel-shaped traps, with openings just large enough for the salmon to enter as they swim against the current. When they try to escape from the weirs, they are drawn into the traps.

14

where man can produce storable surpluses of a basic foodstuff, thereby relieving himself at regular intervals from a day-to-day food quest, can cultures be elaborated to higher levels. As a rule, leisure has been a concomitant of the invention or introduction of agriculture. The North Pacific Coast is unique among areas where man lived on the so-called "hunting and gathering" level in that the inhabitants developed a rich culture, and this circumstance can be traced directly to the nature and abundance of the area's basic food source, the salmon.

Other varieties of fish also ran annually. Herring and smelt schooled offshore in great numbers to spawn along the beaches; olachen ran in the lower courses of the larger rivers from the Fraser northward. None of these species equaled the salmon in importance, but they were taken in large quantities to be eaten fresh or dried, except for the olachen, which is so oil-rich that it cannot be dried. The olachen catch was processed for its oil, which was a luxury product to the Indians. The runs of these three species of small fish occurred in the spring and summer when the previous fall's supply of dried salmon was getting low, and perhaps a little moldy. Hence they were especially welcome.

Wherever the great schools of herring assembled inshore, both the fish and their eggs were utilized. The schools at the spawning season were incredibly dense. Herring could be dipnetted from canoes or impaled on the teeth of the herring "rake," a device shaped like a long slender oar with a row of sharp spikes of bone along one edge of the blade. In recent years sharpened nails have replaced the bone spikes. While one person paddled in the stern of the canoe, another, standing in the bow, swept the rake through the water edgewise, with a paddling motion, impaling herring on the teeth of the rake and shaking them off into the canoe on the follow-through of the stroke.

Herring eggs, encased in a sticky gelatinous substance, are laid on and remain attached in thick layers to seaweed. While the egg-covered seaweed was occasionally collected, the most productive collecting method consisted in placing long rows of fir branches, with the butt ends secured to anchored log buoys, and the tips weighted with stones to submerge them, in favored spawning places. The herring deposited great quantities of eggs on the branches, which could be taken up easily, eggs and all. The eggs were ready for immediate consumption or for drying and storing.

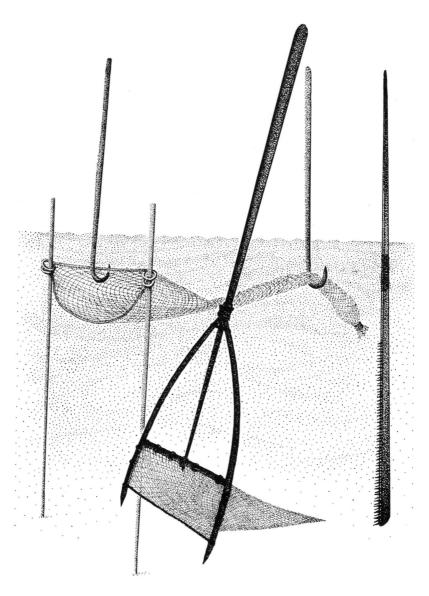

Fishing gear. *Left:* A long tubular net with a funnel-shaped mouth, often used to take olachen. When the tube is full, a hook is used to lift the end, which is untied to dump the fish into a canoe. *Center:* Dipnet, also used to take olachen. *Right:* Herring rake.

The highly prized olachen were taken with dipnets, with the herring rake, and with a long tubular net with a widely flaring funnel-shaped mouth. Smelt were caught in the surf in dipnets as they ran in to spawn on the beach sands.

Fishing with hook and line was considered worthwhile only for large species, such as cod and halibut, for the largest species of salmon, and for the mighty Columbia River sturgeon. To professional fishermen like the North Pacific Indians, such fish as trout were too small and too few to be worth bothering with. Clams, mussels, and other molluscs added variety to the diet. They were abundant and could be collected easily at almost any time of year. At low tide, a sharp-pointed hardwood stick for digging or prying, and a basket to carry the catch, were all one needed to secure a tasty, nutritious meal. That shellfish were nearly a staple in the Indian diet is demonstrated by the tons of shells that mark old occupation sites all along the coast.

### Sea Hunting

While the North Pacific Coast Indians were primarily fishermen, they also hunted. To them, the chase was not a necessity but a source of luxury foods, of hides and pelts, and a way of demonstrating personal prowess. Anyone could catch fish, but only a man of special talents, and one favored by the spirit powers, could be consistently successful in the pursuit of the wary sea mammals or the animals of the forests and mountains.

The sea-mammal fauna included, as has been mentioned, several species of whales, a small spotted seal, the sea lion, porpoise, and sea otter, with the fur seal an infrequent visitor. The abundance of these forms in coastal waters was not uniform, but in general they were plentiful. The extent to which the animals were hunted by the different coast groups is a fairly good index of the degree of Indian adaptation to the habitat. Whaling, for example, was engaged in by only a few groups (mainly Nootkan-speaking tribes), principally members of one linguistic division in the central part and some of their immediate neighbors who almost certainly learned the technique from them. Its practice involved preparation and use of specialized equipment: a canoe large enough to carry safely a crew of several men and

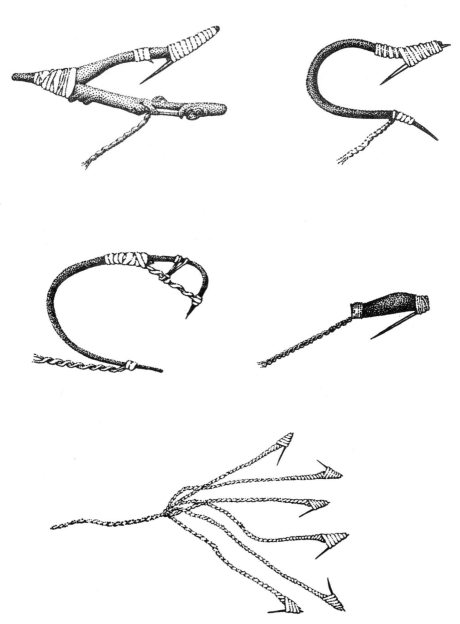

Fishhook types. *Top left:* Northern (two-piece) halibut hook. *Top right:* Wakashan molded spruce-root halibut hook. *Center left:* Haida molded spruce-root black-cod hook. *Center right:* Nootka salmon-trolling hook. *Bottom:* Sharp-angled codfish hooks.

the necessary gear in the boisterous offshore waters, a huge harpoon with a long line and buoys, lances, and miscellaneous small items. The hunt of this largest of mammals involved the maximum development of seamanship in the area. Details of the hunting technique are recounted in Chapter 7.

The purpose of the whale hunt was to procure the oil contained in the insulating thick layer of blubber, the fat in which the body of the animal is encased. As much as possible of the meat was used, but the oil was the chief prize, for the food pattern placed great stress on use of animal fats, which perhaps compensated for the relative scarcity of starches and sugars. Hence almost all the coast groups, those who went whaling and those who did not, made use of dead whales that drifted ashore. Usable, if rank, oil could be rendered out of the blubber even after the flesh had decomposed.

Sea mammals other than the whale were pursued by all Indians of the area, except the villagers on freshwater streams inconveniently far from the animals' normal habitat. Specialized forms of harpoons were used for this hunting. On land, a determined hunter can track a wounded deer all day, and even the next, until he overtakes the weakened, exhausted quarry, but a wounded water animal will escape into the trackless deeps unless the weapon has some sort or retrieving device or one that marks the quarry's movements. An animal killed outright will sink and be lost without such a device. Hence the harpoon was the chief weapon of the sea hunter. The principal exception to hunting with a harpoon was the clubbing technique used on rocky islets where seals and particularly sea lions "hauled up" to rest. An agile hunter with rudimentary weapons could easily dispatch the beasts, for they are clumsy on land.

### Land Hunting

Land animals were hunted and trapped in many ways, depending on the habits of the species and the nature of the terrain. Every hunting and trapping technique known in native North America was practiced by some of the coast groups. Individual stalking, group drives and surrounds with and without use of dogs, spring pole and simple snares, deadfalls, pitfalls, and bow and arrow were all utilized. This abundance of techniques reinforces earlier statements concerning the general economic pattern. The relatively minor importance of land hunting was not the result of lack of knowledge; it was due, rather, to the emphasis on exploitation of sea and river products. Among the major groups along the coast, there were a few villages or tribelets situated at the head of tidewater or on rivers. For them, sea mammals were scarcer and less accessible, land game more readily at hand and hence more extensively pursued. Although such geographically conditioned variation did occur, to the great majority of the Indians of the area sea hunting was of more importance, and in no case did land hunting come to surpass fishing either in interest or as a source of food.

### Vegetable Foods

The North Pacific Coast, although bountifully endowed with fish and game, was deficient in vegetable foods. Except in the southern inland portion where camas (a plant with edible bulbs) occurred and in the extreme south where edible acorns grew, the flora was poor in starch-rich seeds and tubers. It has been suggested that the cultural stress on oils and fats in part at least may have compensated for the scarcity of starchy foods. The tough fibrous roots of certain ferns, the wiry roots of a kind of clover, and the inner bark of hemlock were eaten by many coastal Indians, but these products were neither abundant nor very tasty. Berries did occur in considerable quantity, and there were many kinds: salalberries, huckleberries, cranberries, salmonberries, strawberries, soapberries, among others. When they ripened, all were picked and eaten with great relish. The major deficiency of berries as an important food was the difficulty in preserving them by primitive techniques. Salalberries were cooked down into a thick pulp that was sun-dried in cakes that kept well. Other varieties were put down in whale or olachen oil, a recipe that does not sound savory but which the Indians enjoyed. In springtime, salmonberry shoots were relished as greens. A limited number of other plants, including certain seaweeds, were also eaten.

### Cooking

Aside from berries and the few greens, few foods were eaten raw. There were three basic methods of cooking: grilling over an open fire or over coals, boiling, and steaming or baking in a pit oven. Lacking metal containers that could be put directly over the fire, aboriginal cooks boiled their food by dropping the food and red-hot stones into vessels of water. (See on p. 147 the illustration of the interior of a Nootkan house. Note the box near the fire and the cleft stick to handle the hot stones.) Some groups used watertight baskets for boiling, others, hollowed-out wooden troughs or neatly carpentered watertight boxes. The pit oven was, as the name indicates, a pit dug into the ground. A hot fire in the pit heated a quantity of stones as well as the sides of the pit; when it had burned low, the food was placed over the coals and hot stones, covered with mats and then earth to seal in the heat, and often a fire was built on top to retain the heat even longer. Items that contained considerable liquid, clams and mussels for example, were steamed in their own juices. In cooking other foods, such as clover roots, water was thrown on the heated rocks before closing the pit, to produce steam, or was poured through a tube such as the hollow stem of giant kelp. Other foods, such as meats, were cooked dry, or in modern culinary terminology were baked or roasted.

## TECHNOLOGY AND ART

Although not universal throughout the area, the distinctive art of the North Pacific Coast may be best discussed in connection with woodworking technology, since its basic manifestation was representative carving in wood. Each subarea had its characteristic variations in style, and persons familiar with the art can usually distinguish from which group a given carving comes. Painting, weaving, and occasional uses of other media, such as horn, bone, and stone, were hardly more than extensions of the woodcarving art. Treatment varied from shallow incising to full round. Painting often accented the carving and occasionally was used to decorate uncarved objects, but it was a secondary form of artistic expression.

This art was primarily heraldic, that is, its themes were concerned with the histories, both real and fictional, of family lines, and incidents through which ancestors achieved prominence. Much of the art depicts renowned ancestors and the supernatural beings in human, animal, or monster form, who endowed those ancestors with special gifts and qualities.

The so-called "totem pole" is one application of this art much used in the northernmost divisions, especially among the Tlingit, Haida, and Tsimshian. "Totem pole" may be applied to memorial poles set up in front of a village, portal poles attached to a house front, mortuary poles in a cemetery, and even to the carved posts and beams incorporated in the houses, since all were memorials, or monuments to the dead.

These same commemorative themes were used as applied decoration in full round, in high or low relief, or two-dimensionally, on numerous objects: house facades, feast dishes, canoes, storage boxes, helmets, ceremonial headdresses, weapons, spoons, and almost every other artifact. On all objects they had commemorative significance, representing the same traditional beings and incidents important in family history. Where used most in this fashion, the art became highly conventionalized, losing realism in the treatment of the applied designs. This formalization of the art was deliberate, aimed at satisfying esthetic needs. It was not done because the carvers were incapable of realistic depiction.

In an adjoining area to the south, the shape of an object was often completely modified by decoration: appendages, such as arms, legs, or wings, were added to figures by neatly dowled joints. These objects were less rigidly confined by utilitarian form, or by the limits imposed by the dimensions of a tree trunk, than were the objects made in the area emphasizing applied design. Accompanying this greater spatial freedom was a different departure from realism, one toward an impressionistic suppression of minor detail. These two regional styles were not sharply demarcated in distribution but overlapped somewhat.

In the southern extreme representative art was not found. The carver decorated his products with geometric patterns of completely different inspiration.

### Woodworking

One of the distinctive features of North Pacific Coast culture was the utilization of one of the area's chief natural resources—wood. Woodworking was developed to an extent unrivaled elsewhere in native America. The Indians used principally the red cedar, and in the south, redwood, both of which are soft and tractable, with long, straight, easily opened cleavage planes, and other even-grained woods such as yellow cedar and alder. Douglas fir, true firs, spruces, and hemlock, which are tougher and cross-fibered, and at the same time form the major part of the forests, were little used. They were too difficult to handle with the limited native tool kit. Hardwoods, such as yew, maple, and the like, were used for small objects where hardness and strength were essential.

The native logger and carpenter was equipped with a wide variety of tools: adzes, chisels, wedges, hammers and mauls, drills, knives, and limited sanding materials. Axes and saws were not found in the aboriginal tool kit; instead, the adz, supplemented by the chisel, served as the principal cutting and planing tool. Tough-grained igneous rocks, a form of jadeite, shell (particularly that of certain species of deep-water clams that washed up on the beaches), horn, beaver incisors, and bone were the chief materials for cutting blades. In addition, small amounts of iron were used long before the first direct European contacts.

The source of iron, which was not smelted on the North Pacific Coast, is something of a mystery. I am of the opinion that it must have been traded in a long series of exchanges, via Bering Strait, from some Iron Age center in Siberia. It is known that the Eskimo of the Bering Strait region received iron in small but increasing amounts from the beginning of the archaeologically defined Punuk horizon, dated about A.D. 1000, and it seems reasonable to believe that some of the metal was traded along the coast until it reached the hands of the North Pacific Coast Indians. Another theory is that the iron reached the coast in the wreckage of seagoing vessels that met disaster in Asiatic waters and were washed ashore by the Japanese Current, just as are the glass net floats lost by Japanese fishermen. However, the old-fashioned Chinese junk had no iron in its construction: its members were joined by dowels, not by bolts and spikes. Therefore, only European vessels lost after Magellan's time could be considered as the source of the iron, but there were too few such wrecks to account for all the iron possessed by the Indians at the time of Captain Cook's discovery of the coast in 1778. After Cook's time, when more European shipping plied the Pacific, iron fittings from wreckage that washed ashore were utilized.

The giant red cedar and other trees were felled by laboriously pecking away with adzes and chisels around the trunk. One ethnographer reports the use of fire in felling, but this seems unlikely as a general practice because of the difficulty of getting green wood to burn in a controlled way. Fire was much used, however, to hollow out sections of logs that had been felled and left a few months to season, especially in the manufacture of canoes and large troughs used as dishes and containers; where the fire could be built on an exposed horizontal surface of the dried-out wood, its horizontal spread was controlled by use of wet moss and similar materials. Logs were split in two, or split into a series of thin, wide sections that served as boards, by sets of wedges driven up along the grain of the wood with a maul. Wedges were made with differing degrees of taper, some with one flat and one curved surface, to control the direction of cleavage. These wedges were ordinarily driven with an unhafted stone maul, although a few groups mounted stone heads on long handles that could be used with a full two-handed stroke. Simple drills, consisting of a bit mounted in a straight shaft rotated between the user's palms, served for drilling holes. Fine work was done with small, light adzes and with the knife, a relatively long-handled implement with a small blade set at an angle to the axis of the haft. Sometimes a beaver incisor was so mounted that its natural keen edge could be used, but more commonly a small piece of iron provided the cutting edge. In addition to the use of fire to hollow out sections of wood, boiling water or steam were used to soften wood so that it could be molded slightly or bent across the grain. For sanding, dogfish skin and scouring rushes were used. With these tools and techniques the native craftsman manufactured a host of objects of wood: timbers and planking for houses, huge seaworthy canoes, boxes, dishes, and other types of containers, weapons and implements for fishing and hunting, as well as small delicately carved articles such as dance rattles and masks.

More characteristic of the areal culture than the list of tools used was the way in which they were used. Everything made of wood manifested good workmanship. Within the limits of functional design there was symmetry of form. Corners were squared, although there was no try square in the native tool kit. Surfaces were painstakingly smoothed and polished far beyond utilitarian need and very often decorated. The sea-lion clubs exemplify the point. From a practical standpoint, a sea lion can be clubbed to death with any solid and heavy branch that the hunter can wield. Sea-lion clubs were not, however, rough irregular sticks; they were invariably carved into symmetrical form, smoothed, polished, and frequently covered with low-relief designs. Roof beams—tremendous logs, often two to three feet in diameter and fifty to one hundred feet long—were, where not decorated, trimmed to uniform diameter, and the final adzing done to leave the adz marks in rows, like fluting, the length of the beam, producing an aesthetically pleasing effect. The exteriors of wooden containers and dishes were usually simple geometric forms, sometimes modified into stylized zoomorphic shapes, but always symmetrical both externally and in relation to the hollowed-out portion. In the course of examining hundreds of these objects, I cannot recall an unsmoothed or a lopsided one. In brief, symmetry and neatness were as characteristic of manufactures as the types of the objects.

### Houses

The rectangular plank house was universally used at winter-village sites and usually at other important localities. There were several varients of the basic pattern, each with a definite geographical distribution and only a minor degree of overlapping. Sufficient archaeological research has not yet been done to define the historical relationships of the varients, nor to indicate which is the closest to the original ancestral pattern. However, deviation from a single form is suggested by a number of distinctive features shared by two or more subtypes. These include round-to-oval doorway, double ridgepole, carved posts and roof timbers, walls separate from (not supporting) the roof, gabled roofs, a central pit, and multifamily occupancy and therefore large size, in addition to the basic outline and material. On the basis of the overlapping distributions of these features it seems reasonable to assume that the variants of the rectangular plank house represent local modifications of a single ancestral plan. Plank houses of this type built on pilings or cribwork foundations represent ingenious adaptations to local needs.

Rustic huts of slabs of bark, tentlike shelters of mats, and similar makeshifts were used by a few groups at campsites occupied for brief periods. The semisubterranean earth lodge, so widespread among

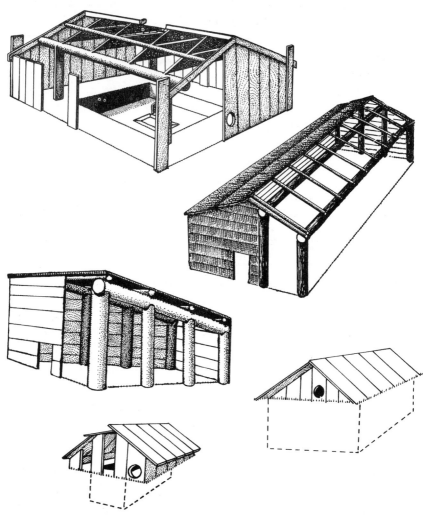

Regional variants of the plank house. *Top left:* Northern type, with mortised members and planking, was nearly square, and the roof had a very low pitch. *Top right:* Wakashan type, with siding independent of framework, was very long (40 × 100 feet), and the roof had a very low pitch. *Center left:* Coast Salish "shed-roof" type, with siding and dimensions similar to the Wakashan type. *Center right:* Chinook-Oregon Coast type, with only the roof and part of the gable above ground. The dotted lines indicate the excavated area. *Bottom:* Lower Klamath type, with three-pitch roof. A little of the siding shows above the ground. The dotted lines indicate the excavated area.

26

tribes of the interior, was used by only a very few coast divisions who had strong ties with the interior and who in all probability were relatively recent arrivals on the coast.

Special structures for storage were atypical. Sufficient space was available in the dwelling houses, even though large quantities of provisions were preserved. Sweathouses were of minor importance except to a few groups at the southern extreme of the area and consequently were rudely improvised and impermanent.

### Canoes

The canoemaker was a specialist everywhere in the area. Because of the importance of woodworking in daily life, every man was something of a carpenter and woodcarver, but only a few had the talent necessary for canoemaking. Dugout canoes of red cedar or of redwood (only rarely were other woods used) were essential to the way of life of the Indians of the North Pacific Coast. Distinctive regional designs were modified, chiefly in proportions and in line, according to the purpose for which the individual craft was intended. The hunter of sea mammals needed a vessel that would glide swiftly and noiselessly through the water; for him the canoemaker shaped a long slender hull with racy lines. To transport provisions and personnel (that is, for craft in which capacity and stability were more important than speed) the "war canoe" with broad beam and bluff lines was designed. Nowhere was the high quality of native workmanship better displayed than in the canoes. Without blueprints, try squares, levels, compasses, or curves, the complex varying shapes of bow and stern were chopped out with the adz in well-nigh perfect symmetry, so that the canoe cut water cleanly, with a minimum of effort, and so that it would not have the unhappy characteristic of falling off toward an unbalanced side.

To make a canoe, a tree that would yield a hull of the desired dimensions was sought, felled, and cut to the length intended for the vessel. Red cedar occasionally grew near the beach or on the bank of a stream where launching would be easy, but such trees were rarely suitable for canoes. Easier access to sunlight causes lower branching and hence numerous knots and other irregularities. For this reason a tree from the densest part of the forest was preferred for its long,

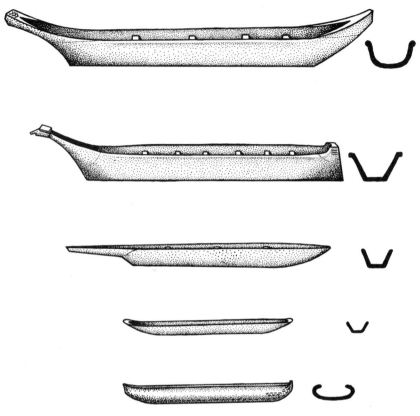

Canoe types. *From top to bottom:* Northern type, Nootka type, Coast Salish version of the Northern type, Shovelnose type, and Lower Klamath type. *To the right of each* is shown the amidships cross section.

clean, branchless bole. Frequently, instead of felling the chosen tree, two deep cuts were adzed and chiseled to about half of the diameter of the trunk, one near the base of the tree and another as high up as the length desired for the canoe. The uppermost cut was made from a flimsy scaffolding of poles. Wedges were driven into the cut to start a split into which a heavy pole was placed. This accomplished, the Indian craftsman went home to other tasks, secure in the knowledge that the section of log would gradually work itself free as the wind swayed the tree and the pressure of the pole constantly widened the split. Advantages of this technique were not only that it saved making two cuts through the entire thickness of the trunk, but also that only the section fell to the ground, whereas an entire large tree could not be felled without extensive clearing to prevent its lodging inextricably among its neighbors. When the section was on the ground, the Indians levered and wedged it into a level working position with the split side down, for work was always begun on the outside of the hull.

After the exterior had been shaped, a series of small holes was drilled to specified depths along the keel line, at the turn of the bilge, and along the sides. Plugs of twigs or withes, usually charred at the tips, were driven into these holes. Then the section was turned over and excavation of the interior begun; as the adz shaved the tips of the plugs, the different color indicated a desired thickness. When fire was used in hollowing the hull, it was used only in the upper rough part of the work. Excavation was always completed with the adz.

Often the canoe hull was only roughed out in the woods. When enough waste had been removed to lighten the section of log, it was dragged to the water and towed to the village beach where the craftsman could work on it more conveniently.

To increase the beam of a large canoe after it had been adzed to proper thickness, the hull was filled with water, which was then brought to a boil by adding red-hot stones. When the hot water and steam had softened the wood sufficiently, thwartlike crosspieces were driven in with great care, the water was allowed to cool so that the wood set in the new form, and permanent thwarts were installed. The operation was a delicate one because the elasticity of the wood had very narrow limits. To spread the hull past these limits could result only in splitting it beyond repair.

Where the canoe was made of half a log, increasing the beam in this fashion increased the interior space slightly. More important, the spreading produced a regularly increasing sheer from bilge to gunwale that progressed symmetrically from bow and stern to amidships and shed water and spray when traveling through rough seas. It also produced a barely perceptible lowering of the gunwales amidships. To make the largest possible canoe from a single log, master canoemakers of some groups derived even greater advantage from this technique by using more than half a log and spreading the gunwales enough to eliminate the inward curves of the original log section. To compensate for a marked longitudinal dip of the gunwales that would result from this greater change in outline, the longitudinal edges of the log were carved with slightly convex curves so that when spread, the gunwales leveled off.

To give added protection against rough seas and increase seaworthiness, many North Pacific Coast canoemakers added separate prow and stern pieces onto the hull, raising these extremes well above the height of the hull section. The joints for attachment of these pieces were fitted with such care that they were barely noticeable. The pieces were secured by sewing with spruce withes through a series of connecting holes drilled along the edges of the joints.

Finally, the hull was sanded and polished and perhaps decorated with paint, inlay, or carvings. The exteriors of canoes to be used for sea-mammal hunting were often singed with torches to remove splinters and minor irregularities, then polished to a glossy sheen with the sandpaperlike skin of the dogfish to reduce water friction so the craft would glide swiftly and silently.

The construction of a canoe, particularly a large one, was a lengthy and arduous task, since the canoemaker worked alone. He recruited aid only for the heavy tasks of turning over the partly finished hull or dragging it to the water. Canoes were treated with great care. When not in daily use, they were drawn up on the beach and covered with old mats and boards to prevent the sun from checking and cracking the wood. On rocky beaches, runways were cleared or constructed for beaching canoes by placing a series of smooth round poles at right angles to the runway, with the ends held in place by large rocks. Canoes could be beached and launched over such runways without damaging the hulls. Some Indians never dragged their cherished vessels even across beaches of smooth sand, but carried them in and out of the water, and kept them ashore on a set of log-and-pole chocks, not on the ground.

The craft were propelled by paddle, and on rivers by pole. Most of the groups used a short-handled paddle with a cross grip at the top, and a more or less elliptical blade. In historic times many groups have used sails, weaving them of mats when imported canvas was scarce, but explicit statements of the earliest European observers indicate that sails were not aboriginal in the area. Unlike the deep-keeled canoes of Oceania, the keelless North Pacific Coast canoes were poorly adapted to sail. The shallow hulls could not be made to beat upwind, and with the wind abeam made more leeway than headway.

Because even the best canoes may take a little water in rough seas
or from rain, a bailer was standard equipment. It was commonly carved
of wood, according to local pattern, but a few groups made bailers
of bark. Anchors were used only occasionally when bottom fishing.
For such infrequent use any rock of convenient size and shape was
picked up and used, and as casually discarded. Rarely an encircling
groove or a line hole was pecked in an anchor stone, which would then
be kept for future use.

### Wooden Receptacles

Woodworkers provided a variety of containers for food preparation,
for storage of food and other articles, and for special uses—cradles,
drums, chamber pots, and sea hunters' quivers. It may be noted in
passing that there were containers of other materials as well, particularly of basketry, but wooden vessels were characteristic of the culture.
The simplest vessels were troughlike trenchers hollowed out of
single blocks of alder, a wood that combines the qualities of softness
and evenness of grain but does not split easily. The Indians preferred
alder because it does not impart unpleasant flavors to food. The basic
dish shape was a rectangle with round ends that slanted outwards and
terminated in a wide horizontal lip. Dishes for everyday use were
normally small and undecorated. The lip and exterior of containers
for feasts were carved in designs in the form of animals and human
beings. These highly adorned dishes were commonly huge, a single
container serving five, ten, or even more persons. Boxes for the storage
of valuables were decorated with inlay and painted or carved in low
relief.

A few coastal groups made storage containers by hollowing out
blocks of wood and fitting covers to them, but the box with one-piece
sides was more widespread. To form the sides of one of these boxes,
the Indian carpenter cut and adzed a cedar board to even thickness.
He then cut three transverse grooves, or kerfs, almost through the
board. These kerfs had to be exactly square in cross section and spaced
at accurately measured intervals so as to fold on themselves to form
a tight seal. The board was moistened and heated at the cuts, or
steamed over hot stones in a pit, until each kerf could be bent at a
right angle; the ends were beveled to meet in a tight joint and were

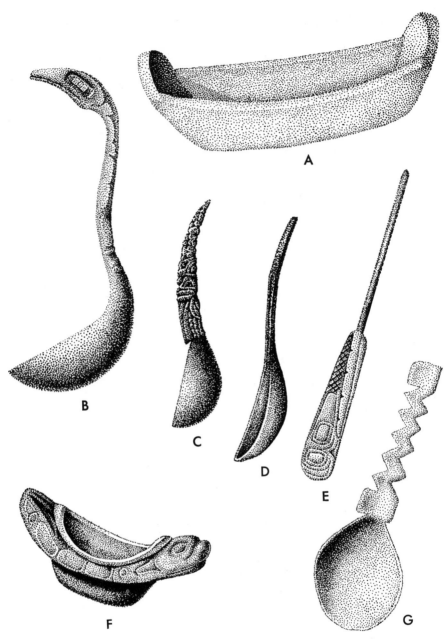

Dishes and spoons. (a) Northern and Wakashan plain dish. (b) Mountain-sheep-horn ladle. (c) Mountain-goat-horn spoon. (d) Alder-wood spoon. (e) "Soapberry" spoon. (f) Northern-type oil dish. (g) Lower Klamath elkhorn spoon.

sewn together through drilled holes with withes, or pegged. For the bottom, a flange was cut around the perimeter of a board to the exact measure of the joined sides, forming a mortise joint, which was held in place by hardwood pegs driven into drilled holes.

Various types of covers were made for these boxes: one type was a thick board excavated so as to fit over the top of the box; another was a thick board grooved like the bottom to fit snugly; and a third consisted of another box that telescoped over the first.

Boxes were made tight enough for the storage of whale and olachen oil, as well as for other materials. They were also used for cooking by stone boiling, for water buckets, and for freshwater containers on sea voyages. Sea hunters' boxes exemplified a particularly skillful application of the box-making technique. For receptacles to stow snugly in the bow or stern of a canoe, the kerfs were slanted to make the finished box wider at the top than at the base.

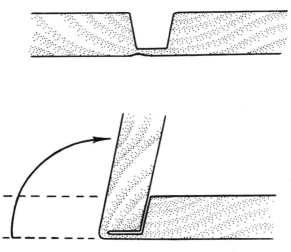

Woodworking technique. *Top:* A kerf. *Bottom:* The plank bent to form a corner of a wooden box.

## Weaving

In the North Pacific Coast weaving was an important craft. Both basketry and textiles show great variety of weaving techniques. (On p. 146 the illustration of a Nootkan house shows a woman at work on a loom.) The principal materials were the tough, flexible roots of the spruce, inner bark of both red and yellow cedar, cattail or tule stems, bark of the wild cherry tree, mountain-goat wool, dog wool, down of ducks and other birds, the "down" of various native plants, and for decoration grasses, fern stems, and the like. Spruce roots were washed, partly dried, resoaked, and split into strips. Cedar bark was stripped from standing trees in long narrow sections. The course outer bark was peeled off and discarded, the inner layer folded into bolts for transport and storage. For matting, the dried red-cedar bark was split into strips; for cordage it was partly shredded by beating, then twisted between palm and thigh. The processing of yellow-cedar bark was more involved. It was soaked first in salt water, then in fresh water, dried, and then beaten across the grain to soften the fibers and partly separate them, transforming the strips of bark into soft, fluffy hanks. Cattails or tules were cut to length, sun-dried, then slightly moistened before being sewn together to form mats.

Mountain-goat wool was a prized commodity. It was plucked from the dried hide, cleaned, and carded with the fingers. The long, coarse guard hairs were picked out and discarded, and the wool was made up into loose hanks. Sometimes a core of yellow-cedar-bark string was added for strength, and the wool was then spun into two-ply yarn. Dog wool was similarly treated, except that a hearting of string was not used. A few Coast Salish groups had a small, woolly breed of dogs that could be sheared or plucked. Bird down and the soft cottony pappus of certain plants were sometimes mixed with wool. In one portion of the area, yarn was made of the down of mallard and other ducks by twisting strips of dried skin with the down attached, or by catching the down into cordage of bark fiber.

The most widespread weaving technique was twining: nonmoving strands, or "warps," are caught together by pairs of transverse strands, the "wefts," which are crossed and twisted about them. In plain twining, single warps are secured by the wefts; in twilled twining, the warps are caught together in pairs, each course of wefts splitting the pair united by the preceding one; and in wrapped twining, one weft is rigid, the other is wrapped completely around each intersection of the warps and rigid weft. Plain twining was used in making spruce-root-basketry containers, hats, and caps. Robes and capes of red- and of yellow-cedar-bark yarn were also made in plain twining. Much of the basketry made by this technique was so finely woven that it was watertight, and baskets were used as containers for liquids and even for cooking by the hot-stone boiling method. The twined-basketry hats were also waterproof. Decoration was applied to basketry by imbrication, that is, by covering the wefts at certain intervals with thin flat strips of colored materials, bleached or dyed grasses, splints of glossy black fern stems, and the like, to produce patterns. Most designs were geometric, but occasionally representative patterns were worked in.

Cedar-bark garments were used by some groups. Thick strands of shredded bark formed the warps, and the wefts were thin, tightly spun cords, widely spaced so that the surface of the fabric was formed by the warps, in contradistinction to the basketry. Shredded red-cedar bark was used for short rain capes of widely flared, truncated conical shape. When the wearer slipped the cape over his or her head, the flared edge came just below the elbows, thus allowing freedom of arm movement, for paddling a canoe, for example. Capes were water-repellent rather than waterproof. The neckband was often trimmed with fur to prevent the harsh fiber from scratching. Robes of shredded yellow-cedar bark were worn primarily for warmth. They were woven on a "half loom," the warps being suspended with the lower ends free. The robe's upper edge and sides were straight, the lower edge convexly curved. Strips of fine fur, such as sea otter, were sewn along the upper edge for ornament, not comfort, since the shredded yellow-cedar bark was pleasantly soft when properly prepared. A few strands of mountain-goat wool were sometimes used as wefts across the lower edge for added elegance, especially where goat wool was scarce.

Much more elaborate, technically speaking, was the "Chilkat blanket" or robe, for many years woven only by women of the Chilkat division of the Tlingit. However, there is evidence that in former times the same kind of blanket was made by other groups as well. These robes and other garments such as unfitted tubular "shirts," dance kilts, and knee-to-ankle leggings were woven in twilled twining with goat-wool wefts and warps of goat wool spun with a hearting of yellow-cedar-bark string. The weaving was done on the simple half loom with the lower ends of the warps hanging free, like the loom on which yellow-cedar-bark robes were made; also like the latter, the warps were cut to varying lengths from edge to center, so that the finished robe had a curved "hemline." Here the similarities end. In the Chilkat robes the weaving was in twilled, not plain, twining; the wefts, not the warps, formed the surface of the fabric, and they were dyed black, blue, and yellow, which with the natural white of the wool gave four colors for development of designs. Men made and painted pattern boards from which designs were copied by women weavers. A peculiarity of the Chilkat blanket was that only at top and bottom borders did the wefts cross back and forth from edge to edge of the fabric. In the decorated field, each major design element was woven as a separate rectangular panel. The panels were subsequently joined by a special weaving stitch or by sewing, and the joints were covered by a sort of false embroidery in which three, not two, strands of wefts were employed. Another element was also introduced around the edges of each color unit in the design. Borders around the sides and bottom of the robe were done in a technique that was more properly braiding than true weaving and that left a long thick fringe.

A different kind of weaving also had a restricted distribution among the Coast Salish. This was done in mountain-goat or dog wool, spun into very heavy yarn with huge spindles, on a full loom. A single long warp was turned back and forth over a string across the center of the loom and wrapped around the two cross bars. A true loom technique of weaving was used: twilling, single weft strands being crossed over two warps and under one. When the work was finished, the horizontal string about which the warps were turned was cut and drawn out, freeing the two ends of the fabric. These robes were often large and usually plain, with at most a colored border.

Yet another type of weaving was exemplified in the "organized" or "nobility" robes. Nothing is known of this technique except what can be deduced from specimens collected in the early decades of the nineteenth century. It appears to have been done by the same groups who wove on the two-bar loom just described; the weave, however, is a variety of twining and could not have been done on a true loom. Since many of the specimens contain yarns or dyes of European origin in addition to those of native materials and colors, some authorities believe that these robes were woven for a limited period subsequent to early contacts with whites. Occasional specimens with a separately woven central panel sewed in along the sides suggest relationship to the Chilkat blanket. Some of the same weavers who wove on the two-bar looms knew this technique, for there are specimens in which the main portion was loom-woven in the standard twilled weave, with borders in the twined "nobility" blanket technique. Such pieces presumably were woven mainly on the loom, then taken down to weave on the borders.

Matting was another type of textile produced over a large part of the North Pacific Coast. Red-cedar bark was a preferred material. The strips of bark, split to even width, and sometimes including a few dyed red or black for decoration, were woven in simple checkerwork or twilled checker. Very long mats were made by working on a diagonal, inserting new elements as needed along one edge. Mats were used as bedding, as furniture, as tablecloths at feasts, as makeshift sails in historic times, to protect canoes from weathering, and as shrouds for the dead. Where flexibility was desired, baskets and walletlike containers were made in the same material and weaves.

Mats of tule stems, especially for mattresses, were made by a number of groups. Some mats were twined together with cordage, and some were sewn by passing a long hardwood needle through a series of stems, then crimping the stems over the needle with a wooden creaser to prevent splitting, before drawing the thread through.

Coiled basketry, which is more properly sewn than woven, was made by a few groups in the central part of the area. Most authorities regard this technique as a relatively recent introduction from the Plateau tribes of the adjacent interior.

### Skin Dressing

In the perennially damp climate of the North Pacific Coast primitive leathers were of little service, since when wet and soggy they stretch out of shape and tear easily, and when dried out after wetting become inflexible. It appears that the standard western North American techniques for preparing buckskin were known but were infrequently used. More buckskin was obtained in trade with peoples of the interior, who were masters at this craft, than was prepared on the coast. Peltries cured with hair or fur on for highly prized robes and sealskins for floats and buoys in sea-mammal harpooning involved a minimum of stretching, scraping, and drying, which left them neither flexible nor durable.

## Work in Stone

There were well-defined patterns in manufacturers of stone and other hard materials. Chipping and flaking of stone to make cutting tools and weapons was not typically a coastal craft. Volcanic glasses and the cherts and chalcedonies from which projectile points and cutting blades can be made in these techniques were rare on the coast; most objects made from them were imported. Neolithic techniques were used to peck and grind tough igneous stones into adz blades, mauls, and pestles, as well as the few mortars and small dishlike receptacles. Where available, slate was ground into knives and projectile points; more frequently shell was treated by the same method to produce cutting implements. Horn and bone were ground into harpoon points and barbs, arrow points, chisels and wedges, clubs and other objects. For the area as a whole, it might be said that craftsmanship in these materials was competent but not outstanding; it was only when horn of elk, mountain goat, or mountain sheep was carved like wood, in the manufacture of spoons, ladles, and small receptacles, that artistic results were achieved.

## Dress and Ornament

The North Pacific Coast peoples, although adjacent to the great area of tailored skin clothing, did not ordinarily participate in that pattern. Usual coverings were robes and cloaks of woven materials or of furs and poncholike rain garments. On pleasant days men went naked except for ornaments; women wore aprons usually of strands of vegetable fibers. Footgear was not in ordinary use, for moccasins are ill-adapted to constant wetting and sandals were unknown.

As one might expect, there was a fairly adequate wardrobe of rain garments. Wide-brimmed rain hats woven of closely twined basketry were used from the north to the Columbia River. One form of hat was a flattened, truncated cone. When worn by persons of high rank, this style was surmounted by four small cylindrically shaped elements, woven in one piece with brim and crown. In another type, crown and brim merged indistinguishably in a convex curve from the small

A man at Nootka Sound, April 1778.

flat area formed by the "starting knot" of the weave at the top. A third form had a concave brim and a small crown surmounted by a woven ball and spike. Still another had a fairly large flat-topped crown and a wide concavely flaring brim. All hats were woven with inside headbands that sat firmly on the wearers' heads, and had chin straps for windy days. The geographical distributions of the several forms overlapped somewhat. The only headgear limited to one sex was the women's basketry caps of the Lower Columbia and the southern extreme of the area. Both were small and brimless, the former, a truncated cone of Plateau type, the latter, reminiscent of Central Californian usage.

Twined basketry headgear. *Left to right:* Nootka chief's hat, Northern and Kwakiutl rainhat, and Wakashan rainhat, occasionally also used by Haida.

The conical rain cape (described in connection with its manufacture), like the rain hat, was worn by both men and women as needed, and had about the same distribution as the hat. Similar garments were sometimes woven in mountain-goat wool for dress occasions. Another rain garment was a square of doubled checkerwork matting made of cedar bark. It suggests a poncho, except that instead of a hole for the head, it had two wide bands of matting that went over the shoulders on either side of the neck to be tied in front or held under the wearer's belt. Robes were worn over the shoulders and over the arms, held in place underneath by the hands when standing or sitting. Where more activity was anticipated, a robe might be worn under one arm with the upper corners tied or pinned over the other shoulder and belted, thus leaving both arms free.

Tailored skin clothing was not ordinarily worn, but some groups who dwelt at the heads of long inlets in the northern portion of the area were familiar with buckskin shirts, leggings, and moccasins of the styles used by their neighbors of the interior. In fact many garments were obtained in trade from the interior, where the Indians were masters at tanning buckskin and at tailoring. Chilkat Tlingit men, who lived in one of the most rigorous winter climates of the coast, wore a sort of trousers with moccasins attached, and their women wore sleeved buckskin dresses. Most divisions using tailored skin clothing reserved it for the wintertime, and in pleasant weather dressed (or, undressed) as did other coast Indians.

Ornaments were regularly worn by both sexes. Daily activity and social rank regulated the amount and splendor of adornment. Dentalia (shells) were popular ornaments and were worn as necklaces, in clusters suspended from holes through lobes and rims of ears, and through a perforation in the nasal septum. Pendants of abalone shell were more popular in historic times when the richly colored shells from the southern California coast were brought in by traders, than prehistorically when only the thin pallid local shells were available. Traditions tell of ornaments shaped of native placer copper, but these were rare. Traders introduced bracelets and neckrings of iron and copper, and in recent times gold and silver bracelets engraved with crest designs in typical northern art style were made by Indian artists.

An ornament of limited distribution was the women's labret, an elliptical object of wood or bone, grooved like a pulley around its edge, and worn in a slit cut through the lower lip. Small labrets were worn at first, being replaced by successively larger ones, until an elderly woman of high rank could wear with comfort a labret nearly three inches long.

Tattooing was another widespread form of adornment, though variable in its application. It was most popular in the north, where youths and girls of high status were liberally decorated with crest designs. Indians of the Queen Charlotte Islands tattooed the entire bodies of young nobles. Southward, this decoration was used more sparingly. In the southern end of the area, the California-type women's chin tattoo was in common use.

Decorative face and body painting was not common for daily use, but on festive occasions it was liberally used, especially in designs symbolic of crests. Northerly groups made use of small stamps to apply repeat patterns. One early source describes a type of painting done by sprinkling tiny plaques of mica over a well-greased ritual performer, so that he sparkled in the firelight. For everyday use, various blends of grease and paint were used as cosmetics on the face to prevent wind- and sunburn.

Head deformation was practiced by many divisions of the central part of the coast, with at least three regional styles, depending on the manner in which the infants' heads were padded and bound to modify their normal form.

## Musical Instruments

Music was an invariable accompaniment of social and religious occasions, as it was throughout most of native America. A song was certain to be among whatever gifts a guardian spirit might bestow; ancestral songs were important features of the ceremonial potlatch (see Chapter 3); dirges sung in the northern potlatches defined the solemn, memorial nature of the proceedings. Most singing had serious connotations, although there is no question that people found it pleasurable, especially the singing associated with certain games. Musical studies have not progressed to the point where areal styles can be discussed, but mention can be made of the types of instruments that accompanied the melody-carrying human voice.

### Drums

The simplest drum was an ordinary plank slightly raised off the ground on a pair of chocks to give it resonance, and played with sticks. Some groups decorated the drumsticks for the principal singers; others used plain hardwood sticks. In a few areas the roof planks served as drums. They were pounded with the upper ends of long slender poles. These drumsticks were equipped with clusters of deer hooves, so the instrument was really a combination drum and rattle.

A different type, found in the central and northern regions, was the box drum, made like the cooking and storage boxes. It differed from utilitarian boxes in proportions: the drum was long, high (or deep), and quite narrow. It was suspended from a roof beam for better resonance. The drummer sat beside it and played it with his fist, wrapped in a protective hank of shredded cedar bark.

The tambourine drum, made by stretching and lashing a piece of rawhide over a circular hoop, had a dual distribution. In the northern sector the instrument was associated with shamanistic (religious) performances. Elsewhere the tambourine was associated with a form of the hand game that appears to have been introduced on the coast in comparatively late historic times. The shamanistic drum was usually painted with a crest or a representation of the shaman's spirit power on the inside. Many of the game drums are painted on the wrong side, that is on the face of the drumhead, where drumming invariably flakes the paint and defaces the decoration.

### Rattles

Rattles of deer hooves, and sometimes of goat hooves, had a very wide distribution. They are typical of aboriginal western North America and thus not particularly distinctive of any one cultural division. However, on the coast they were probably used most by groups with the strongest affiliations to the interior.

Wooden rattles were common. They were usually made of the tractable alder wood, carved in two pieces, which were neatly fitted together to form the container for pebbles. A variety of representative and globular shapes were used by the chiefs, shamans, and dancers.

Circlets of withes, sometimes singly, sometimes concentrically, were used to suspend jinglers of deer hooves, puffin beaks, bits of carved bone, or in a slightly variant form, pecten shells. Rattles of this type were northern in distribution, except for the pecten-shell form, which was associated with one type of masked dancer in the Gulf of Georgia region.

Other objects that might be classed roughly as rattles were dance aprons, half-leggings, anklets, and armbands with attached jinglers that sounded with the movements of the dancer. Another similar device was a split-stick clapper associated with one of the Dancing Societies.

The bullroarer, a flat stick whirled on a string so that it made a booming noise, was another sound-effects instrument of the Dancing Societies.

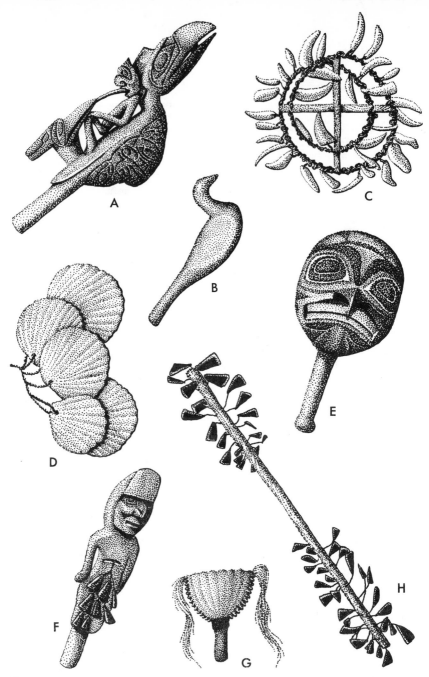

Rattles. (a) Northern Raven rattle. (b) Northern chief's rattle. (c) Northern withe-ring rattle with pendants of puffin beaks, deer hooves, animal teeth, and shells. (d) Pecten-shell rattle. (e) Northern globular rattle. (f) Coast Salish spirit rattle with deer or elk hooves. (g) Nootkan baleen rattle. (h) Plain deer-hoof rattle.

### Wind Instruments

Wind instruments were used for sound effects in the Dancing Society performances, but not for musical accompaniment. Whistles of great variety, from small ones that could be concealed in the mouth to great trumpetlike wooden "horns," were used to represent the voices of various supernatural beings. Some were simple and reedless; others had reeds in the mouthpieces. Most were single, but some were double, to give two tones. Apparently the mechanics of their operation was well enough understood so that they could be constructed to produce any tone desired, but they were not used to carry melodies nor to accompany songs.

The only other wind instruments were a deer call among northern groups, this not surely aboriginal, and a simple bird-bone flute in the southern extreme. This flute was the only instrument in the area on which melodies could be played and which was used purely for entertainment.

### Tobacco

The area as a whole was not part of the widespread North American distribution of tobacco smoking. Only at the southern end was smoking in vogue. There, tubular pipes of wood with inset stone bowls, or entirely of stone, were used to smoke the fragrant leaves collected from plantings in tiny clearings in the brush on sunny hillsides. While smoking was unknown in the rest of the area, a tobacco, probably a true *Nicotiana* was grown by some of the northernmost groups, and, mixed with lime, was chewed by all northerners.

# CHAPTER 3

# Social and Political Organization

## SOCIAL ORGANIZATION

The basic social unit of North Pacific Coast civilization was a group of people defined according to a recognized principle of kinship and associated with geographical locality; the guiding themes of social organization were hereditary transmission of status and privilege, with stress on material wealth. The autonomous local kin group was organized by matrilineal, patrilineal, or bilateral reckoning of descent. These three differing systems had mutually exclusive geographical distributions.

In the northern portion of the area the regulating principle was matrilineal, that is, formal stress on kinship ties traced through the female line. Thus, the northern social units were composed of nuclei of men who lived in the same locality and whose mothers were matrilineally related. These men's wives and young children lived with them and functioned with the group in daily life, but socially were not "members" of the group. Definition of these groups was fortified by systems of matrilineal clan organization in which the maternal descent groups were named and given totemic associations, and complicated by traditional genealogies that purported to trace relationships (matrilineally) between the local groups. In the central portion, the kinship principle was most broadly interpreted: while there was a slight preference for paternal descent, reckoning was really bilateral, so that the local groups were composed of men related to each other either maternally or paternally. In the south, patrilineal reckoning of descent was stressed, although without any formal organization into patrilineal clans.

The localized groups of kin defined who lived together, worked together, and who jointly considered themselves exclusive owners of the tracts from which food and other prime materials were obtained. The local group owned not only lands and their produce but all other forms of wealth: material treasures and intangible rights usually referred to as "privileges"—names for persons, houses, canoes, houseposts, and even for dogs and slaves; crests carved or painted on objects belonging to the group or one of its members; dances, songs, ritual performances, secret procedures and medicines, and a host of other things. Furthermore, the local group functioned in the major ceremonials in which wealth and privileges were used. Politically, too, the local group was autonomous, having its own "chief," administering its own justice, waging war, and making peace. Another distinguishing mark was the name: the traditional history of each group accounted for its name and all rights and privileges belonging to the unit.

## Social Divisions

The members of a local group were divided into the categories of "privileged ones" (chiefs or nobles) and commoners. There was also a class of slaves who were chattels, not really members of the group. In addition to the term usually translated as "chief" or "noble," many coastal languages had a special title for the highest-ranking member of the group. Membership in the division of nobles and that of commoners was hereditary.

It is not accurate to speak of "caste" or "class" in referring to this ranking. Within the nobility there was no uniformity of status, and the same was true of commoners. Rather, each individual occupied a unique position in a graded scale from highest to lowest; no two persons were exactly the same in rank, excepting the slaves who must be discussed apart. The precise place held by an individual, like his membership in the general group of nobles or commoners, derived from birth. The determining principle was primogeniture or its matrilineal equivalent. Highest of the high was the eldest scion of a line of eldest sons (in matrilineal reckoning groups, the eldest son of a line of eldest daughters). Thus, sons of a high chief were not regarded as equals. The eldest brother was of highest rank, but the youngest was in many respects little better than a commoner. However, courtesy required him to be addressed as a noble, because he might someday inherit his brother's position. Since kinship units were not large, each person's place in the social scale was easily known.

On state and festive occasions differences in rank were most noticeable, for those of noble birth wore the finest garb and played the most spectacular roles. But even in routine daily life those of high degree were distinguished by their behavior and by the treatment they received from their fellows. In the large multifamily dwellings typical of the area, the highest-ranking individual and his immediate family occupied a special portion of the house, usually along the rear wall. Other nobility were assigned desirable spaces, while commoners occupied the less comfortable places. The special terms for "noble," "nobleman's wife," "noble child," were customarily used in address, and other marks of deference were accorded the highborn.

The man of high rank usually directed activities in which large groups participated, for example the construction of a weir at an important fishing place; commoners obeyed. Among divisions that hunted whales, only the man of highest rank could own the whaling gear, direct the expedition, and wield the harpoon. However, the highborn were not master carvers or canoemakers, esteemed as those occupations were. In daily dress differences between nobility and plebians were signalized by special articles of clothing and ornament reserved for the wellborn, such as the "chiefs' hats," necklaces, and ear pendants.

In short, the concept of social rank was an active functional principle that regulated a great part of social behavior. In addition, the bonds of kinship were very strong. The noble of highest rank and the lowliest commoner of each group were relatives and recognized each other as kinsmen. Consequently, the two principles of societal organization—social rank and kinship—did not conflict, but modified each other. While the concept of hereditary rank was of great importance, it did not produce a sharply defined class or caste of aristocrats who exploited and oppressed those of lowly birth, as has occurred in other areas where similar social concepts have developed. The North Pacific Coast chief or noble did not grind the faces of the lowborn of his social unit, because they were not his subjects or his serfs: they were his kinsmen, and therefore entitled to special consideration. They were also shareholders in the group's resources and goods.

## The Function of Wealth

A host of objects were regarded as valuables because of their rarity. These included plaques hammered out of placer copper, pelts of sea otter and marmot, wool of the mountain goat and robes woven of this wool, such as those called "Chilkat blankets," and rare shells, particularly *Dentalium pretiosum*. (These shells are the only valuable that can be compared with money and then only in the southern part of the area, distant from the source of supply, where the slender tapered creamy-white shells were minutely graded into sizes with fixed standards of value.) These kinds of wealth are not novel in human culture, although the precise objects of value may have been unique. There are few, if any, parts of the world where objects or materials of some sort, usually rare in nature or difficult to obtain, have not been treasured by local peoples. Peculiarly shaped boars' tusks, pearls, bits of jade, bezoar stones, and similar items have been wealth objects to some human groups at times in their history, though merely curios to other peoples. Distinctive of North Pacific Coast culture is the inclusion of natural resources as items of wealth—the foodstuffs, the materials for dress, shelter, and transport, and the places from which these things were obtained. Each group regarded the areas it utilized as the exclusive property of the group. Group members used habitation sites, fishing grounds, clam beaches, hunting and berrying grounds, forest areas where timber and bark were obtained, through right; outsiders entered by invitation or in trespass. Bounds were defined by natural landmarks with a precision remarkable for people with no surveying equipment.

Even salvage rights along the beaches were subject to ownership deriving from ownership of the land.

Human labor, too, was regarded as a resource to a certain extent, and craftsmen, such as carvers, canoemakers, and weavers of Chilkat blankets, were remunerated for their labor. The products they made were also counted as valuables. Part of the value set on slaves, who themselves formed a category of wealth goods, derived from the labor they performed.

Intercultural comparisons are useful for purposes of explanation, but they must be interpreted with care. Close examination of two cultures may reveal similarities, but if the similarities are superficial, masking different basic concepts and functions, the comparison may be misleading. The wealth complex in North Pacific Coast culture and that of modern Western society appear broadly similar. In both cases wealth and prestige are closely correlated: in both cases wealth and its acquisition occupy a large share of men's thoughts. There, however, the similarities end. Among the Indians of the North Pacific Coast the social units—localized kin groups—were the owners of wealth, not individuals. An individual could regard himself as the owner of personal valuables such as robes and canoes, but major riches such as the lands, houses, and important wealth tokens were group property. Even the objects possessed by the individual were made available to the group in case of necessity. Though the highest-ranking member of each group spoke of himself, or was spoken of by others, as the "owner" of his group's house or houses, its real estate, and most of its treasures, he was the administrator of his group's possessions, not an individual owner.

The prime purpose of Indian wealth was display and ostentatious consumption to demonstrate prosperity and power to others, thus enhancing the local group's prestige. The maximum expression of this use was to give away or destroy quantities of valuables. Wealth at times was used in transactions of the sort presently regarded as commercial. For example, an Indian who had a surplus of olachen grease and an old dilapidated canoe might exchange grease for a new canoe. Without a fixed scale of values, it would be difficult to say whether he made a profit on the transaction, but he satisfied his need of a canoe and at the same time a need of the canoemaker who did not have access to olachen-fishing grounds. If he "bought" the canoe with a copper or with strings of dentalium shells (for which he had previously traded olachen grease), he likewise satisfied needs and distributed surpluses of consumer goods.

Slaves were "sold," that is bartered, for other forms of riches, and among some groups there was the concept of loans, but such business operations were not an end in themselves. Profits were accumulated for the sole purpose of publicly giving them away or destroying them, to prove to envious or reluctantly admiring neighbors that the group was rich enough to be disdainful of vast wealth.

Indians considered the necessities of life—items of food and clothing —as among their wealth goods, but only insofar as they were surpluses. The North Pacific Coast wealth complex represented a unique response to a bountiful environment, which the Indians exploited so efficiently that they produced far more than they could consume in a normal manner. The manipulation of the surpluses is the phenomenon that illustrates the importance of wealth as a social force, integrated to the structure of native society, and providing motivations to social life. In the festivities in which the wealth was utilized, all kinsmen of the group participated. Thus a display of group wealth served as a unifying force in social life, helping as did the kinship ties to contravene any tendencies toward splitting of interest that the system of hereditarily graded statuses might have fostered.

## Slavery

In the Indian view slaves were not members of the society but were outsiders, reduced to the level of chattels. The principal source of slaves was capture in warfare, although in the southern portion inability to pay damages for some offense could be resolved by giving a person into slavery. Captives were often taken in wars between neighboring groups, but their term of slavery was brief, for they were ordinarily ransomed by their kin group. The condition of slavery was regarded as a disgrace to the captives and to their relatives, who promptly offered ransom through neutral intermediaries. There was little haggling over the price. Offers were liberal so foes could not make sneering comments that the captive's kin regarded him as of little value or that the kinship group was a poverty-stricken lot. The painful incident was not forgotten, and worst of all, provided a theme for bitter taunts, which were even more insulting if the slave had been ransomed in a niggardly fashion. Larger amounts were expected and offered in behalf of a person of high rank. In addition, "face-saving" performances involved considerable expenditures to restore the ransomed slave to his former status and to remove the stigma of his disgrace.

Slavery was regarded as shameful to the hapless captive and his people because he had been reduced to the level of a chattel, a thing of less than human status. There was no implication that cowardice or stupidity or other defect of character were involved, because usually only women and children, who were not expected to defend themselves against armed warriors, were taken as slaves. Adult males who by fortunes of war were captured alive usually were mercilessly butchered on the war party's return home. It was recognized that a grown man held as a slave would sooner or later find the opportunity to avenge himself or to escape.

Slaves whose sad plight continued were those captured on raids to places so distant that kin might never know who the captors were. The victims might be kept for many years. They were treated kindly or maltreated at the owner's whim, killed, given away as a grand gesture, or sold. Possession of slaves was prestigeful since it implied success at war or great wealth; to sacrifice a slave on a formal occasion demonstrated a splendid disregard of wealth that only the richest and mightiest could indulge.

It is difficult to estimate the slave population of the area, but it was certainly never very large, for slave mortality was high. Slaves' economic utility was negligible. They gathered firewood, dug clams, and fished, but so did their masters. There is one instance on record of all survivors of a harried tribelet of interior Indians (Tahltan) surrendering and becoming slaves to a coastal group (Niska). Insofar as they could, they learned the language and adopted the customs of their captors over the years, and with the coming of the missionaries were set free. Their descendants live among the former owners to this day, but slave origin is told only in whispered confidence or in anger, for the feeling persists that being a slave was shameful.

## Marriage

Marriage was a social phenomenon in the maximum sense of the phrase, since unions were arranged in accordance with the system of rank, involved demonstrations of wealth, and determined the social status of the offspring. It was a matter of group concern, not of personal preference, because the interests of two groups of kin converged on the couple and on the children to be born. Consequently, marriage is discussed here in connection with social organization rather than as an aspect of the life cycle of the individual.

It was universally regarded as desirable that mates should be as nearly equivalent in rank as possible, which meant that children would inherit the same status, modified only by the principle of primogeniture. Even though children technically inherited status, titles, and so on from only one parent, depending on which line of descent was formally recognized, rank of the other parent inevitably clouded their social position, when, as happened rarely, mother and father were of markedly different status. Thus it was deemed proper for those of high rank to marry persons of high rank, those of intermediate status to marry equivalents, for commoners to seek mates of their own level, and it was unthinkable for a free person of any status to marry a slave.

Wealth played a prominent part in marriage in the form of the bride price, universally required to establish a legal and proper union. The amount given in each case depended on the rank of the principals; more was expected and given for a bride of high rank than for one of low, and in the case of commoners the bride price might be small; but some wealth was always transferred. However, the transfer did not imply that the bride was sold like a chattel or a slave. Her group maintained their interest in her welfare and would intercede for her if she were mistreated. There was a clear distinction between the transfer of wealth connected with acquiring a bride and ordinary buying and selling. In all the languages separate terms were used for the two types of operation.

Among many groups the family of a girl of high rank was under obligation to make a larger return gift to the groom (or to the head of his group) than the value of the bride price. In other words, there was no profit in "selling" a daughter, but by European reckoning, a net loss. The gain was in the prestige accruing to the two groups from the demonstration of their wealth. On the occasion of the "repayment" of the bride price the girl's group often gave privileges—names or crests—to the groom for the couple's offspring, in effect a matrilineal transmission of property in an otherwise patrilineal system.

Both the bride price and the repayment were not to be hoarded by the recipients, but had to be used for potlatching, to make public announcement of the union and of the privileges that had been transferred. Details differed in different parts of the area, but invariably the arrangements were made by intermediaries in very formal fashion. Similarly, the delivery of the bride to her husband and his group was a formal ceremony, accompanied by feasting, and in unions of persons of very high status, elaborate festivities. The kinship structure also came into play in marriage of the lowborn: they could count on their group, through their kinsman the chief, to come to their aid with resources for a modest bride price and at least a minor feast.

It was prestigeful for a chief or chief's heir to seek as wife the daughter of the chief of a distant group, thus implying that none of the immediate neighbor chiefs was high enough in rank. Also for prestige reasons a man of high status might have a number of wives, demonstrating thereby his wealth, since for each he would have paid an exaggerated bride price. Polygyny was not, however, an exclusive prerogative of chiefs. Lesser men might have more than one wife if they wished, although not many did. Among clans of matrilineal organization, the rule of exogamy with reference to either the phratry or the moiety put limitations on choice of spouses. Among these same divisions preferential mating, that is marriage to certain relatives who were at the same time outside the circle proscribed by the exogamic rule, was considered desirable.

For the groups composing one linguistic division—the Bella Coola—an early writer reported endogamy. More rigorous investigation has demonstrated that the so-called endogamy was nothing more than the notion that occasionally it was advantageous to arrange a marriage between distantly related persons to renew the intergroup bonds created by former unions. This idea was occasionally expressed by most other groups who lacked formal clan systems; nowhere was it an invariable rule, nor a common practice, but rather a factor that might be involved under certain circumstances in choosing a mate.

## The Potlatch

The word "potlatch" comes from Chinook Jargon, a widespread trade language, and means simply "giving," in the sense of giving a gift. In each native language there were special terms to designate the institution. The potlatch was common to all groups except those at the southern extreme, and while there were numerous minor differences in details, the basic pattern of the potlatch and its function were uniform.

A potlatch was a ceremonial given by a chief and his group, as hosts, to guests composed of another chief or chiefs with their respective groups, at which the guests were given wealth goods. Essential to a potlatch was the guest-host relation, although the exact composition of the groups might vary. Properly, the local group was the basic unit, both as host group and guest group, but sometimes larger units were involved. Indians distinguished between affairs at which only food was given, to be eaten immediately and to be carried home by the guests, and those at which other forms of goods were distributed. The former may be called "feasts," the latter, "potlatches." The distinction refers to the main event, and a potlatch usually included at least some preliminary feasting.

The overt purpose of both feast and potlatch was the announcement of an event of social significance: marriage of an important person, birth of a potential heir to one of the group's titles, crests, and high statuses, inheritance and formal assumption of one of these titles or crests and its corresponding position, and rescue or ransom and restoration to free status of a war captive. These announcements were not made perfunctorily. When a title was concerned, the announcement included an account of its origin, how it had been acquired by an ancestor, whether bestowed by a supernatural being or captured in warfare, how it had been transmitted down the family line to the person on whom it was being bestowed. Much of the legendary history of the group was recited to prove the right to use the name or privilege. Then the gifts were distributed in the name of the recipient of the title or crest. The first and largest gift went to the highest-ranking guest, the second and next largest to the second in precedence, and so on down the line. Recital of the history of the privilege and the distribution of wealth served to validate its use. The guests were witnesses to the fact that the privilege was rightfully owned and rightfully transmitted to its new bearer. This sanction was the essence of the potlatch and the prime purpose of the wealth. The effect of the procedure may be compared to that of notarizing a document or of registering a deed.

A person might be recognized as the only proper heir to the highest-ranking status, but until a potlatch had been given at which he formally claimed the position and its privileges, he had no right to use them. Nor was he entitled to the deference and honors of the status. For example, he was not invited to potlatches of others nor given gifts. The myriad of rights in North Pacific Coast culture had to be validated in this manner. The rights included those to names and titles, not only names of persons but traditionally owned names for houses and other property, the right to use specific masks and symbols in rituals, the right to perform the rituals themselves, to use carvings, feast dishes, and the ownership of places of economic and ritual importance. Feasts had a similar function. It was usual to announce to guests, for example, that they were invited to eat sockeye salmon from such-and-such a stream, which had been discovered, given to, or captured in war by an ancestor and transmitted to the incumbent head of the group. The public announcement and tacit recognition of the fact by the guest group, so to speak, legalized the claim.

### The Formalities of the Potlatch

Actual procedure of the potlatch was both complex and highly formal. The first step after plans and preparations was the dispatching of an invitation party to the village of the guests. This party was ceremoniously treated, and was given a feast where they could deliver the invitation orally to the assembled group, setting the date on which the guests would be expected. If the villages were distant and the weather uncertain, guests usually arrived by canoeloads a day or two ahead of time and camped nearby or were quartered informally among the hosts, but if so, on the appointed day they reembarked to make a mass arrival. If there were preliminary feasts or ceremonials, these were begun; if not, the guests were ushered into the potlatch house.

Among many groups, guests of high rank were called in order of precedence, each in turn being escorted by ushers to a place of honor corresponding to his rank. When more than one group of guests had been invited, an elaborate protocol had to be worked out, the chief of the highest-ranking group being seated first, and chief of the second-highest group next, then that of the third group, and so on. Then those of second rank were seated. The problem was as complex as that of seating admirals of various navies at a formal banquet in Washington. Men of lower rank and commoners were seated as a group. Just where the line was drawn between the guests individually seated and the rest depended partly on local custom and partly on the elaborateness of the potlatch. When large amounts of riches were to be distributed, more guests were individually seated than at small-scale distributions. Speeches of welcome were made and replied to, supplementing those made on the formal arrival. Men thoroughly versed in the etiquette of the potlatch, the precedence order of the guests, and the family traditions, did the speechmaking for many chiefs, just as researchers and writers assist modern public figures in preparing their public addresses.

The next step was usually the display of crests and performance of dances and songs, not just for entertainment but because these referred to the privileges about to be bestowed. In the northern portion of the area, where major potlatches were strongly commemorative, revolving about the theme of the death of a chief and the inheritance of his title and status, dirges were sung and offerings to the deceased chief and his predecessors were made by burning food and other articles. The new holder of the title was presented, the gifts were distributed, the quantity or nature of each gift was announced by the speaker, and the tallymen busily counted bundles of mnemonic sticks to keep accounts of the presents and the recipients. (Recently chiefs have used secretaries, literate young men with notebooks and fountain pens, instead of the prehistoric tallyman.) Thanks were given by the recipient of each gift, and at the conclusion of the distribution the ranking guest or his speaker made a speech of thanks for all his group not only for the gifts, but for having been shown the prized privileges and having had the new holder of the privileges presented to them.

The foregoing is a synthesized outline of typical potlatch procedure, but there were numerous local differences in detail. For example, groups of the central portion normally potlatched outdoors, rather than in a house. Some Coast Salish were fond of the "scramble" as a method of distributing goods to commoners, but never to chiefs. Goat-wool robes were torn into strips that were tossed into the crowd rather than distributed in more orderly fashion, and contests of various sorts were part of the preliminary entertainment during a potlatch given on the occasion of a marriage. A common form of these contests consisted in a scramble for a wooden ball; the winner was given a prize, apart from the gift he might receive in the formal distribution of presents.

The minor deviations from the basic pattern do not obscure the fact that the potlatch was a formal function with a rigid etiquette, given for a serious purpose, that of validating the assumption of hereditary rights and thereby the whole system of rank. It also validated the social rank of the guest group, whose social precedence was recognized in the seating arrangements, in the use of guests' formal titles, and in the order in which the gifts were given. Reciprocity was expressed in this aspect of the institution. When the roles were reversed and the guests in their turn potlatched, they demonstrated their approval of the exhosts' claims by using the titles they had witnessed and by recognizing the order of rank associated with these titles.

Another function of the potlatch is its effect as a force contributing to the social solidarity of the basic social unit, the extended family-local group, which was also the potlatch unit, whether as host or guest. In some areas there were confederations of local groups into "tribes," although the constituent local groups retained their identity and many of their functions. These tribes occasionally acted as units in potlatch-ing, but this fact does not negate the primary importance of the local group.

The chief of the group was the nominal host and played the most prominent single role because of his position as administrator of the extended family's properties. However, everyone recognized that the whole group—nobles and commoners, whether closely or distantly related to the chief—were hosts. The entire host group assembled on the beach to greet the guests on their formal arrival. All assisted in the preparations, including the assembling of the goods for the distribution. All were identified with their group during the proceedings, if not as stellar performers, as speakers, tallykeepers, ushers, dancers, or singers.

During the potlatch, individuals of lesser rank, including commoners, also received names or other privileges from the group store according to their status. The contributions of parents (of maternal uncles in matrilineal societies) sponsoring low-rank recipients of privileges were often announced, further emphasizing identification as group members. The guests similarly were invited as members of their social unit and treated as a group even though the amount of the potlatch goods given to a commoner guest might be inconsequential. In short, at a potlatch every member of both host and guest groups participated with his social unit and thereby publicly identified himself as a member of it.

Some ethnographic literature on the economics of the potlatch, unfortunately, has confused the potlatch with two other phenomena: the loans at interest and the spectacular rivalry potlatch. For example, it has been asserted that among the Southern Kwakiutl every potlatch gift had to be returned at 100 percent interest. According to this interpretation, if Chief A invited ten other chiefs—B, C, D, E, F, G, H, I, J, and K—to a potlatch at which he presented each with 100 cheap trade blankets, he would thus distribute 1,000 blankets. Chiefs B, C, D, and so forth would be obligated, when they potlatched, to invite Chief A and give him 200 blankets in return. This would mean that if all ten chiefs were punctilious, A would eventually receive 2,000 blankets. But, according to this erroneous view, the obligation did not stop here; it was endless, a sort of commercial chain letter. Chief A would have to repay each of the 200 gifts at 100 percent interest, or in other words to distribute ten gifts of 400, or 4,000 blankets. It is unnecessary to continue this example to the 64,000-blanket level. It is evident that a system in which debts increased endlessly by geometric progression is impossible.

In addition to the fact that a single sequence of potlatches would soon involve tremendous amounts of valuables, as illustrated, Chief A would be invited to other potlatches besides those of B to K, and theoretically each would result in a similar progression. It has been suggested that the quantities of blankets were fictitious, the whole system operating on credit, but there are accounts of eyewitnesses who observed bales of trade blankets and other valuables being distributed.

Internal evidence from detailed descriptions of potlatches and data from informants of groups who potlatched until recent days agree that the loans at interest were quite apart from the potlatch gifts. The amount of each potlatch gift had no relation to any previous gift, except in the general sense that a potlatch gift should be adequate, not niggardly. The amount given each guest depended upon the total amount distributed, modified by the relative rank of the recipient. Guests of noble rank who participated in the potlatch were expected sooner or later to potlatch, "returning" the gifts they had received in much the same way that a modern host expects his dinner invitations to be "returned." There was no requirement that each successive distribution had to be twice as large as the preceding one, or in any exact relation to previous potlatch gifts. Validation of social rank, through formally assuming hereditary privileges, was the purpose of the institution.

It is patent that the potlatch pattern before the introduction of trade goods differed from the pattern after white contact, in frequency and splendor but not in function. During the period for which fullest ethnographic data are available, trade blankets were introduced mainly by Hudson's Bay Company and sold for $1.50 apiece. They became almost an equivalent of currency and were the principal articles distributed in potlatches, where they were used by the hundreds. Before the advent of bales of blankets and other mass-produced trade articles, native wealth was used. These items were scarce, for one of several possible reasons. They were rare in nature, like the nuggets of pure copper from which "coppers" were made. Or they were a long time in the making, like the laboriously manufactured canoes and robes. Or they were difficult to take, like the peltries of the shy sea otter and the marmot. Consequently, even a populous and industrious group would need years to assemble enough wealth articles for a potlatch. Well-informed Indians from groups famous in recent times for their numerous and opulent potlatches often told me of the traditional statement that in prewhite times feasts were comon, but potlatches were infrequent. This does not mean that the potlach is merely an historical phenomenon. It means that the abundance of trade goods gave a new exuberance to the potlatch in the distribution of spectacular quantities of articles. However, even in the epoch of the plethora of imported goods, the Tlingit, Haida, and Tsimshian of the northern part of the area preserved an aspect of the ancient pattern. Of their numerous potlatches the only one considered major was on the death of the chief to honor his memory and to transmit his status and position to his heir. Thus, each chief gave only one major potlatch in his career— that in which he formally assumed his title. If, as seems reasonable, in aboriginal times potlatches were infrequent and could utilize only a relatively limited store of wealth goods, no endless chain of double repayment could have prevailed.

### The Potlatch and Loans at Interest

In spite of its limited practice, the loan at interest is another factor contributing to the misunderstanding of the operation of the potlatch. Simple loans had a somewhat wider distribution. In a number of groups kinsmen *outside* the social unit of the potlatch might lend valuables for the distribution. These loans were repaid, after an indefinite period, in the amount given. Some informants aver that it was in good taste to return a little more than the amount of the original loan to demonstrate gratitude and solvency, but there was no fixed rate of increase. However, loans at interest were strictly commercial transactions, the rate being agreed upon at the time of the loan. The ruinous 100 percent rate was usual for a long-term loan, that is, for several years. Loans for shorter periods called for lower, but still usurious rates: 50 percent for a year or so, and 20 to 25 percent for a few months.

The only connection between these loans and the potlatch was that a creditor could demand repayment of principal and interest only when he was about to give a potlatch, in other words, when he needed the surplus. There are no exact data on the origin of the custom, but there is reason to suspect it may not be aboriginal in origin, particularly because of the differential in rates according to duration of the loan. It is probably significant that loans at interest consisted of trade blankets or money, not of aboriginal value items.

### The Rivalry Potlatch

The spectacular rivalry potlatches came to a peak in the latter decades of the nineteenth century and the opening years of the twentieth. In these affairs, great quantities of valuables were given away or destroyed—coppers were broken, canoes were smashed, money was thrown in the fire, and in the days before the white man's law was enforced, slaves were slain—all to humiliate a rival. The serene, superpolite, and occasionally jovial air of the common potlatch was replaced by an atmosphere of bitterness. Insults were flung and guests were made uncomfortable, as when olachen oil was poured on the fire both to destroy the oil and to force the guests to abandon their seats near it.

Competition between two men for a specific status resulted in the rivalry potlatch. It involved two rivals who were potential heirs for a position, for primacy in the protocol or precedence, or for a particular title with its attendant privileges and prerogatives. First, one would give a potlatch to announce his claims, more or less in the normal manner. Then, the rival would potlatch to the same group of guests, or to additional groups as well. He would deny and belittle the claims of his rival and emphasize his own claims to the status. The first claimant was obliged thereby to give another potlatch to reiterate his pretensions, the challenger replied in kind, and the competition went on and on. Each rival attempted to outdo his opponent's latest effort, giving away and destroying more wealth to demonstrate his economic superiority. The contests were not merely to see which rival had the most wealth; the specific goal was to obtain validation of the claim to the rights in question. The motive for outdoing the rival was to mold the opinion of the chiefs whose places in the potlatch were recognized without dispute, for they were the court of final appeal who recognized or disregarded a claim.

A hypothetical example, assuming alphabetical Indians A to K, may clarify the reasoning. Let us assume that A and B were distant relatives of Chief X who died without direct heirs, that is, brothers or sons. Both A and B desired the position, which included the highest rank among the chiefs who assembled in the potlatch as demonstrated by the right to receive the first gift. Both potlatched, claiming the inheritance, before Chiefs C to K. After a time, Chief G gave a potlatch at which he had claimant B seated in the contested place, addressed him by the title of the deceased X, and gave him the first gift. Claimant A might protest by giving away or destroying valuables, and continue his competition with B. If he did so, however, he invited conflict with Chief G. G could either assist B in assembling potlatch valuables to reassert his claims or himself potlatch again, repeating his approval of B's claim. If the other chiefs supported G's stand, either at once or over a period of time as they gave potlatches, it became useless for A to continue his efforts to gain the title.

If one of the contestants went bankrupt, that is, could not assemble enough riches to equal or surpass the last effort of his opponent, he could no longer press his claim, losing it by default. The claim of the winner was regarded as justified, as in medieval Europe the victor in trial by combat was regarded to have proved his case. This special variety of potlatch was limited in distribution, and its origins are not known. However, several cultural and culture-historical factors contributed to its development.

Among groups that practiced the potlatch, there was also the face-saving presentation, which took place after any public indignity involving a person of high status. If he tripped and fell on a formal occasion, if he were shown to an inferior seat at a feast or potlatch, or if he were captured in war, his only recourse was to wipe away the affront by public announcement of his title and status and by giving away valuables. The elaborateness of the gift giving depended on the circumstances of the loss of dignity: if they were regarded as accidental, due to natural causes, a brief speech and a small gift were adequate to dispose of the matter. However, a deliberate insult—and a clumsy fall in public might be the result of magical machinations by persons of ill will—required a larger distribution of wealth or a full-dress potlatch. This was the *raison-d'être* for the potlatch on the occasion of the ransom or escape of a war captive. His liberation from slavery was celebrated by a reaffirmation of his status and titles, accompanied by a distribution of wealth. Then, as after all face-saving procedures, the disgrace was considered removed and was never again to be mentioned. The rivalry potlatch can be regarded as an application of the face-saving technique: it was the standard procedure when dignity had been injured, in this case, when claim to a status had been challenged.

A variant of the rivalry potlatch involved the status of groups rather than that of individuals. The rivalry might develop when two groups were invited to an occasion where previous custom dictated only one guest group be invited. The addition of guests might be associated with increase in prosperity, as when the introduction of trade goods in abundance stimulated an increase in frequency and scale of potlatching. Inviting new groups immediately raised questions of precedence that could well lead to conflicting claims.

Another factor contributed to rivalry: the confederation of several neighboring local groups into something approaching tribal organization, in which the originally autonomous local groups, although retaining their identities and most of their properties and rights, united in a common village during the winter season. In every such "tribe," the constituent local groups and their chiefs came to be ranked in a graded series, first, second, third, and so forth. Furthermore, there were mergers of tribes into still larger loose confederacies in which all local groups and chiefs were assigned places in a single precedence scale. Such mergers were patently made to order to produce conflict situations and competitive claims. The rivalry potlatch reached its maximum at two sites of early Hudson's Bay Company trading posts, where a number of tribes came to assemble for winter residence.

A third factor that set the stage for bitter rivalries was the sharp decrease in Indian population during the nineteenth century. Decrease was due chiefly to epidemics of diseases such as smallpox and venereal infections, introduced by Europeans, and to the greater efficiency of native warfare following the introduction of firearms. As a result, when the holder of an important title died, there was often no direct heir according to the rules of succession—younger brother, or son, or sister's son among matrilineal groups—and two distant relatives might emerge as competitors for the prestigeful inheritance. It would have been considered ridiculous for a distant kinsman (second or third cousin) to try to assert priority of right over a younger brother or a son. But when the only claimants were both about equally distant genealogically, they became potential rivals. The competitive potlatch afforded them a technique for the resolution of their conflict.

Nearly all specific accounts of potlatch rivalries fall into one of two conflict situations: the attempt to establish or to alter the order of precedence of groups, and the attempt to claim a vacant title and status. One additional category must be noted—the feigned rivalry. Where the rivalry potlatch was common, the people apparently enjoyed the excitement of its bickering, lavish giving, destruction of wealth, and constant threat of open violence. Hence, now and then two chiefs planning to potlatch would arrange in secret to pretend conflict. A common pretext was to allege that their ancestors had been rivals. They gave their potlatches with all the apparent furor and anger that characterized true rivalry, but carefully controlled the spectacles to come out a draw, thus entertaining the public and damaging no one's prestige. On the other hand, many coastal divisions who did not practice the rivalry potlatch regarded such affairs, true or feigned, as ridiculous or in bad taste, not in keeping with the dignified formality of the normal potlatch.

## Coppers

Important items in the potlatch were plaques called "coppers." Placer copper was beaten into a plaque, the upper portion resembling in outline the keystone of an arch, the lower portion a rectangle. The two forms were set apart by the horizontal element of a T-shaped ridge, the vertical stem of which bisected the rectangle. In examples of aboriginal manufacture, the T-shaped ridge is formed of solid metal; in recent specimens of mill-made sheet copper imported by white traders, the ridge is repoussé, visible on the back of the piece as a concavity. Coppers varied from about a foot and a half to three feet in length.

Something of a mystery surrounds the making of the aboriginal coppers. Apparently they came already shaped from the Copper River region, but such metallurgical skill seems beyond the scope of the peoples of that area. The possibility remains that they were archaeological pieces. As they were traded southward, many were decorated with engraving or shallow carving by artists of the northern portion of the coast, as the style of the design attests.

These objects were invariably related to the potlatch complex. When a copper was sold, the transaction had implications beyond that of an ordinary commercial deal in the inherent obligation to use the proceeds of the sale in a potlatch. Among northern groups, the coppers were displayed, then broken during the memorial potlatch for a deceased chief and the assumption of his position by the heir. The copper fragments, referred to as the "bones of the deceased," were given to high-ranking guests. The value of the coppers increased as they were traded from group to group southward, and at the southern margin of their distribution unbroken coppers attained great worth. The price was at least double that of the previous sale.

As coppers lost their association with mortuary rites, they became closely associated with marriage payments and were often given as part of the bride price and bride-price repayment: they were supposed to be sold to augment the wealth distributed in the potlatches made with the bride price and its repayment. In rivalry potlatches the objects were boastfully displayed, then hacked to pieces in order to compel the rival to sacrifice a copper of as great or greater value.

Individual coppers were named, and their histories were well known. In the 1880's when Canadian law made potlatching illegal, police authorities confiscated coppers and other ceremonial appurtenances, which were presented to the National Museum of Canada. However, the Indians regarded the confiscation as unjustified and continued to recognize Indian title to the wealth. Certain splendid specimens of coppers in the museum continued to figure in marriage presentations and potlatch transactions for many years. Particular items came to have fabulous value, for they were safe from the normal destiny of coppers: they could not be broken, but title to them continued to be transferable.

### Diversions

The list of games and pastimes of the area is very long indeed. Athletic contests were popular: wrestling, weight lifting, tugs-of-war, and footraces. (Canoe races are common in the modern American and Canadian festivals in the region, but they were probably not among the aboriginal sports.) Some variant of the widespread game of shinny was played by nearly every group; a level stretch of beach laid bare by spring ebb tides served as a playing field. The hoop-and-pole game was another native American diversion enjoyed by many coast Indians.

A form of the hand game was introduced relatively recently on the coast, spreading rapidly and attaining a vast popularity. This game was played with two pairs of bone cylinders, one of each pair marked, the other plain. Two players concealed the cylinders in their hands while their companions sang and drummed on a tambourine drum. The players tried to guess the positions of the unmarked pieces, of which there were four possibilities: both to the guesser's right, both to his left, both on the inside, or both on the outside. The game was usually called "lahal," and the accompanying songs "did not have words." They consisted of nonsense syllables, possibly because they were originally in an unfamiliar language. Until a few years ago elderly informants could recall the game's introduction. As best as can be estimated, the date of introduction was probably in the 1880's or early 1890's.

Before then, a variant of the hand game, usually referred to as the "many stick game," was played by some of the central and all of the northern divisions, and by groups at the extreme south. In this game a set of sticks consisted of a large number of decorated pieces and one to four unmarked ones, "aces" as some informants refer to them in English. For play, one ace and usually three decorated pieces were concealed in shredded cedar bark in pairs. The object was to guess the bundle containing the ace. There was no singing connected with this play, which was probably considerably older in the area than lahal. Another variant found in the region of the Strait of Georgia and western Washington used sets of wooden disks, which were concealed in shredded bark in two lots, one with and one without a marked disk.

It is not known why lahal replaced the earlier forms of the game, except in the extreme south. It seems dubious that the added feature of singing and drumming, although enjoyed, would account for its vogue. Perhaps the change in odds was the decisive factor. In the older forms with equal odds, a game for only a moderate number of points might seesaw back and forth almost indefinitely. In all these forms of the game, play was slowed down by the fact that only the holders of the pieces could win points. A successful guess won no point, but only the right to manipulate the pieces. The introduced lahal with its two-to-one odds against the guesser made it theoretically possible for a lucky team to tally the usual twenty or twenty-one points in a short time, which perhaps added zest to the play. However, even lahal is not a short game. The individual games I have watched usually took the greater part of the night to complete, and betting by both participants and spectators was heavy.

The hand games were for men. Women of most groups played dice games when they wanted to gamble. Four-piece sets of beaver incisors, each with one marked and one unmarked side, were the most common kind of dice used. Scoring depended on certain combinations of "heads" and "tails" that appeared when the dice were bounced off a basketry tray. The Nootkan-speaking groups resident along the seaward coast of Vancouver Island insist that their forebears had no gambling games until the recent introduction of the hand game and the women's beaver-tooth dice.

Other pastimes were varied. Attempting to make someone laugh by clowning was always enjoyed. Trying to coordinate awkward hand movements with the eyes closed was another. Cat's cradle was, like the others just described, a diversion that could be used indoors to while away a spell of bad weather. But the best indoor pastime was the telling of myths. North Pacific Coast mythology was very rich. Its characteristic tales of tricksters and buffoons, like Raven, Mink, Deer, and Snot-boy, were more entertaining than instructive, and their telling shortened many long rainy nights.

### Traditions

This is a convenient point at which to discuss the historical traditions typical of much of the area. The hereditary mode of transmission of wealth and privileges set a premium on genealogical history. Each local group, that is, each family line, had a traditional history, purporting to recount the origins of the family, its travels, wars, vicissitudes, and victories, all of which was embellishment of the really important facts related: which ancestor had obtained a given property or privilege, and how. Many stories of origin and supernatural experiences of ancestors were lifted intact from local mythology. An important group of the Southern Heiltsuk used the widespread Dog-husband tale as an origin account, claiming to be descended from the principals. To their neighbors the story was merely an entertaining yarn, to them it was a serious historical event. Other groups had more prosaic origins by their own telling: their ancestors were interior Indians who came down to the coast following a certain river.

The Indians did not differentiate between plausible and implausible incidents. All family histories were serious and believable. Unlike myths, histories were not told for amusement. Rather, they were carefully taught to noble children, and pertinent excerpts were recited on occasions when properties and privileges were claimed and displayed, that is, at potlatches.

Most ethnologists who have worked in the area concede a fair measure of validity to the nonfantastic portions for a number of reasons. First, many of the traditions are consistent with each other.

A number of Tlingit groups living in various parts of southeast Alaska refer to themselves as "People from Ganax," and all these groups claim to be related. The origin traditions of all include the origin of the ancestral group who settled at Ganax, prospered, and increased until one by one the daughter lineages split off and went their separate ways. All of the traditions are consistent in relating which subdivision split off first, and the order of the others. The principal crests of all these groups are the same. The major outlines of these stories are several mutually corroborating versions of the same story.

As an instance of slightly different type, the groups of the lower Skeena River had three Dancing Societies in former times: "The Shamans," "Those-who-descend-from-the-heavens," and the "Nutlam." These people assert, in their traditions of these ceremonials, that they acquired all three Dancing Societies from their neighbors to the southward. Internal evidence corroborates these statements. The Dancing Societies are less important among the lower Skeena groups, and the various orders are less complete than among their southern neighbors. Furthermore, the names of the dancers and of many objects of these ceremonials are in the language of the southern neighbors, none in the tongue of the peoples of the Skeena.

Now and then the ethnologist senses a need to reinterpret a traditional episode. The Haisla living at the heads of Douglas Channel and Gardner Canal have traditions that long ago their ancestors came overland from Rivers Inlet and settled the localities occupied by their descendants ever since. Not long after the pioneer settlement, the traditions continue, a wandering clan of Skeena River people came along, and were generously invited to settle among the Rivers Inlet people. However, the locality is closer to and more accessible to the Skeena than to Rivers Inlet. The names of the two principal villages, Kitimat and Kitlope, are in the language spoken along the Skeena, not that of the present occupants. The wanderers who were invited in may accordingly have been those who came from River Inlet; the perhaps revised story puts the tellers in a better light. Despite such instances, which probably represent distortion of historical fact, the great mass of traditional histories when stripped of fantasy episodes— the supernatural adventures of ancestral heroes—are so consistent one with the other, and on points that lend themselves to objective check, that it seems likely that they contain a hard core of historic fact. A possibility for further objective check of the facts lies in the sadly neglected archaeology of the North Pacific Coast. Family histories might be traced backwards in time from known historic villages to the long-abandoned sites their traditions claim they occupied in the past.

## POLITY AND LAW

The fundamental body politic and the basic social unit were the same: the local group consisting of a unilateral lineage or an extended family with its ownership of natural resources, treasures, and intangible rights, its name, its head or chief, and its seriation of statuses of members from highest rank to low. That is, the local group normally governed itself and dispensed its own justice. This political autonomy was in some instances, particularly in the northern and central portions of the area, partly obscured by occasional temporary alliances for military purposes and by more permanent ones for ceremonal and festive ends.

### Alliances

Permanent alliances followed a single pattern: a number of local groups whose territories were contiguous assembled in a common winter village, where each group had its own house or houses. The constituent local groups of such mergers were graded in rank relative to each other by the ranking of their chiefs and higher-rank nobles in a single precedence series. As a rule the unit of highest rank was the group that owned, or originally owned, the site of the joint winter village. These mergers, hereafter referred to as "tribes," were identified by the name of the site at which the groups assembled for the winter. The house sites were given to each group by the original owning group, but the local groups never gave up their autonomy. They continued to own their real estate separately, exploited their economic resources separately, and ordinarily gave their own festivals and ceremonies. Occasionally in recent times the highest-ranking chief gave a potlatch in the name of the whole tribe to obtain the economic support of all groups in assembling goods for the potlatch distribution.

Investigation reveals that such events were staged after agreement and arrangement with the other chiefs of the tribe. There was no authoritarian control of the tribal potlatch by the highest-ranking unit. In other words, all groups participated voluntarily. Since the winter season was the principal period of leisure and major festivals, the chiefs of each tribe commonly met to arrange the order of hosts for feasts or potlatches to avoid complicating confusions. But these arrangements were always made through agreement, never dictatorially. The same was true of the relatively infrequent occasions when a tribe acted as a unit in warfare. The local groups cooperated on a voluntary basis. Instances are not wanting in which one or more of the component units of a tribe remained aloof, neither participating in attack nor being molested in retaliatory attacks of the enemy.

Local geography was always important in the formation of this loose tribal type of organization. Groups who lived "near" each other, whether in distance or in accessibility throughout the stormy winter season, were necessarily those who became involved in closest extragroup contacts. Given the host-guest pattern of feasts and potlatches, nearby groups were almost necessarily in frequent contact, so that amalgamation during the winter festivities was a simple step.

The effective force of local geography is still clearer on the few larger groupings, called confederacies or federations of tribes. In three known instances in the historic period, federations developed when neighboring tribes abandoned their several winter villages to assemble at the major trading posts of Fort Simpson, Fort McLoughlin, and Fort Rupert. In all three cases the tribes were culturally and linguistically homogeneous, and normally on friendly terms with each other. These factors, together with propinquity, led to a degree of consolidation into loose confederacies.

Similar groupings arose in prewhite times among tribes occupying large, ramified inlets, separated from adjacent sections of the coast by bold headlands that were difficult or dangerous to round by sea in all but the calmest weather. These confederacies formed about summer-village sites on or near the outer beaches. Habitable localities convenient to offshore fishing grounds and the best sea-otter hunting and whaling grounds were scarce. The local groups who owned such desirable sites gained esteem and prestige among the tribes by giving their neighbors house sites at the summer village, and by giving them permission to share the use of foreshore and offshore hunting and fishing areas. Like the winter-site confederacies, these were also identified by names; the tribes composing them were also ranked from highest to lowest, but formal organization ended there. As in the tribes, there was no over-all authority or governing power. The local groups were fundamentally autonomous, functioning as elements of the larger body on a voluntary basis.

It must be emphasized that the discussion of the so-called tribal and confederacy organizations treats institutions that were exceptional in the area. Over all of the North Pacific Coast the local group was not only the basic functional unit but in most of the area it was also the largest population aggregate.

## Law Enforcement

### Extragroup Conflict

Law enforcement was another important function of the local group. This sociopolitical unit, consisting of a group of kindred, protected its members against outside aggression. Protection of the group took the form of prompt and drastic action to punish offenses committed against its personnel, the threat of this action serving as a deterrent just as punishment meted out by modern law is intended to deter crime. An Indian group that failed to act decisively in response to an injury to one of its members would be regarded as impotent; consequently, others would commit aggressions against it, convinced they could do so with impunity. While the Indians did not draw the nice modern distinction that we do when we say that our society does not revenge itself on criminals when it punishes them for their misdeeds, their legal actions were inspired by an attempt at social control rather than by a "savage thirst for vengeance." This motivation is not unique to the area but probably is fundamental to most primitive law.

There were two courses open to an offended group. One was to exact revenge by slaying one of the adversaries, and it was deemed proper to take vengeance not on the person of the killer but rather on a member of his group whose status was as nearly as possible equivalent to that of the victim. This concept among the northernmost groups of the coast was carried to the point where only one individual could satisfy the requirements, and that person might be asked to come forth voluntarily to be slain. The alternative was a mass attack that inevitably caused considerable bloodshed and a prolonged feud. The volunteer to be slain was expected to don the ritual finery of his group and come out performing the dance associated with his highest crest until the injured group shot him down. The purpose of this heroic gesture was to prevent further bloodshed and to equalize the losses of both groups so that they could negotiate a peaceful settlement. This procedure was utilized only in cases in which a person of very high rank had been killed. Self-sacrifice in this manner was a behavior ideal, performed to protect one's group and sustain its honor. Some men performed it willingly, others did not. One chief resisted sacrifice by feigning death and then attempting to escape after killing one of his executioners.

The second recourse, usually subsequent to blood vengeance, was to make a settlement through payment of valuables and wealth. This blood payment or wergild system was in vogue among all the North Pacific Coast groups except the Kwakiutl and Nootkans of the central portion. Custom varied in different parts of the area whether wergild could be arranged without loss of honor in lieu of actual blood vengeance for slayings, but wergild was mandatory after killings to make peace possible. When a slaying was avenged, both deaths had to be paid by the transfer of two lots of wealth goods. One payment could not cancel out the other, but both payments had to be delivered physically.

Payments were also made without violent vengeance for offenses less serious than murder. However, the threat of violence was always present if claims of the aggrieved were disregarded. Preliminary negotiations were made through sets of neutral go-betweens. Only after all arrangements had been completed did the two parties to the conflict meet face to face for the formal delivery and acceptance of the blood money. Settlements of these conflicts were usually reached, but never easily. Except in the extreme south, there were no fixed standards for evaluating a human life or the seriousness of an injury. The aggrieved group demanded compensation of an amount as large as they believed the adversaries could assemble, or a little larger to embarrass them. Exorbitant initial demands did not stem from greed or the desire to reap a profit from the death of a kinsman, but showed the high esteem in which the group held its members. The defendants in the claims action had to compromise two conflicting motivations: they wanted to pay handsomely to demonstrate that their wealth was so great that even an exorbitant payment was of no moment to them; on the other hand, they must offer much smaller payment to prove they had no fear of their opponents. Even when both parties really wanted to bring the trouble to an end, haughty attitudes made agreement very difficult for the patient go-betweens. And at times negotiations did break down and were followed by a period of bloody feuding.

### Murder by Witchcraft

Exceptions to this procedure for settlement of murder were deaths attributed to witchcraft. Throughout the area the people were firm believers in the efficacy of black magic. When convinced that they knew the identity of a witch who had caused a death, they sought to kill him or her, regardless of the relative rank of victim and witch. Whether the alleged witch's group avenged the slaying or demanded wergild for it, or both, or neither, depended on whether or not they believed the accusations to be well-founded. There was widespread belief that persons who trafficked with supernatural powers sometimes came under a mysterious compulsion to use their powers to work evil, to the extent that they might become dangerous even to their own group. Therefore, occasionally the slaying of a witch accused of practicing black magic went unavenged, uncompensated, and almost unmourned.

### Intragroup Conflict

Intragroup clashes rarely reached serious proportions. Kinsmen did everything in their power to smooth over such troubles and to prevent disruption of the group. In the rare instances in which blood was shed, usually nothing was done about it. The group would not take vengeance on itself, nor demand wergild of itself, and there was no higher authority. Acts considered serious crimes might be punished by the group, however. There are a few accounts of persons accused of witchcraft being put to death by their own people, usually

by being tied to a stake on the tide flats at low tide and drowned
as the tide rolled in, or by garroting between two logs. Among
groups having unilateral clan organization, clan incest was considered
the blackest of crimes, and offenders were put to death by their
own people to wipe away the disgrace of misdeed.

## WARFARE

In the ethnographic literature distinction is sometimes made between
feuds and war, often on the basis of the scale of the military operations involved. In discussing the culture of the North Pacific Coast,
motives furnish a more useful basis for the distinction. Feuds may
be defined as hostile operations for legalistic purposes, to right a
wrong, or to punish an offense. Wars were hostile operations for
gain. Wars were carried on to secure booty, to capture slaves, and
very often to gain possession of basic resources—lands of economic
importance. However, very long-range strikes, not to conquer lands
but solely for slaves and booty, were sometimes made. Raiders from
southeast Alaska and from the Queen Charlotte Islands sowed terror
and panic among the groups of the Strait of Georgia and Puget Sound
in early historic times, and probably also before white contact.
Weapons, tactics, trophies, and other details were alike in feuds and
wars.

There is considerable evidence that the coast carried the maximum
possible population in prehistoric times, particularly in the northern
half of the area. That is, the ample natural food resources were fully
exploited within the limits of the native technology. The traditions
are replete with accounts of groups driven out of their homes and
lands, and of the hardships suffered before they found new homes.
In many instances, the traditional accounts relate that old established
groups split, and that after an inconsequential quarrel, one of the
daughter groups drove out the other. Perhaps groups increased so in
numbers that their lands could no longer support them adequately.
Population pressures produced tensions, and ill feeling offered abundant pretexts for splitting into senior and junior sublineages.

Shortly before the arrival of the first European explorers several
of the northernmost groups harassed and finally exterminated an
Eskimolike group on Kayak Island in the Gulf of Alaska, although

the victors never properly exploited the locale. Groups from the Queen Charlotte Islands crossed Dixon Entrance into what is now Alaska and settled on the southern part of Prince of Wales Island at the expense of the Tlingit. About the same time, a group of the interior culture who occupied the shores of Portland Canal (but exploited them inadequately by coast standards) were mercilessly harassed and finally enslaved by coast neighbors who took possession of the shores of the Canal and the numerous rich salmon streams.

In southeastern Alaska population pressure and fighting for lands may have intensified during a period of increasing local glaciation, which reached its maximum, according to tree-ring dating, about 1750. Glaciers advanced far down the inlets, rendering large tracts uninhabitable and fishing streams unusable. Indian traditions relate that the Tlingit Hunakwan sharing a winter village in Glacier Bay scattered to live at their various fishing stations when a glacier destroyed their village. But population pressures are probably older than this late glacial phase, for along the coast south of the scene of this glacial activity there were wars for land, also. These wars were bitter struggles. As long as one member of a group remained alive and free, he could assert his claim to the properties in question. Therefore, aggressors aimed at extermination of the enemy by killing or enslaving all members.

Slaves and booty were also incentives to military adventures. Throughout the northern half of the area ceremonial rights and other privileges could be taken in war by capturing the masks and other ritual paraphernalia associated with them. However, the ability to stage a captured ceremony, complete with names, songs, dances, and other features, meant that the captors had witnessed the performance often enough to be thoroughly familiar with it, or had enslaved a person who was coerced into teaching the complete routine.

In the northern half of the area wars were frequent, hard fought, and produced large numbers of casualties. Whether or not to wage war was a matter for local-group decision, though alliances were made in order to put larger forces in the field, and sometimes tribes agreed to fight as a unit.

## Offensive Tactics

Chiefs were the nominal commanders of war parties. Some chiefs took actual field command; those who did not, delegated responsibility to their warriors or war leaders. Each group had one or two war leaders. As a rule the position was hereditary and of low rank, but if a man were successful, he might be allotted higher names and privileges, thus raising his status or that of his descendants.

Some chiefs and war leaders wore armor: cuirasses of rods bound closely together with leather or sinew thongs, or of thick leather. The northernmost divisions used wooden helmets and visors. Other warriors wore no protective devices on the grounds they hampered movement too much. Weapons were those suitable for close combat: clubs, bludgeons, and heavy daggers.

Part of the preparations for war involved secret rituals by the war leader, but there were practical preparations as well. I have heard a number of accounts by Indian informants describing the training of a combat group in which the war leader made his men practice dodging arrows and spears, and disembarking from canoes under fire. However, attacks in which these skills were useful were far less common than the surprise attack usually staged at night. The massive wooden houses with loopholes for defensive fire gave excellent protection against primitive weapons, and in the early historic period against musketry, so that frontal attacks were frequently failures. Such strategy was therefore reserved for strikes on camps and temporary stations, at which the flimsier habitations could be rushed successfully. When attacking winter-village quarters, fortified "refuge" positions, and even the more important fishing stations, the usual night raid was effective. The attackers, faces painted black, or red and black, their long hair knotted atop their heads to afford less convenient handhold, beached their huge war canoes around a point, out of sight of the target village. A canoe guard party was left to protect the means of retreat in case of a successful counter attack. The remainder of the force proceeded to the village via trails through the woods. On the black stormy nights that favored a venture of this sort, the raiders might join hands to form lines, so that warriors unfamiliar with the trail might not get lost. Silently and cautiously

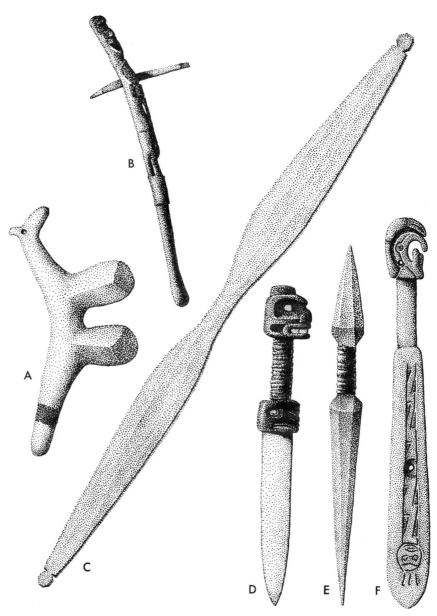

Weapons. (a) "Slavekiller" of stone (archaeological). (b) Two-piece "slave-killer" (wooden handle, horn point). (c) Bow, general coastal type. (d) and (e) Northern fighting knives (iron). (f) Wakashan war club (bone of whale). *Note:* Bows were four and one-half to five feet long. The other weapons are drawn to the same scale.

they advanced. The risk of discovery was always great. Sentinels were posted if an attack was expected. In addition, a few people were likely to be up and about during the night: fishermen who trolled on night tides, amorous youths and others, or persons engaged in ritual training.

Once at the village and undiscovered, the force split up according to assignments. Attack strategy included which houses were to be struck and by whom; individual warriors were assigned specific victims, each creeping to the sleeping place of a chief, noble, war leader, or man noted for his bravery. The precise locations of the sleeping places was important intelligence for an attack. If not already known to the raiders, the information was sought from captives or neutrals when planning the raid. The most delicate part of the operation was the entry into the house, the raiders slipping one by one through the narrow low doorway, then feeling their way to their stations, trying not to give a premature alarm by falling over a box of food or stepping on a sleeping dog. At his assigned station, each waited the signal. When the men were assumed to have reached their positions, the war leader shouted his war cry, leaped upon his own assigned victim with club or knife, and the attack began. Pandemonium ensued, with a wild mixture of war cries, screams and groans of victims, cries of frightened women and children, sounds of blows and struggles. In all this confusion the advantage was with the attackers who were in position and did not interfere with each other. The village residents who were not killed or seriously wounded at the initial blow blundered about in the dark and were as likely to come to grips with one another as with the foe. Women, children, and the less valiant of the men got in each others' way as they ran to the secret exits. But escape was not possible if the raiders knew the locations of the exits. It is small wonder that a properly executed night raid produced heavy casualties.

When the last victim was slain or captured, the successful raiders beheaded the dead, tied up the captives, and looted the house. Sometimes they set the house afire to destroy it and all booty they could not carry off. They then made their triumphant return home. The trophy heads were displayed on poles in front of the raiders' village, or on a prominent point nearby, so that all who passed would observe the proof of the warriors' prowess.

Though uncommon, daylight attacks were occasionally made in beginning a war, or after a long period of military inactivity—in other words, when the enemy were expected to be off guard. The approach might be made by land, as in a night attack, or by a frontal attack disembarking from the war canoes on the village beach. This latter tactic was less frequent and usually used against sites at which the habitations were poorly constructed and therefore could be charged successfully. In such actions bowmen gave the landing troops cover with volleys of arrows. Sometimes the task force attacked simultaneously on two sides of the village or camp in a pincers movement. As a variant, a diversionary attack might be made by a landing force on the beach while a large party in the woods struck from the flank or rear.

A strategy of treachery that was favored for its efficacy was simulated peacemaking. It was deemed appropriate when the victims of a lengthy campaign were severely damaged and wary, living in small scattered groups and continually shifting from camp to camp so that they were difficult to find for an attack, or had assembled in an impregnable defensive position. If the timing was right, that is, if the peace overtures were made when the victims were disheartened and anxious for hostilities to end, they might be expected to take the bait. Preliminary arrangements were made through intermediaries, or through captives released for alleged humane motives and bounteously supplied with presents of food. A beleaguered group was chronically short of food since its members could not fish or hunt as usual because of constant fear of attack. Finally, a meeting of the two sides was scheduled, and the ceremonial procedures for peacemaking and a great feast were planned. Each warrior of the aggressor group was assigned a victim, with whom he was to consort until the designated signal for attack. Then he whipped out a weapon concealed under his robe to strike down his companion. A similar technique was used to capture the last survivors of the interior Indians living along Portland Canal; the only variation on usual procedure was that most of them were reduced to the ignominy of slavery rather than slain.

Despite the fact that they were highly skilled waterfarers, the North Pacific Indians did most of their fighting on land. Rarely, and by pure chance, enemy forces met while embarked and engaged each other with bows and arrows. Even then, the weaker party tried to get to a beach, to make a stand ashore. The only common naval operation was the pursuit of an embarked party by a larger force. The famous "war canoe" of the North Pacific was for approach, for retreat, or pursuit by an overwhelming force; it was essentially a transport, not a ship of the line.

### Defensive Tactics

Defensive measures varied. Groups anticipating attack posted sentinels who stood alert watches the first few nights but then began to sleep at their posts. This defect was recognized in offensive strategy. After an initial attack, aggressors often delayed follow-up operations to allow time for the defenders' sentinels to become bored with their dull assignments.

More effective were the defensive positions in common use in time of war. Nearly every group had such a place. Steep-sided hills or islets were much favored, the ideal being a site with a single difficult and narrow access route, where a few warriors could hold off a large enemy force. The natural features of such a locale were often supplemented with barricades or palisades of logs. Man-made fortifications were used alone where no natural defense position was convenient. The defect of defensive positions was that they could not withstand a protracted siege. When food stores were low, the defenders had to venture forth to replenish them, often traveling considerable distances to fishing grounds bountiful enough to supply the entire group in the course of a hasty provisioning expedition. A compensatory factor was that attackers, fighting at a distance from their home base, had logistical problems too; they could not maintain a constant tight siege for a very long period.

The ultimate defensive strategy, when defeat was near and when defensive positions could no longer be provisioned, was to break up into small units that scattered to temporary camps in the woods, eking out a hand-to-mouth existence as they hid from their relentless foe. A number of small groups known as the Xaihais living in the region north of Milbanke Sound were reduced to this condition early in the historic period. They were being ground to bits by stronger ruthless neighbors to the north and to the south. Their modern

descendants relate tales handed down from those bitter times when
their forefathers ate most of their food raw lest smoke by day or the
glow of fire by night reveal the locations of their impoverished camps
to roving war parties. Both sets of enemies were trying to exterminate
these people, to take possession of their rich fishing and hunting
grounds. That there were survivors at all is due to the Pax Britannica
that put a stop to native warfare, not to the success of this sort of
defense or to compassion on the part of the foe.

# CHAPTER 4

# Religion and Ritual

## CONCEPTS OF THE SUPERNATURAL

A lack of systematization of belief was characteristic of religion in the North Pacific Coast—a characteristic shared with other areas in western North America. Although social life revolved about minute gradations in rank, the Indians did not endow their deities with a divine counterpart of graduated status. A few classes of spirit beings were believed to exist in large groups with chiefs and commoners like people, but these were animal spirits that lived in schools and packs, like salmon, olachen, herring, and wolves, and they formed a special category of supernatural beings. Most of the native gods were democratic and equalitarian, whatever their other characteristics. Beliefs in an afterlife and in other worlds were unsystematized.

A distinction must be drawn between mythology and actual belief. For example, a widespread myth with an Orpheuslike theme related the adventures of a man who rescued his beloved from the Land of

the Dead. The typical story described his route through somber
forests, over perilous mountain passes and a Styxlike river, and something of the existence led by the spirits of the dead in that Hades.
But the people who told the myth for entertainment did not believe
that it necessarily described the destination of the souls of the departed.
They believed that the spirits of the dead remained near the place
of death, to the peril of the living, or that they turned into little owls
that hooted in the forests by night.

Most of the coast groups had the custom of addressing a brief
stereotyped morning prayer to a deity or deities commonly associated
with the sky or the sun. These beings were remote, inactive, and
vaguely conceptualized. The custom might be construed as the tag end
of diffusion of belief in a Supreme Being in which the form had been
adopted but not the real meaning.

More important to the Indians were the supernatural beings who
inhabited their own world: the forests, the mountains, the beaches,
the waters, and the nearer reaches of the skies. These were the gods
with whom human beings might come in contact, to their benefit or
disaster. A great many of these were guardian spirits, familiar to
most American Indians—beings who could confer blessings, good
fortune, and even a measure of supernatural power on man. Many
were animal spirits, at least they assumed the form of animals; others
were monsters of weird and terrifying aspect. It seems that monsters
were more numerous on the North Pacific Coast than in other parts
of western North America. There were huge cave-dwelling man-
eating birds with tremendous sharp beaks; there were frightful sea
monsters in the ocean deeps. On the highest mountain peaks dwelled
thunderbirds, who kept reptile-like lightnings as a man kept dogs, and
who flew off with whales as easily as an eagle flies away with a trout
in his talons. Ogres and malevolent dwarfs shared the forests with
animals and animal spirits. A huge hand emerged from the ground,
shaking a rattle, but no one dared imagine to what horrendous form
it was attached. Giant quartz crystals possessed a life of their own:
they glowed with a blinding white light, vibrated with a humming
sound, flew through the air, and killed ordinary men and animals with
a mysterious charge. These are but a few of the myriad of terrifying
supernatural beings who peopled the native environment. All were
dangerous to mortals, but most of them could confer valuable gifts too.

Animal spirits of a special class were believed to live in groups similar to those of human beings. The core of this belief related to the salmon, who dwelled in a huge house, similar to the houses of the Indians, far under the sea. In their home, the salmon went about in human form. When the time came for the annual runs, they put on their robes of salmon skin and converted themselves into the fish that were the staple of the area. The run was thus conceived to be a voluntary sacrifice for the benefit of mankind, and when the bones of the fish were returned to the water, they washed down to the sea where each fish became reassembled and came back to life.

Many groups of the coast extended this concept to other fish, like the olachen and herring, and less commonly to hair seals and, curiously, to a noneconomic species of animals, wolves. Wolves were regarded with mixed awe and dread by most Indians of the coast, although they were not dangerous to man because of the abundance of game. There are no authenticated records of coast wolves attacking anyone. They were feared for their presumed supernatural powers. As a matter of fact, the two animals that were actually dangerous—that would attack a man even without provocation—the grizzly and the brown bear— were not objects of such great awe, although they were usually ceremoniously treated when killed.

## RITUAL CLEANLINESS

To the Indian, these many supernatural beings were natural phenomena, a part of his normal environment with which he had to cope and which he would exploit if he could. The basic requisites for dealing with the spirits were ritual cleanliness and knowledge of certain ritual acts.

Ritual cleanliness was achieved by partial fasting on a limited diet of dried foods, use of emetics and purges, frequent bathing and scrubbing of the body with branches until it was painfully scrapped clean, and continence. Some of my informants have referred to this procedure in English as "training," an apt term, for in many ways it resembled the training routine of an athlete preparing for a contest. Many men "trained" at intervals, a certain phase of each moon or certain seasons each year, according to their private hereditary routine, for a great part of their lives without ever having a supernatural encounter.

Such training was considered beneficial: it gave general good luck and well-being—the spirits were well disposed toward such a man, even though they might not reveal themselves to him. The difference between routine training and an overt spirit quest was not always great—a matter of intensity, perhaps, and of aim. If the trainee did encounter a supernatural being, he sought to control it. In the spirit encounter as conceived by people of other parts of western North America, the spirit was believed to take compassion on the weary self-tortured seeker after power. On the coast the concept was that the seeker controlled the spirit. He was protected from harm by his ritual purity, and by an appropriate act he compelled it to yield. An interesting parallel in a folk tale from a far distant area is Aladdin and his wonderful lamp. In the Westernized version the djinn did not serve Aladdin because he felt compassion for him; he served because Aladdin possessed the lamp and had learned how to rub it in the magical way that *compelled* the djinn to appear and do his bidding.

The magic gift depended in part on the type of spirit and in part on the interests of the seeker. There were local differences in belief, and probably some individual differences in conception as well. Among some groups the trainee sought a particular type of power by incorporating special secret procedures in his training ritual. One sought hunting power, another, war power, yet another, curing power. Among other groups, curing power was the principal type sought; other sorts of power were believed to be encountered more or less by chance. There were also differences from region to region whether most individuals made deliberate spirit quests, or whether only the exceptional individual sought to obtain power while most men contented themselves with occasional training for the general well-being it was thought to bestow, and as protection in case of an unsought encounter with a supernatural power.

This is an appropriate place to stress the fact that in native concept all the varieties of incorporeal property related to social status, the things termed privileges—names, crests, songs and dances for public display, and the rest—were originally obtained from supernaturals by chance or deliberate encounter by an ancestor. The only exceptions were a few privileges derived from creation myths, that is, ones claimed to have been established at the time of putting the world in order, which thus also had a supernatural origin.

At the public assumption and validation of one of these privileges, that is, at a potlatch, the tradition of its origin was related along with the account of its transmission to its current possessor via normal inheritances and transfers in marriage. Only in case of capture of privileges in war might the origin tradition be omitted. It was at this point that social origin and religious belief fused, or that religious concepts were secularized, as one may choose to view the process.

## SHAMANISM

Among most groups of the North Pacific Coast, an individual who obtained supernatural power for curing had to go through a novitiate, during which he or she performed before relatives. The novice needed practice in controlling his newly found powers. This novitiate was frequently accompanied by restrictions, including seclusion and dietary tabus, and by purification procedures or treatments by an established shaman. Less widespread was the belief that any spirit encountered had to be followed by ritual cleansing because a person fresh from contact with the spirits was enveloped in an aura of spiritual potency that might react dangerously on children and others inadequately prepared to cope with it.

The curing shaman was the most spectacular exponent of the phase of religious belief that involved direct contact with spirit powers, because he gave more public demonstrations of his prowess. There were two universal theories of disease in the area: disease by intrusion of foreign objects and disease by soul loss. Disease-producing objects —splinters of bone, duck claws, pebbles, or among some groups, luminous supernatural pellets—were believed to be sent by malevolent spirits to go about doing harm of their own volition, or to be sent by evil shamans. It seemed logical to believe that the person who had the power to remove the diabolic objects from the body of their victim could manipulate them any way he wished. And the shamans did not discourage these suspicions.

Curing by a shaman was staged as a public performance in the house of the patient with his relatives, friends, and neighbors in attendance. It is clear from accounts that a shamanistic curing may have been aimed at restoring the health of the sick person, but it also had a high entertainment value. Informants of some years back, who had themselves witnessed curing sessions in the isolated portions of the coast where shamanism was practiced until the early years of this century, described performances in detail—the gestures of the shaman, each variation from his customary routine, the reactions of the patient, and the like. It was obvious, listening to their descriptions, that the people were enthusiastic and expert witnesses who found in curing sessions topics for conversation for days afterward. This aspect of shamanism was not unique to the North Pacific Coast.

The scene as it was customarily staged—the huge house, thronged with people, lighted only by a blaze in the principal fireplace, for curing was normally done at night, the suffering patient and his anxious family, the somber figure of the shaman—had all the elements of drama. The patient was usually very ill, for the Indians, like many other people, went through their stock of home remedies before calling the doctor.

The performance proceeded through a series of subclimaxes to its peak. After a preliminary examination, the shaman decided whether or not to take the case. To be successful in his calling he had to be a fairly good judge of human health. For obvious reasons, a shaman, many of whose patients died, was rarely consulted. It was bad form to lose a patient. Further, bad feeling ensued; the usual interpretation of the mourners was not that the shaman had been *unable* to cure, but that he had succumbed to the bribery of some secret enemy and had let the patient die, or had even speeded his death. There was also the danger that a close kinsman might go berserk in his grief and attack the practitioner. Hence, if the shaman thought the sick person would not recover, he might refuse the case, alleging the infirmity was not the type that his spirit powers could handle. If he refused, he avoided difficulties, but he also lost his fee. Some shamans worked out a standard routine for taking difficult cases. The practitioner would make his preliminary examination, questioning the patient where he hurt, poking and thumping him, and then, in all but the most responsive patients, would shake his head sadly and say to the family, in effect, "It's a pity, but I'm afraid your kinsman is too far gone; he will probably die no matter what I do. I could have cured him without a doubt if you had called me in time, but now his ailment has progressed too far. Of course, if you wish, I'll do what I can, but I can't promise to save him." He then let himself be persuaded to attempt a cure. If he put on his act convincingly, the hedge protected him both ways. If the patient died, the shaman had disclaimed responsibility; a recovery was even more to the curer's credit. Had he not made clear the sick person was in the very jaws of death when he undertook the case?

Among most groups an additional more detailed diagnosis followed. The shaman sang over the patient, accompanied by assistants and relatives of the patient. Standard practice was to begin singing in quiet tones at slow tempo, gradually increasing the volume and the beat, to build up nervous tension. By singing the songs his supernatural helpers had taught him, the shaman called them to him. As his spirit powers approached, the shaman became frenzied and danced about his patient in wild figures. The songs and dances of supernatural source and import, the clatter of his dance rattle, and the proximity of his spirits inspired him more and more. Among the northernmost groups he put on masks representing his various familiars. Over most of the area one or more of the supernaturals were believed to take possession of the shaman; among other groups the familiar spirits, visible to him alone, came close, advising him. Finally he learned, or could "see" the cause of the ailment. Here again, the shaman had an opportunity to choose whether to continue. The infirmity might still turn out to be a type beyond his speciality. For example, not all shamans could recover a lost soul. And many groups believed that ills produced by witchcraft could not be cured by any shaman, but only by the witch himself, if he could be forced or induced to undo his spell.

If the shaman continued his cure, he once more began his singing and dancing until he attained a state of exaltation. He extracted intrusive objects in various ways: with the hands, by sucking with the mouth, or through a tobacco pipe. There were not only local differences in the techniques and manipulations for extraction, but individual shamans had their special operative techniques. Removal of the disease-producing item was the final climax. Would the practitioner announce that the objects had been sent by an evilly disposed colleague, and if so, would he hint broadly enough to remove all doubts about the identity of the sender? Some coastal divisions believed that objects could be destroyed to bring harm to the sender; others, that a more powerful shaman could "send" them back to cause

the death of the sender; but the objects were always displayed before
being disposed of. Some sleight-of-hand manipulations must have
been involved in these displays.

I recall a description of the illness of a high-ranking chief of bygone
years, who tried one shaman after another without finding one who
could relieve his suffering. At length a slave offered to cure him,
asserting that he had shamanistic power. He performed his diagnosis
with professional competence, but as he was achieving inspiration to
extract the disease object by sucking, he was watched closely by a
war leader. As he approached his patient, the slave passed one hand
across his own face as though wiping his mouth, whereupon the war
leader sprang forward, grasped him by his long hair, and yanked him
backward. With a powerful hand he forced the slave's jaws open and
extracted from his mouth two splinters of bone tied together with a
strand of human hair. My interpretation of the incident was that the
slave shaman had provided himself with an object and was caught as he
rather clumsily prepared to "remove" it from the sick chief. The
Indians, however, concluded that the slave intended to inject the
objects into the chief to complicate his illness and to finish him off.
They, therefore, hustled the slave out of the house and down to the
beach, where they killed him.

Soul loss was a mysterious malady to which North Pacific Coast
Indians were subject. There was a general, not very clearly formulated
belief in a subsidiary soul, whose departure from the body did not
cause immediate death, but rather lassitude and wasting away, which
was fatal if the errant soul were not recovered in time. Not every
shaman could perform the feat of soul recovery; those who could were
specialists. Sometimes an intrusive-object shaman recognized the disease and referred the patient to a colleague who had the special power
required to cope with the complaint.

There were many ways to recover a strayed soul. Perhaps the
least pretentious was that in which the shaman sent his supernatural
helper to fetch it. Another pattern involved a search by the inspired
shaman himself, who usually was able to find the soul, which he
captured in a handful of eagle down near the village. Among other
groups, soul recovery was the best show of all. The shaman with his
helpers manned an arrangement of painted boards that represented a
supernatural canoe, and acted out the perilous journey to distant

lands or other worlds in quest of the lost soul, until they finally found it and fought their way back to restore it to the patient.

Another theory of disease might be designated "spirit disease." According to this school of thought, if a person was ritually impure when he encountered a supernatural being, or did not perform the proper ritual act, he might fall victim to a fatal illness. Among some groups holding this view the disease was a contamination by the spirit's power; according to others the spirit itself took possession of its victim. Some shamans claimed power sufficient to remove contamination, or even the spirit if it had not completely possessed the patient, but cures were not common. The course of the disease was violent; most sufferers died before a shaman could treat them.

A discussion of shamanism raises the problem of who the shamans were, and more important, why certain people became shamans. The profession was open to both males and females, except in the southern extreme of the area, where only women exercised the profession. Among the northernmost groups shamans wore their hair uncombed in a wild tangle mixed with paint and bird down. Elsewhere a shaman not engaged in a cure could not be distinguished by his dress from his fellows, but nevertheless every member of the calling was known not only to neighbors but often to distant groups. Their fame was widespread, even though the profession was recruited from among those of low or intermediate social rank. It was exceptional for a man or woman of high status to become a shaman.

The classic overt motivation for undertaking the arduous quest for shamanistic power, for performing the nerve-racking and physically exhausting séances, and for tolerating the constant menace of an untimely end, was to gain wealth goods. Informants say that youths were counselled by their elders to become shamans in order to get rich. Yet analysis shows that this goal was not a practical one. Shamans were paid for curing, but payments were of no great consequence except when the patient was a chief, or member of a chief's immediate family. No shaman could make a living at his calling as physicians do today. A shaman had to fish, dig clams, and rustle firewood like anyone else. And on infrequent occasions that he received a handsome fee for curing a person of high status, he was under obligation to turn over the lion's share to his elder kinsman, the chief of his group, when a potlatch was planned. For these contributions the shaman and his heirs received recognition and esteem beyond that to which their low status normally would have entitled them, but they did not accumulate great stores of wealth. The real reward the shaman reaped was the prestige he acquired—a special sort of prestige, made up more of awe than admiration, and compounded with fear and sometimes hatred. The importance of the curing sessions as public spectacles made a public figure of a nonentity. Shamanism was the surest route to prestige for one who found himself doomed to low status in a rigid social system. The war leader, the successful sea hunter, the skillful canoemaker and carver, all attained a measure of special recognition, but the shaman overshadowed them all.

During the historic period, some administrators of Indian affairs, all missionaries, and many missionized Indians regarded shamans as cold-blooded frauds who chose the calling to mulct their fellows of masses of riches—thereby taking at face value the false motivation of shamanism as a manner of enriching oneself. In spite of shamanism's basic premise, the manipulation of supernatural powers by a human being, it is difficult to believe that the shamans viewed themselves as deliberate hoaxes. Such a trade secret would leak out sooner or later. Indians were constantly suspicious of their shamans, but suspected them of malpractice, not fraud. There may have been isolated instances of deliberate impostors—the slave shaman who was caught at his trickery may have been such a one—but such cases seem to have been very rare.

Accounts, not only of nonprofessionals but also of the few ex-practitioners I have encountered, suggest that most shamans believed in their own power. There is no evidence that shamans were recruited from the ranks of the emotionally unstable, as has been inferred in other primitive areas. Given the cultural theory of supernatural power, they were persons who accepted certain stress-produced sensory reactions as manifestations of the spirits, and learned to enter into the self-induced hypnotic state of the inspired shaman. How did the shaman rationalize such blatant deceits as the sleight-of-hand tricks he used? He probably believed that the agility with which he performed them was really the gift of his tutelary spirit.

## WITCHCRAFT

Belief in witchcraft as a common cause of illness and death was widespread. The term witchcraft is used in these pages to refer to ritual acts to bring harm or death to a person magically, a procedure distinct from that of shamans who "sent" the same sorts of disease objects they extracted for hire, for ill will, or because their spirit powers compelled them to do so. Disease caused in this manner derived from the shaman's power to handle disease objects. Witchcraft, however, was a ritual procedure. The techniques of witchcraft were thought to have been revealed originally by supernatural beings, but subsequently passed from one generation to another as family secrets. Articles intimately associated with the intended victim—bodily excreta, hair, a fragment of a worn garment—might be placed in a grave, or wrapped up with a bit of human bone for special disposal.

Many groups associated frogs with malevolent powers, and one specific technique involved stuffing spittle, excrement, hair or whatever had been in contact with the victim, into a live frog's mouth. The mouth was sewn shut, and the frog attached to a supple rod by a cord. The rod was planted at the edge of a rapids, so that the current dragged the frog downstream until the elasticity of the pole jerked it back upstream. The continual jerking of the frog was supposed to cause the victim of the witchery to fall prey to violent convulsions and finally to die. Probably prayers, or formulae, and ritual acts accompanied these preparations.

Witchcraft was generally regarded as a very serious crime, and it was difficult to detect. A few shamans claimed powers of clairvoyance, but even they could not always locate the diabolical contraption and identify the maker. Most people knew a good deal about witchcraft, but even willing informants disliked discussing their knowledge in too much detail, lest they give the impression of having professional knowledge of the black arts. Suspicion, based on circumstantial evidence, was the means of "identifying" witches, just as in the Salem witch trials.

## RITUALISM

The contrast of witchcraft and shamanistic malpractice offers a convenient introduction to another area of attempts to control supernatural forces. Without ever having direct contact with spirits, an Indian could learn to perform many procedures that produced desired results by a sort of compulsive magic, just as in the case of witchcraft. The complexity of the ritual procedures varied greatly as did the purpose for which they were performed. The ritual training associated with the spirit quest, or performed for personal good luck and well-being, was one of this type of rites. While the general training pattern was universal, each family line had special secrets, handed down from generation to generation, involving the form of the prayers, the kind of plants for scrubbing the body, the phase of the moon when the training should begin and end, and so on. Individual rites for individual purposes were those of hunters of land game or sea mammals for success in the chase, or the rituals of the canoemaker so the hull would not split as he worked on it. War leaders had secret proceedings to give them strength and fortitude, and to ensure military success. Other rituals were of broader interest, to produce a bountiful run of salmon or olachen, to cause dead whales with masses of oil-rich blubber to drift ashore, or to bring about other results in the public interest. Procedures were often lengthy and complex, and known to a few persons only. Such persons are referred to as ritualists, or priests. A great deal of North Pacific Coast religious activity was performed by priests, with or without assistance of fellow group members.

## FIRST SALMON RITES

Of all the priest-conducted rites of group interest, the most important was associated with the arrival of the first salmon each year. Because the salmon were regarded as beings who voluntarily sacrificed themselves for the benefit of man, it was important that they be treated well. Although salmon beings left their material bodies behind, they were immortal, and if offended, might not return the following year. The first catch of the year in important fishing places was given an elaborate welcome, so that the salmon beings would be well disposed toward the humans who fished there.

In detail there were almost infinite variations of procedure of the First Salmon rite, but the basic pattern involved the taking of the first fish by the priest or his assistants, who carried it in a special manner to an altar on which it was laid in the presence of the assembled group. Throughout the rite there was constant reference to the run and its continuance, and the first fish was usually placed with its head pointing upstream so the rest of the salmon would continue upstream and not turn back to the sea. The first fish was treated as an honored guest of high rank: the priest sprinkled it with eagle down or red ochre or other ritual material, and made a formulaic speech of welcome, followed by songs or chants of the type to greet a visiting chief. The fish was cooked by the priest or an assistant to the accompaniment of prayers and songs; then each person present was given a sacramental taste. If the fish was small, several might be caught so that everyone could be served a first taste.

After the performance, people might begin to fish for themselves. Often there were restrictions on use of the salmon for a certain period. For example, among some groups fillets could be dried at first, and whole fish roasted for immediate use, but the complete skeleton—backbone with head and tail attached—had to be returned to the water in one piece. Later backbones and heads could be separated for smoking and preservation, but it was still necessary to return the bones to the water. It was believed that salmon permitted themselves to be harpooned or clubbed in the normal manner of taking, but should not be further mistreated. Many groups told a story to children about the terrible fate that befell a naughty boy who poked out a salmon's eyes in play. In rivers in which several species ran, the first of each species might be given identical treatment, or the earliest species might receive the most elaborate attention, the others more perfunctory handling.

In dilute form the observance was performed beyond the limits of the North Pacific Coast—in the adjacent Plateau hinterland and in central California as far south as salmon run—but these peripheral practices do not obscure the fact that the ritual and the basic concepts about which it was developed were typically North Pacific Coast.

Similar rituals in honor of the first herring and the first olachen may be assumed to represent extensions of the First Salmon pattern to other genera that, like the salmon, appeared suddenly and in vast numbers each year. These rites followed the same general pattern of ceremonious handling and formal welcoming by a priest.

Some animals were accorded special treatment, although the rites were minor performances as compared to that for salmon. Bear, mountain goat, and whale (whales by only the few groups killing them) were ritually treated, but the ritualist was the hunter, not a priest. Frequently the procedure consisted of a formal welcoming of the immortal quarry that voluntarily permitted itself to be taken.

The chief of each group was usually the principal ritualist, and he "trained" and performed the rites to bring success to group endeavors. He performed a rite in preparation for the construction of the group's major salmon weir and traps, and likewise to cause dead whales to drift ashore on his group's beaches. The exact nature of his rites, the songs and prayers he used, in brief the entire routine, was hereditary family property, carefully taught to each heir-apparent by his elders.

The peculiar relationship conceived of as existing between a hunter and his quarry is pointed up by the nearly universal belief that not only the hunter's actions affected his luck, but those of his wife could aid his success or cause his failure. Some preparatory training procedures required the hunter's wife to accompany him in his arduous ritual bathing. It was universally believed that during the hunt, her activities controlled the actions of the game. If she moved rapidly and made quick, nervous gestures, the game would be nervous and wary, running away from the frustrated stalker. If she moved about quietly and slowly, or lay quietly on her bed during the hunt, the quarry would be quiet and let itself be approached. These concepts referred particularly to game that was difficult and wary—mountain goat, marmot, hair seal, sea otter, and whale—although some groups included additional species in the list.

## CEREMONIALS

There were two fundamental ceremonial patterns, which had mutually exclusive geographic distribution. The more widespread, found from the northern British Columbia coasts to the Columbia, revolved about the theme of the supernatural experience; the other, completely different, was based on a complex of concepts and observances fundamental to areal religious thought, those expressed in the First Salmon ritual. This latter complex has been called the World Renewal ritual, and was limited in distribution to the Yurok, Karok, and Hupa of northwestern California. Its central theme was belief that a race of prehuman spirits had set the world in order and brought the salmon and other staples to the area. A formulist symbolically re-enacted the procedures of the spirits, repeating by rote the magic prayers, speeches, and acts believed to have been performed on the first occasion by the spirits. His quiet secretive procedures (the formulaic prayers were hereditary and jealously guarded property) were accompanied by performances in which dancers displayed wealth goods. One of these dances, the White Deerskin Dance, featured the highly valued pelts of albino and other oddly colored deer. The other, called in English the Jumping Dance, served to display scroll-like deerskin headdresses with appliqués of the bright red scalps of the pileated woodpecker. These and other valuables utilized were the riches of the people, as ordained, native theology maintained, since the beginnings of the world. One can scarcely escape the impression that there must have been some connection, albeit remote, between these wealth-display performances and the more northerly wealth-distribution (potlatch) pattern. The combination of esoteric procedures by the formulist and the public wealth-display dances were believed to renew the natural resources of the groups performing the rites.

The other major ceremonial pattern in the area, referring to supernatural experiences, may be divided into three distinct categories, which comprise a series in complexity of elaboration of the basic theme. However, chronological significance cannot be demonstrated. The three forms are:

1. The Spirit singing complex, in which each performer displayed songs, dances, and sometimes supernatural powers in the form of sleight-of-hand feats, which had been bestowed upon him in the course of a personal encounter with a guardian spirit.

2. The Crest dance, in which a performer displayed songs, dances, masks, and other ceremonial properties, which had been bestowed on an ancestor of the family line in an encounter with a supernatural being.

3. The Dancing Society complexes, in which not only the gifts be-

stowed on an ancestor by a spirit power were displayed, but the entire history of the ancestor's supernatural adventure was dramatized.

Viewing the three types of ceremonies as parts of a series assumes that classes 2 and 3 represent amalgamations of the concept of acquisition of spirit power with the principle of hereditary transmission of special rights and privileges; the difference between 2 and 3 is essentially a matter of presentation: in type 2 performances the details of the ancestor's supernatural experience were recited, in 3 they were acted out. There were four varieties of Dancing Society performances. That is, there were four Dancing Societies that differed chiefly in the type of supernatural beings with whom the ancestors had dealings, and the gifts received.

## LIFE CRISIS OBSERVANCES

Important religious beliefs of most primitive peoples, and some not so primitive, relate to the observances at crucial stages in the life of the individual. Commonly the more important of these observances are correlated with physiological changes in the life cycle: birth, puberty, and death are major occasions for special treatment. These critical stages, and others less sharply defined in the progress of the individual from the cradle to the grave, were times to protect the individual and his group by special ritual among all North Pacific Coast peoples.

The concept underlying such rites was that the person at the moment of change was in a peculiar condition of ritual uncleanliness offensive to supernatural beings, and simultaneously imbued with magical power capable of causing good or evil. The people whose village was overrun by the glacier at Glacier Bay some two centuries ago blame the movement on a pubescent girl, who was bored with her long confinement and peeked through a hole in the wall of her cubicle at the glacier up the valley. She held up bits of dried salmon from her meager repast and chirruped to the glacier as to a dog. Because of the magical potency of her condition, the glacier responded to her call like an obedient dog, with disastrous results.

While many persons and things might be affected by an individual in one of these critical states, fish and game were considered most susceptible. Fresh fish and all meats were tabu to the person, and diet was limited to old dried fish. Seclusion, out of the sight of fishermen and hunters, was the rule throughout the area, and even approaching a salmon stream was forbidden.

### Rites at Childbirth

On the occasion of birth, the father as well as the mother was in the dangerous state requiring seclusion, dietary restrictions, and the like. The newborn infant was also given special treatment, but for different reasons: in its weak condition it had to be protected from malign influences; in addition magical ways were used to ensure its health, well-being, and good fortune later in life. One object treated with magical techniques was the detached umbilical cord; another was the basketry or wooden cradle after the infant had outgrown it. Typically, the seclusion of the parents was terminated by a purificatory procedure involving ritual bathing. These rites were private ones, not occasions for public ceremony. They were attended by the principals, a few close relatives, and often by a ritualist, who if not a member of the family, was paid to direct the proceedings.

The ritualist, with his purifying techniques, was an important figure in all the crisis rites. Among a few divisions of the central portion of the area persons who had inherited the right to a certain type of mask and dance gave a public performance to cleanse those in critical stages of life.

During childhood several occasions were considered propitious for minor observances for the youngster's well-being. Shedding the first tooth and the first fish or game taken, are examples of such times; however, they were not considered as critical episodes in the life cycle, and involved few tabus and restrictions.

### Puberty Rites

The onset of a girl's puberty was the first major crisis through which she passed. Throughout the area, a pubescent girl was secluded and could not see other people nor be seen by them, except the elderly female relatives who attended her. The duration of seclusion varied in different sectors of the coast, but typically was lengthy. The picture of normal treatment is slightly complicated by the fact that seclusion of girls of high rank was used to prevent premarital sexual relations, which were disgraceful to the girl and her entire group. The seclusion of the daughter of a chief might commence considerably before her physiological puberty and continue until her marriage had been arranged.

Food restrictions were severe. A little of the oldest dried salmon was all she was usually allowed, although in the southern part of the area where oaks grew, she was permitted a little thin acorn gruel. Should she violate any food tabu, it was believed that disaster would surely follow. If, for instance, she should eat fresh salmon, not only would she be seriously harmed by the food and the fisherman who had caught the fish permanently lose his luck, but the offended race of salmon would probably never again enter the territory of the group to allow themselves to be caught. Use of the scratching stick was universally required; the drinking tube, a hollow bone or reed, was required by many groups for the pubescent's use for ritual reasons. These implements, the scratching stick accompanied by the tabu on touching one's body with one's own fingers and the drinking tube, were manifestations of the basic concept of contamination at "life crises" among most native American groups and among aborigines in many other parts of the world. On the North Pacific Coast, there was a host of other special rules as well, which varied among the different groups. Finally, when the wearisome seclusion was concluded, a public debut was given. As in so many other customs, there was great variation in the details of procedure from one coastal division to another, but everywhere the essence of the performance was a purification rite. A private or semiprivate purificatory ritual, involving bathing, dressing in new garments, and the like, was held, and at the public performance a symbolic cleansing was given the girl. An elaborate hairdressing was often a key part of the public rite.

Wherever the potlatch complex was in use, a potlatch was given in honor of a girl of high rank at the end of her seclusion. For her distant cousin of lower status a feast would serve the same purpose: to make public announcement of her new status as a mature woman, to announce her new name and any other privileges to which she might be entitled. This potlatch or feast was in a sense a social adjunct to a religious observance, and not an integral part of the puberty rite. In the same fashion social recognition via potlatch or feast followed termination of other crisis rituals, but it was not a part of the ritual.

Concluding the puberty rites, the girl was regarded as a young woman, eligible for marriage. Her subsequent menstrual periods were occasions for attenuated repetition of the puberty seclusion, with similar dietary restrictions, usually for four or five days, depending on the pattern number of her group. A self-administered and brief purification concluded the restrictions. During her menses she was not thought of as being in as critical a state as at puberty, but her presence could communicate a malignant influence on hunters and fishermen, and could endanger the very lives of shamans and others in close contact with spirit powers. Should she eat fresh salmon or approach a salmon stream, the run would stop immediately. Hence her behavior at these times was of vital importance to all the group.

Properly speaking, there were no boys' puberty rites on the North Pacific Coast. However, among groups who stressed the guardian spirit quest, the arduous routine of bathing and fasting began more or less at the time of puberty. In view of the fact that the youth was expected to be exposed to the potentially dangerous contacts of supernatural powers, a few groups added such symbols of crisis situations as the scratching stick and drinking tube to his spirit quest procedures. And he was secluded even when he was not searching for a spirit power in the woods, to protect him from malignant influences of the incontinent and the ill-disposed.

Among a number of coastal divisions boys began to prepare at an early age for the severe test of resistance and fortitude that was the spirit quest and the "training" routine they would follow through adult life. At eight to ten years of age they began by taking a daily bath in the sea or river. The Japanese Current that warms the coast is of tropical origin, but the waters that wash inshore are dense, chill waters of the deeps off the continental shelf. Winter and summer water temperatures are cold and to bathe in the sea or in river water from a glacier required considerable conditioning.

### Rites at Death

The inevitable end of the individual life cycle was the occasion for another set of crisis rites. Precautionary measures, purifications and the like, were for the living, relicts and others who had been in close contact with the deceased. Most of the peoples of the area had a morbid terror of the dead, deriving from the common belief in the evil powers of ghosts. No matter how kindly and beloved the departed had been in life, once dead he was feared, for his ghost was thought to be malevolent and dangerous particularly to his own family. (It may be noted in passing that while warriors who killed in war or feuds among some groups were required to go through subsequent purificatory rites, these were brief and perfunctory. Warriors beheaded and mutilated the corpses of their victims, toyed with the heads, and so on, with little fear of the dead or their ghosts, certainly with less fear than the kin of the same slain persons.) Thus, over most of the area, the dead were hustled to their final resting places. To deceive the ghost, the body was passed through an improvised exit in the wall or roof so that the ghost could not find the doorway to re-enter the house, or so that the living might not have to use the same exit as the dead.

Only in the northernmost part of the coast were bodies permitted to remain in the house. The body of a dead chief might be set up in state, surrounded by his treasures, for several days, while traditional family dirges were sung by the mourners. The period of seclusion was lengthy, and restrictions were severe on relatives, particularly on the immediate family. Purification rites were needed to terminate the restrictions and to restore the relicts to normal life.

Methods of disposal of the dead varied widely from one part of the area to another: in wooden storage boxes, in caves, suspended from trees, set atop memorial poles, or in canoes raised on scaffoldings, and cremation. There were particular forms of burial for the dead of special categories: shamans in some places, and twins in others. In areas of the potlatch complex, a mortuary potlatch was given on the death of a person of high status. Among the northernmost divisions a cycle of feasts and potlatches was associated with a chief's death, including the mourning and memorial rites at his demise, and the successor's formal assumption of the status.

# CHAPTER 5

# Population and Culture Subdivisions

THE FOREGOING CHAPTERS HAVE described the fundamental patterns of areal culture without distinguishing between population units or cultural subdivisions, in order to bring out the basic unity of North Pacific Coast culture. To round out the picture we now consider the composition of the native population, and the regional specializations of areal culture patterns.

## LINGUISTIC DIVISIONS

The considerable diversity in linguistic distributions may be listed easily from north to south. The northernmost language division, which occupied most of the Alaska panhandle, was Tlingit. Part of Prince of Wales Island in Alaska, and the Queen Charlotte archipelago to the south, were inhabited by speakers of the Haida tongue. Both Tlingit and Haida have long been considered by linguists to be related to Athapascan, spoken by interior groups of the Yukon and

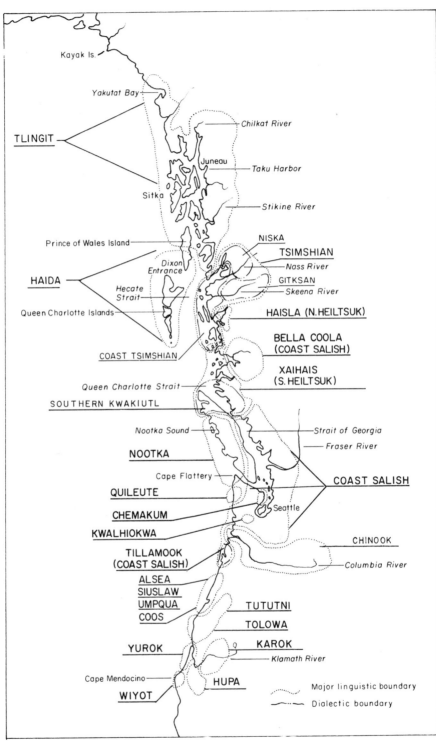

The North Pacific Coast—Linguistic Divisions

McKenzie drainages, and by scattered enclaves southward along the coast. As far away as the desert Southwest of the United States, Navajo and Apache also spoke forms of Athapascan. Another division of this NaDéné (Tlingit-Haida-Athapascan) stock, Eyak, has recently been identified in the Copper River region, just north of Tlingit territory, and Eyak is reported to be as divergent from Athapascan as are the other two members of the stock.

There is evidence of minor changes in linguistic boundaries in late prehistoric times. The Yakutat Bay people, now thoroughly Tlingit, may have spoken an Athapascan dialect until nearly the beginning of the historic period. Presumably this language change, and probably cultural changes as well, came about through trade contacts with Tlingit-speaking neighbors of the Cross Sound region. The Tagish of the interior lake region adopted Tlingit speech, presumably also fairly recently, but they adopted almost nothing of coastal culture, retaining their rude interior patterns until modern times. The Haida occupation of Prince of Wales Island is the result of an intrusion from the Queen Charlottes about the middle of the eighteenth century.

South of the area of Tlingit speech on the mainland and offshore islands, the Tsimshian dialects were found. There were three of these: Niska, of the Nass River in British Columbia; Coast Tsimshian, of the outer coasts at the mouths of the Nass and Skeena Rivers and the lower portion of the Skeena; and Gitksan, spoken by groups along the Skeena above its narrow awesome cañon. The Niska division was augmented, apparently in late prehistoric times, by a Tlingit group forced from their northern home by population pressure, who were given tracts on the lower Nass, and who soon became Niska in speech and custom. In the early historic period, this same group became the chief aggressors in a campaign with other Tlingit- and Tsimshian-speaking units against some Tahltan bands who spoke Athapascan. When they captured and enslaved the last survivors of the Tahltan bands, they also claimed their victims' lands along the western shores of Portland Canal, thus extending the boundaries of their newly acquired Niska speech. South of the Skeena, a coast Tsimshian division, the Kitisu, waged a bitter war against their neighbors to the south, but the extent of their gains has not been recorded.

According to both Tlingit and Tsimshian traditions, ancient linguistic distributions were quite different: Tlingit-speaking groups held the lower Skeena and the adjacent coasts, and were pushed out by the ancestors of the Coast Tsimshian, who presumably split off from their Gitksan relatives upstream long ago. In defeat the Tlingit retired northward to the Panhandle region, which, traditions indicate, these early Tlingit found unoccupied. There, their number was increased by interior groups who came down the Stikine to the coast. Insufficient archaeology has been done along the northern coasts to corroborate or disprove this folk story. The theme that the Skeena was a major route in migrations of peoples from the interior to the coasts recurs in Haida traditions, which relate that important ancestors of the modern Haida came from the Skeena River region. There is no indication whether they preceded the Tlingit or split off from them. When they arrived on the Queen Charlottes, they found the "old Haida" who, traditions maintain, had lived on the islands so long that they had no folk memory of having lived anywhere else.

To the south of the Tsimshian, a considerable number of groups spoke varieties of a language known as Kwakiutl, and an isolated enclave spoke a Coast Salish dialect, Bella Coola. The northernmost form of Kwakiutl was Haisla, which was spoken by groups of Douglas Channel and Gardner Canal who were cut off from the outer coasts by the Kitqata Tsimshian. These people claim that their ancestors came overland from Wikeno (or Owikeno) Lake at the head of Rivers Inlet, far to the south. The possibility that they may have infiltrated and peacefully dominated a Tsimshian outpost has been mentioned in another connection. Nearest to them, although separated by the Kitqata and Kitisu Tsimshian, were a number of small groups known as the Xaihais, who spoke the Heiltsuk variety of Kwakiutl, and then the Heiltsuk proper, or Bella Bella, of the Milbanke Sound region, and the Wikeno of Rivers Inlet and Wikeno Lake.

The Haisla tradition of having come from the Wikeno Lake region finds at least partial confirmation in the fact that the Haisla and Heiltsuk dialects differ only slightly. Recently an ethnographer successfully used a Rivers Inlet interpreter when working with Haisla-speaking informants. The differentiation of Haisla from Heiltsuk is more properly cultural than liguistic. South of Rivers Inlet, from Smith Sound to Yucluta Rapids, and from the northwest tip of Vancouver Island, including Cape Scott and Quatsino Sound, along the northeast coast of the island to Seymour Narrows, the shores were inhabited by speakers of Southern Kwakiutl, a language related to Heiltsuk but markedly divergent from it.

Adjacent to the area of Kwakiutl speech, along the sheltered waters of the Strait of Georgia, on the lower Fraser River, ringing Puget Sound, and occupying most of western Washington state, were groups speaking dialects of Coast Salish. These dialects are closely related to but distinct from Interior Salish dialects spoken in the southern interior of British Columbia and east of the Cascades in Washington. Two outlying pockets of Coast Salish were Tillamook on the Oregon coast south of the Columbia River, and Bella Coola on upper Dean and Burke Channels, and the lower Bella Coola River on the central British Columbia coast. The speakers of Bella Coola were cut off from the outer coasts by the Heiltsuk, and separated overland from their nearest linguistic relatives by many miles of extremely rugged terrain. Studies in glottochronology, which attempts to derive temporal significance from linguistic divergence, interpret the differences of Bella Coola from other forms of Coast Salish as the result of prolonged separation. Whether the findings of glottochronology are accurate in terms of years, the general interpretation of a long separation of the speakers of Bella Coola from their linguistic kindred is corroborated by both anthropometry and cultural data. There is no evidence that Coast Salish formerly had a more extensive distribution along the coast. On the contrary, such archaeological data as there are from the lower Fraser-Strait of Georgia region, indicate that there, at least, the Coast Salish were relatively late emergents from the interior, replacing an older coastal population.

On the oceanward shores of Vancouver Island, from Cape Scott to Nitinat (a village at the mouth of the river from Nitinat Lake), and across the Straits of Juan de Fuca on Cape Flattery in modern Washington, lived speakers of the Nootkan tongue. This language has long been recognized as related to Kwakiutl, the two forming the Wakashan stock. Some modern linguists believe that Wakashan and Salish are distantly related, and that with Quileute-Chemakum, two small isolated linguistic groups found on either side of Cape Flattery, they are ultimately related to the Algonkin group of languages, but these relationships still require precise definition.

The lower Columbia River, from The Dalles to the seacoast, was the residence of groups speaking Chinook, who separated the Salishan Tillamook from their relatives to the north. The Chinook language has no close affiliates, but is grouped by some linguists into a larger language entity called Penutian. Tsimshian, too, is classified as Penutian, but the greatest number of native languages of this superstock are found from the territory of the Chinook southward, in western Oregon and central California.

The central Oregon coast was inhabited by speakers of a variety of independent languages, sometimes allocated to the Penutian group: Alsea, Coos, Siuslaw, and Umpqua. In southwest Oregon and extreme northwest California were a number of Athapascan-speaking groups, usually lumped under the name Tolowa-Tutuni, two of the larger divisions. These were not the only Athapascan-speaking peoples on the coast. Some distance up the Klamath River in present-day California were the Hupa, who spoke another dialect of the same tongue, and in the nearby central California culture area, other Athapascan speakers were found. And to the north, in southwestern Washington, were the Klatskanie-Kwalhiokwa, who became extinct so long ago that little is known about them except that their language was Athapascan. Early in the historic period, part of the Klatskanie moved across the Columbia to the Klatskanie River in northwest Oregon, where they apparently soon dwindled to extinction.

In northwest California, were the Yurok and Karok, neighbors of the Hupa on the lower Klamath River, and the adjoining Wiyot along the coast to Cape Mendocino. Yurok and Wiyot are Algonkin languages; the affiliation of Karok to other American Indian tongues is not certain, although some authorities suggest its inclusion in a superstock known as Hokan.

All this linguistic diversity suggests that the area was populated by groups from various parts of the interior of the continent in a succession of migrations. Local variation and specialization of areal culture patterns probably stems from the differing cultural heritage of the groups settling on the coast. However, it is vain to speculate on what the sequence of settlement may have been, for we have no absolute or relative measures of the time represented by the linguistic distributions. For example, even if we accept the glottochronological estimate of the time represented by the divergence of Bella Coola from other forms of Coast Salish, there is no assurance that the linguistic divergence correlates with the migration of the Bella Coola to their present

4. Bella Coola mask,
7 inches wide by $10\frac{3}{4}$ inches
high.

1. Kwakiutl mask (Alert Bay), $52\frac{1}{2}$ inches long, $9\frac{1}{2}$ inches wide, and $8\frac{1}{2}$ inches high.

2. Kwakiutl mask (Quatsino Inlet), 21 inches long, 12 inches wide, and 14$\frac{1}{2}$ inches high.

3. Bella Bella mask, 27 inches wide by 11 inches high.

5. Skokomish basket (southern end of Puget Sound), 14 inches in diameter.

7. Quinault basket, 12 inches in diameter.

6. Haida basket, 13½ inches in diameter.

10. Haida rainhat, 15 inches in diameter.

9. Chief's hat, provenience unknown, $11\frac{1}{2}$ inches high.

8. Hat, *probably* Nootka, 14 inches in diameter.

11. Kwakiutl house post
(Rivers Inlet), 35 inches
wide by $9\frac{1}{2}$ feet high.

12. Yurok carved paddles, 36 inches and 43 inches long.

14. Totem pole,
provenience unknown,
61 inches high.

13. Tlingit figure, 33 inches high.

15. Gitskan medicine man's kit.

16. Shaman's box, *probably* Tlingit, 13 inches long.

18. Kwakiutl feast bowl, 5-foot "wingspan."

19. Kwakiutl feast bowl, 77-inch "wingspan."

20. Bella Bella frog bag, 17 inches wide by 21 inches long.

17. Kwakiutl shaman's wand, 18 inches high.

22. Dentalium money string, provenience unknown, 28 inches long.

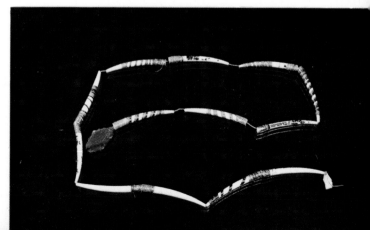

21. Yurok spoon, 7 inches long.

23. Yurok carved mauls, $6\frac{1}{2}$ to 7 inches long.

24. Hupa elkhorn purse, $5\frac{1}{2}$ inches long.

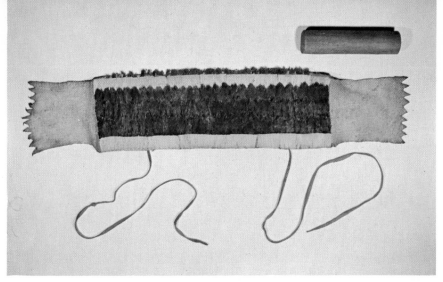

25. Scalp mosaic headdress, provenience unknown.

27. Haida box, $13\frac{1}{2}$ inches wide by 14 inches long.

26. Wooden carved bowl, provenience unknown, $13\frac{1}{2}$ inches long.

28. Carved box, *probably* Kwakiutl, $26\frac{1}{2}$ inches long, $15\frac{1}{2}$ inches wide, and 15 inches high.

29. Chilkat blanket.

30. Chilkat blanket.

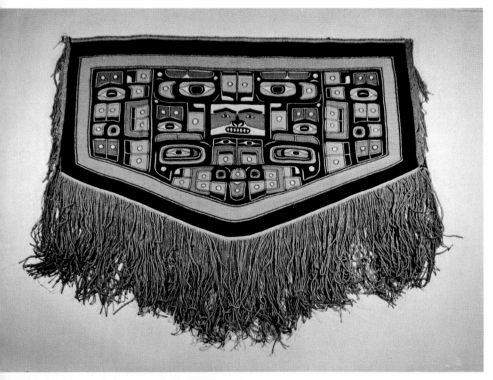

32. Tlingit shirt, or armor.

31. Tlingit elkhide armor.

34. Copper, provenience unknown, 21 inches high by $29\frac{3}{4}$ inches long.

33. Haida copper (Nass River) $27\frac{1}{4}$ inches wide by $43\frac{1}{4}$ inches long.

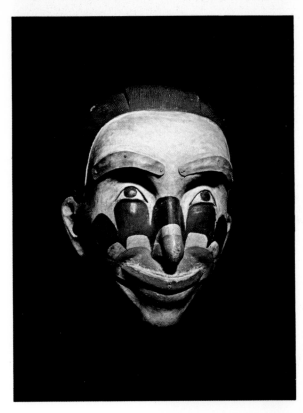

38. Haida mask.

36. Tlingit mask.

35. Tlingit mask.

39. Tlingit mask.

37. Haida mask.

home. Ancestral Bella Coola may have been a distinct variety of Salish long before any Salish-speaking person ever saw salt water. Eventually, when enough careful archaeology has been done, working backwards in time from horizons known to have been formed by specific groups, the sequences of arrivals on the coast may be unraveled and new meaning read into the ethnographic culture patterns. Meanwhile, linguistic divisions are best used as classifiers in discussing cultural specialization and variation. Since the local groups and even the sociopolitical units called "tribes" were small and numerous, it is more convenient to use the linguistic groupings in descriptions of local patterns. In point of fact, many of the regional specializations of culture correlate roughly with linguistic divisions or blocks of linguistic divisions. Hence, in the following chapters the "Tlingit" or the "Chinook" or the "Tolowa" mean "the groups of Tlingit speech," or those of Chinook speech or those speaking the Tolowa variety of Athapascan, without implication that these language divisions had any social or political unity.

## NEIGHBORS

The peoples who bordered the North Pacific Coast area did not participate in its culture, although here and there they borrowed traits and even complexes. They, too, are conveniently described in terms of linguistic aggregations. It has been remarked that the neighboring inland cultures were "lower" or "simpler," that is, less complex or less elaborate. The mere business of keeping alive in rigorous, inhospitable, inland climes may have taken all the people's time, leaving them neither leisure nor energy to develop craftsmanship, art, ceremonialism, and other refinements that typified coast culture. Yet something more was involved than environmental inhibition; there was a factor of cultural choice as well. Certain crafts were competently executed by the groups of the interior. In the north, tailored skin clothing might be a necessity, but most interior groups made it better than pure necessity required, with ornamented yokes, fringes, and other adornments. Porcupine-quill embroidery in the north, and coiled basketry and soft woven bags in the Plateau region were neatly and artistically made, indicating the people could be capable craftsmen. The fact remains that aside from these manufactures they had little interest in the decorative arts. Salmon swarmed far up the great rivers that transected the Coast

Ranges: the Copper, the Stikine, the Skeena, the Bella Coola, the
Fraser, the Columbia, the Klamath. Many interior groups utilized
salmon but none exploited the resource with the same efficiency as
the coast peoples. Hence something more than environment is needed
to account for the differing emphases of coastal and interior cultures.

There were differences in frequency of contacts between coastal
and interior groups. The Tlingit, especially those inhabiting the mainland, were in frequent communication with their Athapascan neighbors,
particularly for purposes of trade. While trade was intensified in the
historic period, especially in connection with the quest for furs, it
was also carried on prehistorically. Coastal groups sought dressed deer
and moose hides, ermine pelts, tailored skin clothing, coppers, and
possibly jadeite for celt blades. It is still not known if the pre-European
iron received via western Eskimo sources was traded up the Yukon
and over the passes to Tlingit country, or was mainly traded along the
shores of the Gulf of Alaska. But there is every indication that there
was a considerable prehistoric traffic between the Tlingit and their
Athapascan neighbors.

Among the Tsimshian, the Niska had occasional contacts, chiefly
with Tahltan, the Gitksan were in frequent contact with Carrier,
while the Coast Tsimshian had very few dealings with interior Indians,
except those they met on visits to the Nass or upper Skeena. The
Bella Coola were well acquainted with the Chilcotin, who came down
their river valley; the Heiltsuk and Southern Kwakiutl, although their
territories in part bordered on those of interior groups, seem to have
had almost no inland contacts. Their mainland rivers head in the Coast
Range, and there were no easy routes across the rugged terrain that
separated them from the interior.

The Coast Salish had considerable contact with their Interior Salish
kin, chiefly via the Fraser River, but also over the mountain passes
east of Puget Sound. Along the Fraser, there was a blending of cultures
not found elsewhere in the area. Some of the Fraser River villages
were difficult to classify as coast or interior. The Chinook of the
Columbia plied a vigorous trade with inland peoples, Salish, Sahaptin,
Shoshonean, and occasional adventurers from more distant groups such
as the Klamath, since The Dalles was a rendevous and trade mart for
a vast inland area. Along the Oregon coast there seems to have been
little contact inland. The coast hills are not such a serious bar to com-

munication as the Coast Range in the north; perhaps the Calapuyan bands had little the coast groups wanted. Similarly, the Yurok, Karok, and Hupa profess scant knowledge of and few contacts with the central Californian groups upriver and south of them.

## PHYSICAL ANTHROPOLOGY

The data on anthropometry of the North Pacific Coast leave much to be desired. The earliest measurements were made after nearly a century of white contacts and miscegenation, and, in the north, after several decades of the Pax Britannica that made possible more frequent contact and intermarriage among the Indians themselves. South of the Canadian border the data are very poor indeed. However, the information available suggests that the historic Indian population consisted of several distinct physical types, indicating varying sources of the native population, just as do the linguistic distributions. All the physical types are variants of the American Indian form of Mongoloid.

Beginning in the north, Tlingit, Haida, and Tsimshian were characterized anthropometrically as a distinct group, marked by tall stature, relatively short trunk, and long arms and legs. The head was large, and relatively broad, with correspondingly broad face. The nose was low, concave in profile, with low root and broad alae. From north to south, this type appears to have had some differences, perhaps representing dilution, which may be noted in stature: from Tlingit, 173 cm., Haida and Coast Tsimshian, 169 cm., to Niska, 167 cm.

Farther south the "Kwakiutl type" included Heiltsuk, Bella Coola, Southern Kwakiutl and Nootka. In this form, stature averaged medium (166 to 162 cm.). Bodily proportions differed sharply from those of northern neighbors: trunks were very long in relation to arm and leg lengths. Broad deep chests and wide shoulders were typical. The head was large and relatively broad, rather like that of the northern type, but the facial proportions differed, being not only broad but very long as well, with massive broad jaws. The nose form defined for this type was distinguished by great length, narrowness, and a highly convex profile, although a low-bridged concave form was also observed.

Professor Franz Boas, who pioneered the researches in physical anthropology in this area as well as those in linguistics and in ethnography, reported that he found no objective means for distinguishing Coast from Interior Salish in physical type. Salishan-speaking peoples from coast and inland groups conformed to a single physical type, which also was distinct from the Northern and Kwakiutl types. Stature was medium, heads were relatively broad but absolutely smaller than in the other two forms. Faces were broad, but, relatively and in actual measurement, very short. Noses were heavy, convex in profile, with a heavy long tip. Skin color, both on exposed and unexposed areas, was notably darker than that of either of the other types.

Archaeological investigations in the lower Fraser region have revealed that prior to the modern Salishan type, there was an earlier population characterized by long narrow skulls with narrow faces, and apparently short stature. Insufficient excavation has been carried out to make possible comments on the distribution of this early form.

South of the Canadian border, there are few data other than some on stature, which shows great irregularity. In southwest Oregon and northwest California there appears to have been a strong admixture of a long-headed California type that modified the brachycephalic pattern of most of the recent coast population.

## SUBDIVISIONS OF AREAL CULTURE

Although the description of North Pacific Coast civilization in preceding pages has stressed areawide culture patterns, frequent reference has been made to local differences within the framework of the general patterns. Detailed plotting of the distributions of the various local specializations shows four regional divisions or culture provinces, which are not, however, uniform:

(1) Northern province consists of the Tlingit, Haida, and all the Tsimshian. The Haisla are borderline, and are included as a marginal component of this province.

(2) Wakashan province includes Heiltsuk, Bella Coola, Southern Kwakiutl and Nootka, with provisional inclusion of the Comox groups of the Strait of Georgia Salish. Their inclusion or exclusion depends ultimately on whether or not the heavy overlay of Southern Kwakiutl traits that distinguished them from their linguistic congeners was a prehistoric acquisition, or a postcontact development. The Chemakum

and Quilente neighbors of the Makah (the Cape Flattery Nootkans) should be counted as marginal members of this subarea.

(3) Coast Salish-Chinook province includes all Coast Salish (except the Comox), the Chinook, and at least the Alsea on the Oregon coast.

(4) Northwest California province centers on the Yurok, Karok, and Hupa of the lower Klamath River, with the Coos, southwest Oregon Athapascans and Tolowa, and the Wiyot, as marginal components.

The separation of the area into subareas is probably the result of the way the region was settled over a prolonged period, and the delineation of subareas according to major criteria shows many parallels. The migrations of peoples of diverse origins are thus expressed in correlated linguistic divisions, cultural provinces, and the distribution of physical types.

Distinctive features of the cultural subdivisions are presented in four sketches of specific groups in chapters that follow. Each group described was typical of the culture province in which it was situated: Coast Tsimshian of the Northern province, Nootka of the Wakashan province, Chinook of the Coast Salish-Chinook province, and Yurok of the Northwest California province. Each sketch emphasizes the specializations of areal culture patterns that distinguish the four cultural subdivisions. Chapter 8 describes Kwakiutl Dancing Societies.

# CHAPTER 6

# The Opulent Tsimshian

## Ancestors

The lower Skeena River was the home of the Coast Tsimshian division of the groups speaking the Tsimshian tongue. These people were culturally typical of the Northern province of the North Pacific Coast, and this thumbnail sketch attempts to point out the distinctive features of that subarea in the course of describing Coast Tsimshian life. According to tradition, the ancestors of these people, and of their Gitksan and Niska relatives, came from a legendary site—Temlaxäm, or "Prairie Town"—somewhere in the interior, very long ago. The tales relating this phase of Tsimshian history have a strong interior flavor. They tell of times when the people were snowbound, and suffered famine; they refer to living in semisubterranean earth lodges of the interior type. It seems reasonable to accept these tales in a general sense; the Tsimshian had to reach their historic home by moving either from the interior or along the coast, and there is no evidence to support the possibility of coastal migration. After suffering innumerable vicissitudes, the ancestral Tsimshian began to establish themselves in villages below the Skeena River cañon. These villages were associated with salmon-fishing grounds on streams entering the Skeena, and continued to be important economic sites to the Tsimshian until modern times. So bountiful was this new land in comparison with their old sites in the interior that the Tsimshian traveled no farther for a long time.

## Tribes

The entire division of Coast Tsimshian was composed of fourteen tribes. Three of these moved to the outer coasts where they established permanent homes and acquired new territories, chiefly at the expense of the Tlingit and the northernmost Heiltsuk. These three were, or became, the Kitkahtla of Porcher Island, the Kitqata of the region around the mouth of Douglas Channel (where they cut the Haisla off from the outer coasts), and the Kitisu, farther south where they were the chief aggressors in endless wars against the disunited groups of northern Heiltsuk or Xaihais.

Nine of the remaining groups began to push northward from the mouth of the Skeena, driving out the Tlingit, until they held the mainland to the head of tidewater on the Nass and to the mouth of Portland Canal, and the adjacent islands. Each tribe chose a separate site and built a winter village on the islands flanking Metlakatla Pass, off the modern city of Prince Rupert, since the winters are much milder there than on the river. These Metlakatla Pass sites are now enormous shell middens; either the Tsimshian spent many winters there, or, as is more probable since there are more than nine large archaeological sites, the locality was intensively used by predecessors of these people.

The two remaining tribes, the Gitselas and the Gitsam-xelam, lived the year around in their villages at the entrance to Skeena River cañon. Like the three southern tribes, they maintained close contacts with the Metlakatla Pass groups. These last-named consisted of the Gitsilasu, Gilutsa, Gicpahloas, Gitando, Ginadoiks, Gitlan, Ginaxangik, Gitwilgiyots, and Gitsis. The element Git, Gic, or Gi' (sometimes rendered with a "k") means "people of——"; the latter portions of the tribal names refer to the village sites on the lower Skeena, suggesting that these groups achieved their sociopolitical identity while residing in that locality.

## The Year's Cycle

These groups controlled one of the most favorable districts of the coast. It was vast and had abundant resources. From their pleasant winter village sites, where they enjoyed the milder temperatures of the outer coasts but were sheltered from ocean storms, they moved in the spring to Red Bluff on the lower Nass, which was the scene of the heaviest annual run of olachen of the area. They caught the oil-rich fish in great quantity, aboriginally with only the herring rake, but the schools of fish were so dense that a full canoe was normally obtained in a very short while.

Just prior to the historic period, a new device was introduced, a net with a wide funnel mouth and a long tubular section tied shut at the end. The mouth of the net was prepared with withe rings that slipped over stakes set in the river bed to hold the net in place under water. When enough fish had entered, the after end was pulled up with a ring and pole; the ring shut off the tubular section and prevented escape of the fish. The tip was untied and the fish dumped into the canoe. This net came to be used wherever olachen were fished on the coast. It is called yakatl (or yagatl) by Tlingit, Tsimshian, Nass, Haisla, Heiltsuk, and Southern Kwakiutl; only the Bella Coola have their own name for it. According to native tradition, the net was invented by a Haisla girl, who conceived the idea after watching a bullhead (a large-headed, widemouthed fish, whose form the net resembles) swallowing baby trout. From the Haisla, the net was introduced to the Tsimshian and Nass, and by them to Tlingit who owned olachen streams (especially Unuk and Chilkat Rivers), and the device was also diffused southward along the coast.

Canoe loads of olachen were thrown into large pits and left to "ripen," that is, to partially decompose, which made the oil easier to render. When the fish had attained the proper degree of ripeness, they were scooped into wooden boxes, water was added, and the mass brought to a boil with red-hot stones. Oil was then skimmed off the top and allowed to cool. As it cooled, it thickened and became "grease." The emanations from the huge pits of rotting fish combined with the vapors from the cooking boxes produced, it is reported, a remarkable atmosphere, but the Indians were not squeamish in those days. Modern Indians, in deference to whites, now render grease from fresh-caught olachen, but the old people complain that it does not have the same rich flavor it used to have. The people were happy in this busy stench-laden activity, for the olachen grease constituted one of the great riches of the Tsimshian tribes. The substance was a highly regarded foodstuff north of the Strait of Georgia, and grease from the Nass was famed far and wide as the best.

The Haida, in whose islands no olachen runs occur, came to the Nass to trade with Tsimshian and with the Niska farther upstream, who also reaped a rich harvest of the fish. They brought huge canoes wrought from the finest red cedar, elaborately carved boxes, flaky white dried halibut, and their famous chewing tobacco to trade. Tlingit too came in numbers, as ready to fight as to trade, for they were usually on bad terms with Tsimshian, but wanted the grease. Even Sanyakwan Tlingit, in whose Unuk River olachen ran, admitted that Nass grease was of superior flavor to their own. The Tlingit also brought a variety of trade goods, the most prized being the copper plaques that their northernmost divisions obtained from the Copper River natives. Later, the Coast Tsimshian took grease inland to trade with their Gitksan relatives for furs, dressed deer and moose skins, and porcupine-quill embroidery, which the Gitksan had obtained from the Carrier.

The olachen camps at Red Bluff represented one of the peaks in activity and excitement in the yearly round. When the run was over and the last boxful of fish had been tried out, the people loaded their canoes with their newly acquired trade goods and with boxes of grease for their own use or for later trading ventures. Even though many canoes were large, more than one trip was sometimes necessary to get all the people, grease, and possessions back to Metlakatla Pass.

The canoes of the Coast Tsimshian enabled them to move about freely and exploit adequately their sea-coast environment. Although designated the "Northern type," the canoe was the standard model of all coast groups including the Southern Kwakiutl, and with minor modifications, of many Coast Salish near the Strait of Georgia and Puget Sound. This vessel was made with a vertical forefoot and sloping counter. Separate prow and stern pieces (described in Chapter 2 in the section on canoes) fended off wave crests that otherwise might come aboard. In cross section, the bottom of the hull was slightly flattened for stability. The sides followed the natural curvature of the log, but any tendency to tumble home was eliminated from the log by the spreading operation, also described earlier. These craft were made in a variety of sizes and proportions. Some war canoes for transporting personnel and freight were huge: forty to fifty feet in length, six feet in beam. Since these were the vessels used on festive occasions, the prowpiece was often surmounted with carvings, and the hull above waterline was elaborately painted. As remarked, some of the biggest and finest of these canoes were Haida-built, but the Coast Tsimshian also had competent canoewrights who made fine craft. Canoes for fishing and other everyday use had the same lines as the war canoes, but were smaller. Special long, slender craft were custom-built for sea hunters to glide swiftly and silently through the water. All canoes were propelled with crutch-handled paddles that had elliptical blades tapering to a slender point.

As a rule, the people did not tarry long at the Metlakatla Pass villages on their return from the Nass. Halibut fishing and sea-mammal hunting were engaged in briefly before it was time to go to the Skeena to ready the weirs and traps for the salmon runs. Salmon fishing in the streams was not an exciting occupation, but drudgery. It was not the skillful or lucky man who put up the big catch, it was the industrious one. Men and older boys tended the traps or harpooned or dip-netted, then carried the fish back to camp. The womenfolk hunkered over their cutting boards, sliming and gutting the fish, then slicing them thin with mussel-shell blades. The fish were spread with wooden skewers to dry. There was wood to get—spruce and fir knots to keep the fires going, and half-rotten alder to make the smoke that gave the fish a pleasant flavor. Fish were smoked in large plank structures. Men helped their wives rustle wood, and gave them a hand at turning over yesterday's catch, moving day-before-yesterday's fish higher on the drying racks, and hanging up the fish just prepared. There were skewers to be prepared for next day, a damaged harpoon tip to be repaired, or other chores to tend to. The period of salmon fishing was a busy season, with no time for play. Berrypicking permitted some breaks in the routine, but after salmon

season, there was more time for this pursuit. Local groups went berrying on the hillsides along the Skeena; others owned berry grounds
elsewhere.

When the supply of dried salmon was safely in the big winter
houses on Metlakatla Pass, there was not much time until the onset of
winter. Some hunting, both on land and on water, was done at this
time, and canoes and houses were repaired in preparation for winter.

## Houses

In the winter villages, the Coast Tsimshian built well-carpentered
structures in the best of the Northern province tradition. These huge
houses were constructed of massive timbers hewed from red cedar.
Four square cornerposts were slotted to receive the "plates," or side
beams. They also supported the paired plates that formed low gables
at front and rear. Subsidiary posts, usually elaborately carved, supported the typical double ridgepole, and often still other posts and
beams divided the span between the paired ridgepoles and the side-
plates. Sills were mortised into the bases of the cornerposts at front
and sides; upper sill faces and the undersides of roof plates had match-
ing slots into which planks were fitted vertically to form the walls.
Roofing consisted of double rows of overlapping planks. An ingeniously suspended plank smokehole cover could be rotated on a
horizontal axis to one side or the other of the central smokehole
to keep out wind and rain.

Houses were a little less than square, fifty by fifty-five feet being
average size and proportions. A central pit, approximately five feet
deep and thirty feet square, formed the main living space, where
women cooked at the central fireplace and people ate or lounged.
One or more sets of steps led into the pit, which was usually lined
with wide cedar-plank retaining walls. Some houses had narrow platforms around the principal pit, serving as subsidiary steps and benches.
Traditions tell of great houses of bygone days that had ten levels or
platforms, but no such enormous structures have been observed in
the modern period. The upper platform, at ground level, served
for storage and for sleeping places.

At the rear of the house the chief and his immediate family occupied
one or more cubicles formed of especially selected planks, which

were often elaborately carved and painted with designs referring to family crests. People of lesser rank had family spaces along the side walls. Boxes and baskets of food and other gear formed casual partitions between the spaces of individual families. The house walls were often lined with cedar-bark mats against winter winds that whistled through the cracks between the planks. The lower levels and sleeping places were usually floored with planks. The large rectangular fireplace was boxed and filled with sand and with the beach cobbles that were used for the stone-boiling technique of cooking. The principal entryway to the house was at the center of the gable end facing the beach. Both rectangular and oval doorways were in use at least in recent times, although oval entries may have been more frequent anciently. Some houses had portal poles, tall shafts of red cedar with carvings depicting the inhabitants' major crests, the gaping mouth of the lowest principal figure forming the doorway. Portal poles were not as common among the Tsimshian as among the Haida. However, the whole house front was often painted with designs relating to family crests.

The winter houses were the Tsimshians' principal homes, which the people worked most of the year to fill with food and valuables so they might spend the winter in feasts and festivities. These houses were symbols of the people's wealth. Only a prosperous family group was considered capable of building such a structure, and in a sense this was true. Primitive methods of logging and lumbering required numerous man-days of labor in the preparation of timbers and planking; consequently surpluses of food had to be prepared to maintain the labor force while they performed this work. In addition, both foods and treasure had to be accumulated to "pay" other groups to perform certain tasks (carving, painting, and setting up the house), and for the festivities deemed necessary on completion of the structure. The many houses in the nine villages on Metlakatla Pass represented a concentration of riches almost beyond belief to neighboring peoples, whose winter villages, consisting of similar houses, were scattered and remote from one another.

In 1834, Hudson's Bay Company established a trading post called Fort Simpson, and it was not long until Tsimshian groups began to construct winter houses nearby. The advantages of living close to the post were manifold: not only were trade goods constantly available, but the Tsimshian were also in a position to intercept other groups who came to trade furs, thus gaining a middleman's profit with little effort. Hence the sites on Metlakatla Pass were abandoned, and all nine tribes settled at Fort Simpson. The migration was expedited by moving all serviceable planking and timbers from the old sites to the new. Feasts and potlatches were celebrated one after another with furs, canoes, coppers, trade blankets, guns, and many other articles distributed in splendid profusion. Only a rich people like the Tsimshian could have accomplished such a move in so short a time. When all nine tribes were assembled at Fort Simpson, they numbered about four thousand people.

## Clan Organization

The tribes were not equally divided numerically, but they all had an identical formal social structure, according to which each tribe was composed of four matrilineal clans. The names of these clans and the principal crests associated with them were the same in all nine tribes, and in fact among the other Coast Tsimshian as well. Thus, each tribe was comprised of the following: Laxgebu (Wolf People), Laxsgik (Eagle People), Gicpodwuda (Blackfish clan), and Qanada (Raven clan).[1] Analysis of functions makes clear that each of the four clans of each tribe was basically a local group. A complicating factor is that the rule of exogamy, fundamental to formal clan organization, was extended from these basic units to all clans with the same name. Accordingly, a man, for example, of the Qanada clan of the Gitando was not only prohibited from marrying a Gitando woman of his clan, but also from marriage with any woman of a Qanada clan of any other tribe, or even of corresponding divisions among the Niska and Gitksan. The clans were even equated on the basis of similarities of crests with clans of the Tlingit and Haida, permitting extension of the exogamic rule to those neighboring groups. In the older literature, the term "phratry" is sometimes used to refer to the combined clans of same name and crests of the Tsimshian, that is to say, all the Qanada of all the tribes, or all the Eagle People. However, these "phratries"

[1] Gicpodwuda (People of ———) is an untranslatable term. Members of the clan are usually referred to in English as the Blackfish (or Killerwhale) clan after one of their principal crests. Qanada is similarly untranslatable.

were not functioning social entities in any sense beyond that of their limitation on choice of mates.

The individual clan unit within each tribe, as remarked, was basically a local group, and it had all the attributes and functions of a local group as described in Chapter 3: its members were regarded as close relatives and were ranked in a continuous series from the clan chief down; they jointly owned lands of economic importance, house and camp sites, and a host of privileges—ceremonial names or titles for chiefs and their lesser brethren, house names, ritual performances, songs, and the like. Perhaps most important were the crests, the animal or monster figures associated with each clan. The principal crests—Wolf, Eagle, Blackfish, Raven—and certain accompanying ones, such as Frog with Raven and Beaver with Eagle, were represented in each of the fourteen tribes of Coast Tsimshian, but minor crests were peculiar to certain clans. Most honorific titles for chiefs and house names referred to the principal crests of the clan. The carved house posts and portal poles, the paintings on chiefs' rooms, on house fronts, canoes, and wooden boxes, the carvings on food dishes and mountain-goat horn spoons, in brief, the decoration of almost every object, represented one or more of the clan crests of the owner.

The neat and orderly fourfold division of the Coast Tsimshian tribes suggests a possible arbitrary and artificial development after the arrival of the groups on the coast. It is probable that alien influence, particularly from the Tlingit, affected the Tsimshian system. For example, the name of one clan, Qanada, which is meaningless in Tsimshian, is related to the Tlingit place-name "Ganax" (said to mean "safe, or sheltered, place"). Ganax was claimed as a traditional home site of one of the important Tlingit lines, whose several related branches, each of which eventually became an independent local group, call themselves "Ganaxadi" or by a variant form, "Ganaxtedi," both of which terms mean simply "People from Ganax." (There was also a place called "Ganax" in the Queen Charlotte Islands which was important in the tradition of certain family lines.) Among the related Niska there were no Eagle People (Laxsgik) except at one place, where a Tlingit clan-local group settled after having been driven out of their original home.

The Gitksan also have a threefold division: Xanada, Laxgebu, and Fireweed People (Gichäst, equated by them with Gicpodwada), except at one village, in which there is an Eagle People (Laxsgik). According to tradition they moved in from the Nass, and were of Tlingit origin. It is not known whether this group split off from the formerly Tlingit Laxsgik group at Gitlaxdamks, mentioned above, or was descended from another set of Tlingit wanderers.

However, the Tsimshian system was not simply a copy of Tlingit society, which was based on a twofold division, or moiety system. Through matrilineal descent reckoning, all the Tlingit belonged to either the Raven or the Wolf (in the north also referred to as Eagle) moiety. In every Tlingit "tribe"—and these "tribes" were much less firmly integrated than among the Coast Tsimshian—both moieties were necessarily represented, but there might be only one Raven clan-local group and three or four Wolf-Eagle clan-local groups, or vice versa. The Haida had matrilineal moieties, like the Tlingit, but with no clustering of local groups. Each Haida clan-local group had a separate village, which had no connection with any other except for traditional relationships between two or more daughter groups. Incidentally, there was a group of Haida local units whose names contained the element "Gitins," meaningless in Haida, but suggesting derivation from the Tsimshian stem "Git-," "People of ——"; possibly the ancestors of these groups were of Tsimshian origin. At any rate, it is clear that there has been considerable interchange among the three northern linguistic divisions, not only of concepts and nomenclature but also of population.

However established, the Tsimshian system could be maintained indefinitely, despite disease, unbalanced sex ratio at birth, or disastrous enemy raids, by adoption of children from a more numerous clan-local group into one threatened with extinction, or by adoption of children from a corresponding division of another tribe. Both methods have been used to keep noble titles active in recent decades when the population suffered decline.

The Coast Tsimshian tribal groupings were more solidly unified than those of any of their neighbors, even including their Niska and Gitksan kin. The four component clan-local groups of each tribe were ranked in order, although the sequence differed from one tribe to another. The nine Fort Simpson tribes seem to have come closer than comparable divisions on the coast to developing a national sense, even though on occasion they found themselves in conflict. This feeling of unity was greatly enhanced after their settlement at Fort Simpson, but its roots seem to extend back to an earlier day. Perhaps the attitude developed while the ancestors of the Coast Tsimshian fought their way to the outer coast, or perhaps it was already in existence and was the factor responsible for their military successes.

In the matrilineal descent system among the Tsimshian, boys were brought up by their biological parents until the age of nine or ten, when they went to live with their maternal uncles, whose clan and tribal membership, and whose status they would inherit. The Tlingit who observed the same custom rationalized that the real fathers would not have the heart to force the youngsters through the rigors of the training program, with daily bathing in icy waters and whipping with bundles of branches to restore circulation to numbed skin. A girl, however, stayed with her parents until marriage, when she went to live at her husband's home.

## Potlatches and Life Crises

The life of the individual Coast Tsimshian was punctuated with frequent feasts and potlatches, as was expected among a people of vast wealth. Like other groups that participated in the potlatch complex, they viewed the crises of life as events of twofold significance. First, observances were necessary for the wellbeing of the individual and those close to him. Second, after the perilous phase had been successfully weathered, the sociological significance of the fact should be made public, affirming or reaffirming membership in the group, defining or redefining specific status in the complex social system.

The most splendid potlatches, involving conspicuous waste and gifts of spectacular amounts, were celebrated in honor of those of highest rank—the heirs or potential heirs, that is, the sons and daughters of the eldest sisters of the chiefs of the clan-local groups. Those of lesser status were more modestly presented to the public, or were included in secondary roles in the festivities for a kinsman of higher rank. The major Tsimshian potlatch was a memorial to a deceased chief and the validation of his heir's titles and status. At the same celebration, those of lesser status could be presented as group members. The time for their debut was adjusted to conform to that of the major event, which was planned well in advance: the first naming of recently born infants, the ear-piercing of both boys and girls, and the lip-piercing of prepubescent girls for the first, small labret, or the completion of a pubescent girl's restrictions.

According to Tsimshian custom, the time of a girl's coming out was flexible. At her first menses, a maiden was secluded in a cubicle prepared in the house or camp. She was subjected to nearly a total fast for four days. Girls of highest rank were sometimes given a double dose: after four days the pubescent was given a modest meal of old dried salmon, and then went through a second four-day fasting period. She was ritually bathed, and her hair dressed by her mother and her father's sisters before a period of secondary seclusion, which was subject to less stringent restrictions. Principal tabus were on eating fresh salmon and certain species of game, and on going about. This period was usually said to last "a year," but really lasted until the end of the next salmon-fishing season. It could be lengthened or shortened if a major potlatch was scheduled, so that group affiliation could be formally affirmed simultaneously with privileges bestowed on other members of the group.

The death of a chief set in motion a complex chain of events. His widow or widows cut their hair short and soot-blackened their faces in mourning. They were secluded in a cubicle for four days and nights while the people assembled and sang the dirges of the clan each night. Other mourners cut their hair, women short, men to about shoulder length, and painted their faces with special mourning patterns of the family. The mourners who were members of the dead chief's clan-local group were semirestricted and called upon other divisions to perform various tasks in connection with mortuary rites. Although father's clan was not stressed as much by the Tsimshian as by the Tlingit, members of the clan-group of the dead chief's father were charged with many important tasks. They prepared the corpse. The body was set up in the place of honor at the center rear of the house, surrounded by family crest symbols and valuables. His coppers stood on end in splendid array in front of the body. The clan-group of the father of the deceased also prepared the funeral pyre and took care of the transportation and cremation. Ashes and bits of unburned bone were carefully collected, put in a decorated wooden box, and secreted in the woods to prevent their being used in black magic. Cremation was the universal method of disposal of bodies in the early historic period until missionary influence caused abandonment of the custom, but some Coast Tsimshian informants insist that anciently box burial in caves was customary, as among many Wakashan-speaking groups to the south.

A chief lying in state.

The heir and his advisors asked another group to prepare a memorial pole, and sometimes the occasion was utilized to build a new house or to make major repairs to the old house. The groups who performed these tasks were supported with provisions by the mourning group, who served them nightly feasts while the work was in progress. The work was done at convenient times during the year and was suspended for the olachen fishing on the Nass and salmon fishing on the lower Skeena, because it was essential to lay in food stores. With these interruptions, preparations for the great potlatch might last for a year or more. Ceremonial gear had to be refurbished or renewed, songs and dances taught and practiced. Vast amounts of provisions had to be laid by for the feasting. Hunters and trappers ranged far in search of valuable furs. Trading parties moved canoe loads of olachen grease and other goods to neighboring peoples or carried boxes of grease on their backs over the mountainous trails to trade with the interior "Stick Indians," as they were disparagingly called. Formal invitations were issued to guests by parties dressed in finery and singing special songs. Several features of the Coast Tsimshian potlatch procedure vary from the generalized areal procedure described in Chapter 3. Presentation of group members of lesser importance was made first, before that of the dead chief's heir. Later in the proceedings a masked dancer, representing an ancestral spirit and carrying a copper, instructed the new chief to break the copper and present pieces to the guest chiefs. "Breaking" was done with a chisel. The generally somber tone of the mortuary potlatch was relieved by dances of age-mates—youths, middle-aged men, old men, young married women, old women—of the clan of the deceased chief.

The formal potlatch distribution was given as "payment" for the mortuary tasks—the cutting, carving, and setting up of the memorial pole, the house-building—or for any special task, such as ear- or lip-piercing performed on junior members of the family. These "payments" were gifts scaled to the social rank of the recipient, not to the task performed. When a task like carving a memorial pole required the skills of a specialist, the chief to whom it was assigned "subcontracted" the job, paying the artisan who did the actual work. When the stores of wealth had been distributed, the guests departed with their gifts, and the heir was firmly established in his new position, satisfied that he had discharged his obligations to his predecessor and the family ancestors and had satisfactorily demonstrated the wealth and power of his family by the splendor of his potlatch. In the early days of Fort Simpson, rivalry potlatches were given by Tsimshian chiefs, but few details are known about them. They were said to have been bitterly contested, but never became firmly rooted in the potlatch pattern.

## Dancing Societies

The Dancing Societies were known to the Coast Tsimshian, most of the groups possessing performances of the Nutlam and of the Ones-descending-from-the-heavens (Dluwulaxa, or Mitla). Many of the individual spirit representations in these performances were known by their Heiltsuk names, making their origin fairly obvious. A few groups possessed the right to perform some of the dances of the Shamans series, but only the Southern Coast Tsimshian (Kitkahtla, Kitqata, and Kitisu), had this complex in its entirety. Performances were valued as distinctive and important privileges, but among the Fort Simpson groups at least, never attained the importance of the crest displays. The Dancing Society complexes were diffusing north-ward from their probable center of origin among the Heiltsuk when historical factors, principally Christian missionary activity, caused them to be abandoned. The Gitksan had the Nutlam and the Ones-descend-ing-from-the-heavens cycles, but are said to have owned none of the Shamans series performances. Southern Tlingit groups had few indi-vidual masks and dances, which they apparently performed in-completely and out of context.

## Art

In addition to being famous for their riches, the Coast Tsimshian were outstanding exponents of the Northern style of decorative art. One of the distinctive regional styles was that of the three northern-most linguistic divisions. This Northern style was highly conventional-ized applied art. It was used to decorate utilitarian objects, from spoons and dishes to house posts, from halibut hooks to storage boxes, from canoes to shaman devices for entrapping lost souls. A distinctive trait of the art style related to its applied nature: the patterns, whether painted or carved, were adapted to the form of the object they em-bellished. The themes were representations of the animals, birds, fish, or monsters that were the crests or supernatural beings important in family legends. The adaptation of design in application to an object usually required more or less distortion.

Several techniques of application were used in painting and low-relief carving, which usually involved a conceptual splitting of the figure into two symmetrical halves, as though sliced from head to tail and spread flat around the decorative field. Such treatment produced an exact symmetry, which was an esthetic necessity to the artists. Although carving in high relief or in full round did not require this kind of adaptation, even high-relief designs were modified to conform to the shape of the object they decorated. However, carvings in full round or high relief were infrequent. Totem poles and spoon handles, which may appear to be in the round, are in low relief, that is, the design is wrapped around the cylindrical or half-cylindrical basic form. As a result of this characteristic, designs were confined within the limits of the form to which they were applied. This is true even when appendages were mounted on the carving, as was sometimes done in representations of a bird's beak or the dorsal "fin" of the killer whale. Such attachments extended beyond the basic shape of the object, but the design as a whole was dominated by the outlines of the pole or spoon handle or whatever.

The static quality that such limitation of field might have given the designs was countered by several conventional techniques. On elongated objects series of figures were overlapped, or interlocked, so that the observer's eye is carried from one part of the total design to the other. Rhythmic sequences of large and small figures augmented this effect of movement in many Northern style designs. Another device that gave an esthetic effect of motion was the use of lines of varying width. Almost all wood carving was painted with accentuating lines, wider at the middle and tapering toward the ends. The Coast Tsimshian made such frequent use of another manner of suggesting variation of the decorated field that it often serves to distinguish their work from that of their Tlingit and Haida neighbors. Large and very small figures were combined, not only in lineal sequences, but in internal sequences, using the tiny figures as filler. All large open areas of the principal design—eyes, ears, flippers of sea mammals, limbs of animal and human figures, especially at the joints—were covered with carved and painted small elements, such as tiny faces or the conventionalized "eye" motif. This tendency to fill all spaces with small figures was found in all Northern style art, but was especially characteristic of Coast Tsimshian work. This type of treatment is also typical of the Chilkat blanket designs, and is one reason many

Totem pole.

authorities are inclined to credit the tradition that this type of weaving diffused to the northern Tlingit from a Tsimshian source.

Another characteristic of the Northern art style is the conventional-ized depiction of the themes. The creatures used as crests were painted and carved with limited realism. Heads and bodies of land animals, and the occasional human beings portrayed, were of about the same form and proportions; those of birds differed chiefly in being shown with wings. Aquatic forms with fins and flippers were a little more distinctive. A particular animal was identified by a specific conventionalization, which was used and recognized everywhere in the geographical range of the art style. For example, Beaver was always depicted as a generalized animal with prominent incisors, a wide scaly (cross-hatched) tail, and raised forepaws, sometimes holding a horizontal stick to the mouth. Bear had a long snout, protruding tongue, and prominent claws. A birdlike figure with a long, straight beak represented Raven; if the beak was shorter and strongly hooked downward, Eagle. Most of these recognition traits were fairly obvious; however, to correctly identify monsters, like Sea Bears and other wierd fancies, one needs familiarity with the traditions of the family group for whom the carving was made.

From the purely artistic standpoint one might argue that this rigid conventionalization inhibited truly creative artists, confining them to the level of their mediocre brethren. However, in mask-making the artist had more freedom to give rein to his talent. Masks were free of the restraints of applied art and permitted greater scope in rendering many minor or special beings whose distinguishing features were not universally standardized. In addition, realistic portrait masks of living persons were made when a ritual called for the appearance of a double of some performer. Masks of this kind are realistic sculpture of considerable merit.

Among the Coast Tsimshian there were many masters of this art. Some of them carved many memorial poles for neighbors, particularly the related Gitksan, and far to the north, a famous painted screen of a Chilkat Tlingit house was apparently done by a Tsimshian. Every Northern province chief had to have at least one Raven rattle. Its artistic merit lies in the graceful, streamlined form, which overcomes the gimcrack effect of little figures on the Raven's back and unrelated design on the underside. The rattles were made by carvers of various divisions, but the best were said to be Tsimshian. The same was true of headdresses that featured a flattish, delicately carved and inlaid maskette attached to a headband surmounted by sea-lion whiskers, with a trailer of ermine skins down the back. Even their neighbors who were often at odds with the Coast Tsimshian considered their artists outstanding.

# CHAPTER 7

# The Nootkan Whalers

## Mokwina and the Noble Lady [1]

The big cedar dugout slid over the long sea, the tapered forefoot slicing through the green water. With effortless strokes six paddlers drove the craft on a southeasterly course parallel to the shore, the sheen of sweat on their naked bodies the only sign they had been paddling since before dawn.

The only apparel were wide-brimmed basketry rain hats for protection from the afternoon sun, and black paint covering their faces. Usually deer tallow and red clay were applied to prevent sunburn, but today Chief Mokwina had ordered black paint to show their anger, for they had cruised fruitlessly in search of whales for three days. Only the seventh crewman, the elderly steersman, had not complied. He had painted his face dark red with wavy black lines, a

---

[1] A synthetic story based on several accounts of whale hunts by various Nootkan informants, *not* a single verbatim account.

133

design of secret magical significance. Although a commoner, he knew much about whaling ritual, as well as the practical aspects of the hunt, for he had been trusted aide and steersman of the chief's father before him. He had often listened to the story of Mokwina's ancestor, whose guardian spirit encounter many years ago was the source of valuable secret knowledge about whaling, in Mokwina's family. (Traditions relate that the art of whaling had been acquired in ancient times by two or three groups who lived the year around on the shelterless outer coasts, and who eventually transmitted the knowledge to others, usually as part of the bride-price repayment.) Mokwina called him "uncle" as a sign of respect and fondness.

Chief Mokwina squatted in the bow of the canoe, glowering over his box of charms and spirit tokens. Only he and his steersman "uncle" knew the mysteries the box contained. Rumor had it that the skull of his paternal grandfather, painted with whaling scenes, was one of the key pieces. The grandfather had killed twenty-three whales while he had borne the title "Mokwina," and the present chief was trying to surpass his record. But neither skull nor any other charm was producing results on this hunt. During the arduous days of Mokwina's preparatory training, whales were seen daily, spouting and lolling lazily on the surface close inshore. One had even played for several hours directly in front of the summer village of Yukwot. Mokwina had been tempted to break his training ritual to try for it, but he was at a crucial point in his training routine and it took time to arm and stow the harpoon line and floats. The whale might depart during this process, bringing bad luck to the whole season's hunting. However, the whale had remained in the vicinity, and Mokwina thought bitterly, "Perhaps that was the whale my deceased grandfather called for me. Could it be that I offended the Whale Spirits by not trying for it? Offended or not, just let me close one, and she'll find that this Mokwina can drive a harpoon as deep as could any of his forefathers!"

Angrily he fumbled among the objects in the box until he found what he wanted: a string of human teeth from which hung two killer-whale tusks. He tied this token about his neck. The old steersman recognized the piece, clapped his hand over his mouth, then nodded reluctant approval. The string of grisly ornaments was used in the ritual, but he had never seen it worn on a hunt. Ordinarily the

Whale Spirits were beseeched and cajoled. Displaying the object implied a defiant challenge. The teeth had been battered from the heads of slain enemies. The tusks symbolized those ruthless foes of the giant whales, Wolf Spirits gone to sea.

The chief replaced the lid on his charm box. Over his shoulder he said, "My uncle, aren't we in deep water here?"

The steersman replied in the low flat tone that did not carry far over water, "My chief, the mountain peak of the Ahousat Thunderbird is coming in line with the steep edge of Sealion Rock. We are coming to the edge of very deep water here. The 'noble ladies' should be feeding and playing in shallower water on a day like this."

Sea Hunters knew the "noble ladies" were whales, but it was tabu during the hunt to mention them by name.

"Steer in to the edge of the kelp beds, then come about, and we'll cruise back down the coast."

As the bow swung to the port, the steersman waved his paddle overhead so the sunlight flashed on the blade to signal a change of course to the two escort craft. A whaling canoe, manned and outfitted in every respect like that of the chief, was captained by Mokwina's next younger brother. The third vessel was a sleek sealing canoe with a crew of three, nearly as long as a whaling canoe, but just barely broad enough to accommodate a man. Its trim lines and carefully burnished hull slipped through the water so easily, its crew kept station on the chief's craft by lazy irregular strokes.

Mokwina climbed to his usual lookout position, standing with a foot on either gunwale just astern of the prow piece, and swaying easily to the roll of the canoe. The whale hunter was a striking figure: he was not tall, but burly, with a broad muscular back, deep chest, solid belly, and short thick legs. His physique and truculent bearing gave him a formidable air that made it seem slightly less fantastic that puny man should seek and attack the mightiest creature of the animal kingdom.

In the quiet voice used during the hunt, a bow paddler called for the drinking water. The steersman shoved the container forward with his paddle to the nearest crewman, who passed it on. The container was a small wooden box with a close fitting lid lashed down with cordage. A small access hole lessened the danger of spilling water in rough seas, and a plug and drinking tube were attached to the lid in good seagoing fashion. The paddler pulled the plug, inserted the tube, the leg bone of a crane, and murmured one of Mokwina's towing chants, "Noble lady, the fresh water at our village of Yukwot is sweet." After taking a few sips through the tube, he drove the plug back into place with the heel of his hand and passed it back aft.

The canoe was nearing the kelp beds when a whale surfaced on the port bow, not fifty yards away. A sighting so close was unusual, and it was a shocking spectacle. Where there had been nothing but green sea and the background of Vancouver Island's shore and mountains, suddenly a shadow appeared beneath the water and an enormous gray mass burst the surface. The creature spouted, then lay quietly so that only her head and back were above water. Her flukes moved gently from side to side. Mokwina scrambled down from his perch on the gunwales and seized the harpoon from its proper position: butt on the floor of the canoe, slightly to starboard, and armed foreshaft resting on the prow piece. The Nootkan whaling harpoon, complete with shaft, foreshaft, and head, was nearly twenty feet long. The heavy seasoned yew shaft was three or four inches in diameter, and tapered to its ends. It was made in three sections so skillfully joined that it appeared to be a single flawless piece of wood. Two pieces of elkhorn formed a slot for a blade of giant mussel shell, which was held in place with a coating of spruce gum. The two pieces of elkhorn and shell were lashed together, the lashing also forming a lanyard with an eye splice for the main line. (A similar harpoon head for salmon fishing is illustrated on p. 12.) When the shell broke on a strike, as often happened, the elkhorn pieces remained as barbs. The shell cutting blade was easily replaced with a spare, but Mokwina treasured the elkhorn base, which had belonged to his father and to his grandfather.

Mokwina snatched up the heavy object with one hand, gesturing wildly with the other for the crew to close the resting whale. The signals were superfluous. The crewmen were already paddling as hard and as silently as they could toward the quarry. But before they could put the chief alongside, the whale sounded, flipping her tail flukes as she dove. Mokwina signalled his men to stop where the whale had disappeared and stood waiting, the unwieldy harpoon in his hands, point to his right. The crew held their crossgrip paddles poised, the steersman steadied the bow of the canoe. All eyes searched the water anxiously.

The shadow appeared beneath the water once more, to the right of the anticipated heading. The whale broached, spouted, and went down again before the paddlers could get the canoe under way. The chief snarled in rage. Resting the harpoon on the prow, he used hand signals to maneuver the canoe into position. There was another tense wait of several minutes.

When the whale came up, she was so close that the hunters felt the spray from her spouting on their faces. Her tail flukes were abeam of the canoe's prow. But she was to the left, the wrong side. The harpooner could strike only to his right, and the bulky 40-fathom harpoon line and its four inflated sealskin floats were coiled in two parts that could run only over the starboard side. Cautiously the paddlers backed water until the canoe crossed behind the gigantic beast, then drove forward close to the animal's left side. They barely lifted the long tapered paddle points out of the water, so the drip from the blades would make no sound. When they had placed Mokwina abreast of the whale's left "flipper," they stopped and steadied the canoe. The strike had to be made at very close quarters for the harpoon was too heavy to throw.

The chief stood tense, holding the harpoon almost horizontally, high over his head, his toes curled over the gunwales. The steersman watched carefully. When the whale's tail flukes were closest to the canoe in their pendulumlike swinging, they were least likely to strike it in frantic reaction. Rather, they would swing away from the canoe. At that precise moment he called, "Now!" The first starboard paddler touched the chief's leg with his paddle tip. The chief pivoted at the waist and drove the harpoon with all his strength just behind the whale's flipper. A solid jar told him the harpoon had driven home deep and firm. He dropped from the gunwales to a crouch on the floor of the canoe, to avoid being struck by the harpoon shaft as the cetacean rolled wildly.

The paddlers on the port side backed water hard as their mates drove forward, veering the canoe off sharply from the whale. The animal lunged forward in a spasmodic movement, then sounded, carrying the harpoon line of tough twisted cedar withes and its four sealskin floats over the side.

As the line uncoiled, only the first float disappeared from view, indicating relatively shallow water. The other three zigzagged wildly as the creature fought to free herself of the harpoon head. However, the sharp blade of mussel shell had shattered on impact, letting the heavy lanyard pull the pair of elkhord barbs slightly crosswise to the route of entry. The harpoon head was too deeply imbedded in muscle to be torn free by the resistance of line and floats or even by the whale's struggles.

The cedar-bark string that held the long yew shaft of his harpoon was strong enough to hold the head in place when he made the strike, but now, as intended, it broke during the whale's struggles, and the shaft came floating to the surface, astern of the whale. Mokwina ordered his crew to turn off course to recover it, then changed his mind, as the sealing canoe came knifing through the water to make the recovery. It was the task of this speedier vessel to carry the harpoon shaft directly to Yukwot as notification of a successful strike. At the village, the harpoon was leaned against the wall over the chief's sleeping place, where his principal wife lay covered with a mat of cedar bark. She was from a noble family at Clayoquot, and had been trained from childhood in the rituals proper to a chief's wife. She understood the importance of her role and was meticulous in performance. She had been lying motionless since the whaling party's departure before dawn, to make the whale tame and quiet. During the hunt she represented the animal and controlled its movements by her own: if she made quick brusque movements, the whale would, too. She, therefore, lay as quietly as possible to assure the hunters a docile whale. When the harpoon shaft was placed over her, several women assistants seated around her began a chant, extolling the beauties of the village and inviting the "noble lady" to visit them.

Meanwhile, the hunters pursued the "noble lady." Two paddlers inflated spare floats, bending them to short coils of line and then to lanyards of spare harpoon heads which the chief passed them from his charm box. Mokwina rigged a spare harpoon shaft with a head and a short length of line buoyed by a single float.

The chief's younger brother waited at his station some distance to the left. He was said to have the honor of striking the second harpoon. However, in practice, whoever was in a better position made the strike. This time Mokwina was closer when the whale surfaced, and he jabbed the harpoon high on the back. The strike was badly placed, but by luck it held. The chief's brother closed with the whale and placed his harpoon deep in the side, near Mokwina's first strike, and like the first, this blade carried a complete 40-fathom line with four floats.

The titanic struggle, the drag of lines and floats, and the repeated attacks of the whalers each time the beast surfaced—all combined to tire her. The hunters would not give her adequate breathing time, and her dives became shorter, her surges less violent. The remaining harpoons and spare floats were soon placed, adding to the burden the weary animal dragged through the water. Her dives became shallow, she surfaced longer, breathing heavily, and payed no attention to her tormentors when they tried to make her dive. It would not be long until the kill.

Mokwina still scowled. For some time the whale had been on a seaward heading; her first wild lunges had been away from land, and now she had settled on a course straight out to sea. The weight of the harpoon lines in her left side should have swung her around, but the great beast resisted this drag and continued a straight course. Vancouver Island's shoreline was far away; indeed the foreshore was out of sight. Only mountains loomed above the horizon. To kill the whale so far out meant at least two days and nights of wearying towing, and hence Mokwina's scowl. The whale's behavior meant some member of the party had been lax in his ritual preparation—in dietary or continence restrictions. If every crewman had complied to the letter, the stricken whale would head for Yukwot and let herself be killed in the cove in front of the village. Family tradition reported an ancestor, many generations ago, whose crew trained so rigorously that he did not bother to pursue a whale after harpooning her, but instead set course for the summer village, confident that the whale would come in to be lanced just off the village beach. But those were the people of olden times; nowadays a whaler had to put up with a crew of irresponsible rascals.

The chief looked back at the mountain peaks to compute his position. The whale was still swimming strongly, and land was far away. Mokwina steeled himself to ask for advice.

"Uncle," he said, "something has gone wrong. This noble lady does not want to go to her home at Yukwot. One of our comrades could not resist the temptation of fresh tasty land meat or the shine of a pair of bright eyes, so we must all suffer for his fault. Do you remember a charm of my father's that would make the noble lady turn home?"

The old man spat onto a wad of shredded cedar bark, which he tucked into a woven bag. It was dangerous for whalers to dispose of excreta in the open sea where so many dangerous spirits roved. "Well, chief, I remember the first trip I made, as a paddler for the noble chief, your late father. He struck a noble lady early in the morning; she headed to sea just like this one, and she ran all day, until we could see only the tips of the snow-capped peaks on the horizon. Then your noble father commanded us to lay alongside the very head of the noble lady, and he poked her in the eye with the butt of the harpoon shaft, not hard enough to hurt, but gently, until she turned toward shore. I do not know what prayers or charms he spoke so she would not smash the canoe, but I saw him poke her gently in the eye and make her turn inshore."

"The noble chief my father was a great hunter. Put me alongside the noble lady's head when she surfaces." The crew obeyed with such dexterity that the canoe glided alongside the whale's head at the moment she came up to breathe. Although the whale no longer paid attention when the canoes moved in to the harpooning position, to move in farther forward, along the head, was dangerous. As the canoe come into her field of vision, she paused, lying quietly in the gentle sea, her great unwinking eye fixed on her foe. Mokwina stood on the gunwales, and with the butt of the harpoon shaft, gingerly touched the whale close to the eye. He could think of no charm to say except the words of the towing chant, "Go gently, noble lady, toward the sandy beach." Nothing happened. Emboldened, the chief jabbed a second time, hard, in the beast's very eye. Reaction was immediate and shocking. The creature splashed her mighty flukes, reared her bulk out of the water, and lurched at the canoe. The frenzied efforts of the paddlers barely hauled clear of disaster. In the excitement, the crew was not sure if the whale was trying to crush the canoe or to seize it in her jaws. The vessel heeled over wildly. Mokwina was thrown sprawling over the port gunwale, half out of the canoe. The harpoon shaft hit him a vicious blow across the back and simultaneously knocked down the starboard bow paddler.

The whale did not dive. The steersman shouted to hold the canoe close to the beast, but behind the head, where the animal could not see it. Apparently searching for her enemies, she circled left. As she turned across the canoe's bow, Mokwina snatched up the killing lance, and in wild fury, thrust it deep into the great baleful eye. They heard a horrid muffled bellowing as the whale dove. The buoys showed she was turning away from the painful wound, and headed back toward shore.

The chief waved to his younger brother to pursue on the new course, then took stock of his situation. A bad crack had been split in the bow, but fortunately above the waterline; it took water only on crossing a swell. The injured paddler sat on the floor of the canoe, blood dripping from a broken nose, rubbing a badly bruised arm. He would be of no further use on this trip. The harpoon shaft was floating astern, sprung at one of its joints. It could probably be repaired, and so was recovered. The lance was nowhere to be seen. It was either embedded in the whale's eye socket, or had gone to the bottom, weighted by its long elkhorn blade. The chief gave the order to continue after the whale.

Near sunset, the whale gave out. She had been swimming slowly on the surface for some time. Now she lay quietly, just the top of her head and back out of the water, moving only when the harpoon lines went slack with the drift of the inshore current. She was near shore now, several leagues northwest of the entrance to Nootka Sound, where Yukwot was situated. It was plain she would go no closer. The time had come for the kill.

The first step was to render the animal helpless. The hunters in both canoes used lances with wide chisel-shaped blades, and stabbed repeatedly until they severed the principal tendons controlling the flukes, in effect hamstringing their prey. Next, all the sealskin floats on the harpoon lines were moved close around the creature's head to lessen the danger of sinking. The principal harpoon lines were unbent from their lanyards to be used in towing. Finally, using his brother's killing lance, Mokwina jabbed vindictively between the proper pair of ribs and into the heart. The whale rolled, spurting blood from her blowhole, and died.

A special duty of the injured crewman, now performed by one

of his mates, was to dive with sharp mussel-shell knife and cut slits
behind the whale's lower jaw and through the upper lip, so that
the mouth could be tied shut. It was believed that the quarry would
fill with water and sink while being towed unless this was done.
The tow lines were attached to this hitch, and the laborious business
of towing began.

The next day had dawned when the whalers came in sight of
Nootka Sound. A halibut fisherman saw them, and sped the good
news to the village in his light canoe. A fleet of canoes came out to
assist in the towing; some brought dried salmon and drinking water
for the weary sea hunters. As the whalers rounded the point of
Friendly Cove, they could see the throng of people on the beach,
shouting and chanting. Many hands seized the tow lines to beach
the quarry, and Mokwina's wife came to the water's edge to greet
the whale in the time-honored ritual.

"Oh, noble lady, welcome to our village. We have been waiting
long for you to honor us with your visit. I bring you sweet water
and sacred food." So saying, she dashed a cup of fresh water on the
dead whale's muzzle, and then sprinkled a handful of sacred eagle
down over it.

Young men waded out to Mokwina's canoe and carried it out of
the water on fir poles so that its polished hull might not be scratched
by the gravel of the beach. Mokwina stood in the bow, singing one
of his spirit songs, until the craft was lowered onto a set of log
chocks in front of his house. He entered the house, walked its length
to his personal sleeping place, and sat down heavily beside the successful harpoon shaft. One of his wives brought him a dish of boiled
halibut, but he waved her aside. Approvingly he noted the great
house was in a bustle of activity. One of his younger brothers and
an uncle were passing out blubber knives of large mussel shell
to young men of the house. Men were erecting a sturdy rack of
stout poles on which Mokwina's own special cut of blubber would
be hung for ceremonial treatment. Women were assembling cooking
boxes for rendering the blubber and heating cooking stones in the
fires. Slaves brought loads of firewood for the central hearth. At
Mokwina's order an elderly aunt brought a small wooden vessel of
whale oil and a hank of shredded cedar bark, with which she helped
him remove the black paint from his face. Then she repainted him

red with two black triangles whose points met across the bridge of his nose, a pattern of the Thunderbird who had taught the secrets of whale hunting to the chief's ancestors. She and one of his wives combed out his long hair with their fingers, greased it liberally with whale oil, and sprinkled it with eagle down. Mokwina put on a new yellow-cedar-bark robe adorned with four thick strands of mountain-goat wool and strode outside carrying the harpoon shaft.

The entire Moachat confederacy was assembled on the beach. Chiefs and subchiefs of all local groups, in festive finery, sat in their formal place sequence on planks along the upper edge of the steep slope of the beach. A visiting chief from the Nuchatlat had been seated in a place of honor. People of lesser rank stood or sat beside the row of chieftains, men on the right, women on the left. Mokwina's own group stood by to cut up and distribute the blubber. His speaker hastened to his side and informed him that all was in readiness. Usually the chief liked to make his own speeches, but today he felt too weary for the effort. Instead, he leaned against the harpoon shaft and gave occasional cues to his speaker, who half shouted in the staccato style that is the mark of good oratory. As the speaker related the origins of whale hunting in the chief's family, men cut the special piece of the blubber reserved for the successful whaler—a piece just behind the head, a fathom down either side, and a fathom wide. They hung this cut over a rack like that set up inside the house (to which it would be moved later), adorned with eagle plumes and decorated with red paint. Next, a group of women, led by the chief's principal wife, chanted a song and sprinkled offerings of eagle down on the huge slice of skin and fat. Then the men began to cut the blubber in fathom-long strips. The first was given to the Nuchatlat visitor. Each local chief in order of rank was presented with a large slab of blubber. Next, strips of standard fathom length but narrower width were given to special individuals who did not sit in chiefs' places, and none of whom were of Mokwina's own local group: the carver who had made the successful harpoon shaft, a crewman, and others who had performed special services. Members of Mokwina's own kin group—the old steersman, his younger brother, paddlers and crewmen of the hunt would receive pieces of blubber or oil in private. Signalizing Mokwina's hereditary whaling technique, the whole procedure was like a potlatch, except that it was held outdoors, which was not otherwise Nootkan custom. The Indians called it a "feast" and considered the meal, when the cutting and cooking were done, the finale of the distribution. When the gifts had been made and blubber carried to Mokwina's house for subsequent feasts and distribution to the household, the remaining scraps of blubber and meat were presented to commoners en masse. In a wild scramble they stripped the carcass, while flocks of screaming sea gulls circled and darted, snatching up bits. In stripping the rich fat, someone cut through the gut, and gas formed from the decomposed contents of the huge stomach escaped with a rush, saturating the air of the whole village with its stink. By afternoon only the bones and offal over which the seabirds wheeled remained of the "noble lady."

### The People and Their Environment

Nootkan-speaking people and two divisions of the linguistically related Southern Kwakiutl, the Quatsino and Klaskino, held the storm-lashed seaward side of Vancouver Island. The southeasternmost groups were the Nitinat of the island and the Makah, across the Strait of Juan de Fuca on Cape Flattery. The coastline of the island is broken. Abrupt rocky headlands and sand beaches where the surf breaks heavily even in summer separate deep enclosed bays and sounds, from which branch long narrow fiords. The seaward passes of bays are narrow in proportion to the volume of water inside, and hence racing tidal currents and tide rips form. The mighty Pacific rolls in against the island ceaselessly, and when the southeasterly storm winds blow, from early fall till late spring, they produce cross-seas of great size and violence. For this reason the Indian winter villages were buillt in sheltered coves on the upper reaches of the inlets. Only summer offshore fishing and whaling stations were near the outside coasts.

Not even reasonable guesses can be made from early sources about the size of the Nootkan-speaking population at the close of the eighteenth century when historic contacts began. An estimate based on the number of local groups is at least 10,000 persons. If the estimate is correct, Nootkans were about equal in numbers to the aboriginal Tlingit, and equal to the combined total of all Tsimshian-speakers, which would mean that Nootkan territory was somewhat more densely populated than that of the northerners. The southwestern seaward side of Vancouver Island is colloquially referred to as the "West Coast." As a habitat it was an extreme example of the areal pattern. Rainfall was heavier than on many other portions of the rainy North Pacific Coast, the forests were larger and denser, the game and fish populations more abundant.

Nootkan communities displayed the complete typological range of the North Pacific Coast political structure. In the central and southern regions of Nootkan territory, local groups functioned independently even of close neighbors. The northern Nootkans, from Nootka Sound to Cape Cook, included a few completely separatist local groups, but most local groups were confederated into tribes with common winter villages. There were in addition several confederacies of tribes that were prehistoric in origin, two of the largest being those of Nootka and Kyuquot Sounds. These confederacies were characterized by common summer villages close to the outer coasts, for convenience to offshore fishing, seal, sea-otter, and whaling grounds. As recounted in the Mokwina story, the Nootkans had a highly developed whaling complex. Like other North Pacific Coast peoples, they shifted residence several times a year to localities of basic economic importance and occupied their principal home sites during the winter season when the food quest was virtually at a standstill.

## Houses

The main Nootkan housetype was especially suited to this way of life. Like other North Pacific Coast houses except the Northern one, the Nootkan walls were structurally separate from the framework, whose function was to support the roof. The siding consisted of panels of red-cedar planks slung horizontally on withes looped between pairs of vertical stakes. The boards overlapped, making a better seal than if untrimmed boards had been placed edge to edge. This siding, while not very stable and not contributing to roof support, was easy to dismantle and reassemble. The Nootkans erected house frames at all their principal stations and moved wall and roof boards from place to place as needed. Thus, a single set of planks served them the year around. As a rule, a local group would have permanent house frames standing at three sites: the village at which they wintered, at a locality convenient for summer fishing and sea-mammal hunting, and at their principal salmon stream. For a few days' stay at a temporary camp, the people usually took along a few planks for makeshift shelters.

The massive house frames consisted of four huge cornerposts that

House at Nootka Sound, 1778.

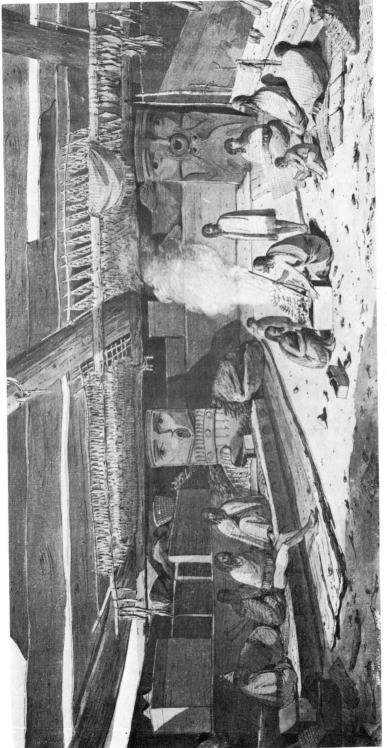

House at Nootka Sound, 1778.

147

formed a rectangle, twenty or more feet wide by fifty to one hundred feet long. Longer structures had subsidiary posts to help support the span of the one-piece side beams that ran from front to rear of the house. Double or single ridgepoles were supported at either end by pairs of posts with cross supports. Ridgepoles raised the centerline of the roof and gave a slight pitch from center to eaves. Over this framework a secondary set of beams and rafters of large poles was lashed with withes, then covered with the roof planks. A standard plank varied from one to five feet wide, depending on the size of the red cedar, but was always two fathoms (native measure) long. A Nootkan house was complete when each slope of the roof consisted of two ranges of planks, liberally overlapped. Heavy poles weighted down with large stones were laid over the planks to keep southeast storm-winds from blowing them away.

The principal house posts were sometimes the natural round of the log from which they had been cut. In many winter houses, they were carved into representations of crests, or more often of family ancestors. As mentioned in Chapter 2, huge longitudinal roof beams were adzed to an even diameter and finished with fluting. An hereditary privilege might call for the end of the ridgepole to extend beyond the facade of the house and to be carved with the design representing sea-lion heads. The siding surrounded the basic framework and floor area like a fence. Its architectural function was to provide shelter. The floor was at ground level, with no central pit or flooring. The doorway was in a gabled end wall, away from the southeast winds. A roughly rectangular space was left between panels of planking, but there are a few early history references to round entryways, apparently cut through special wide planks.

Living spaces along the walls and across the rear of the house sheltered an entire local group. When such a unit expanded and needed two houses, it was well on the way to sociologic fission. The chief and his family occupied the right rear corner, his immediate subordinate, the left rear corner, the third- and forth-ranking chiefs, the front corners. Centers of the sidewalls were assigned to persons of intermediate status, while those of low rank occupied in-between spaces. The house chief might have a plank-walled room in his corner of the house, but usually, like other members of the group, he occupied a space marked off by storage boxes, baskets, and miscellaneous equipment. Sleeping places were wide red-cedar planks, raised slightly off the ground on poles or small logs to keep them dry. Cedar-bark mats were the usual mattresses. A few groups with access to shallow lakes where cattail reeds grew wove mattresses of the stems. Each family had its own hearth in front of its sleeping and storage space. A huge central fireplace was reserved for use on festive occasions. Overhead racks provided storage space for bulky possessions, dried and drying fish, strips of whale blubber, and the like.

Nootkan housewives of former days apparently were not very tidy. Some early explorers complained in their descriptions of these houses of the typical atmosphere: a composite of the odors of kitchen refuse that littered the floor, smoke, only part of which leaked out between the roof boards, drying fish, and rancid whale oil that dripped from the blubber on the drying racks. To the Indians these odors were not objectionable: they emanated from the wealth of foodstuffs and from friendly family fireplaces. And the rank scent of whale oil represented success at bringing down the mightiest quarry of all. (The Indians, however, gagged at the odor of cheeses offered them aboard the explorers' ships; only in recent years have their descendants been able to bring themselves to eat this substance.)

## Fishing and Hunting

The Nootkans exploited efficiently most of the fish and game resources of their homeland, but set special store on certain products: they prized spring salmon and to a lesser degree, coho, for size and flavor, sockeye, which run in a few streams only, for flavor and rarity, but the dog salmon (chum) was the staff of life. This fish runs in the fall, later than on the Northern coasts. When salmon fishing was over, autumn storms began, and the people transported their loads of planking and baskets and bales of dried fish to the winter village. They lashed two large canoes together like catamarans with a space between that was decked over with house planks. These "rafts" formed ample and stable platforms for freighting stores of fish home. The only danger lay in a storm or heavy seas en route. Through the winter there were days when cod and other bottom fish could be caught, molluscs collected on low tides, and occasionally land game hunted. Elk, deer, and black bear, but neither mountain goat nor grizzly bear, occur on Van-

couver Island. Late fall to winter was also a good time for waterfowl
hunting. On dark overcast nights the hunter's canoe carried a fire in a
sandfilled box. Birds resting on the water were caught in the shadow
thrown by a screen in front of the fire. These winter food quests were
not required for subsistence, but they lent variety to the daily fare of
dried dog salmon.

The next major food source was herring that appeared in early
spring. There were no olachen runs in any stream in Nootkan territory, but enormous shoals of herring that spawned in sheltered coves
provided a major staple. The same "rake" used for olachen by mainland groups was used on herring, which were eaten fresh and dried.
Floats were attached to submerged branches, which received herring
spawn, a favorite food. These simple devices had to be moored with
great care so the ebb tide would swing them out to deep water and not
leave them aground. Herring season was also an excellent time to troll
for spring salmon, using herring for bait. And as hair seal and sea lion
harried the shoals of the small fish, they were caught. For some groups
the winter village was a convenient center of operations for this fishery;
others shifted to summer sites. Occasional groups owned herring-fish-
ing and egg-collecting grounds too far from either summer- or winter-
village sites; such families had permanent camps where they had set up
small house frames.

In the early summer, mass moves were made to the sites near the
open sea. Halibut fishing and sea-mammal hunting were the order of
the day, although both animals were available and sought most of the
year. In the inlets there were banks where a good catch of halibut
was often made in winter and spring. But the best halibut grounds
were those on the long gently sloping beds off the outside beaches.
The same was true of sea mammals. While all species might be encountered in the inlets and fiords at any time, the best hunting was on the
outside coasts where sea lions hauled up on rocks in fine weather, and
hair seal congregated. When the sea was calm, sea otter were often
found resting in beds of giant kelp along the outer coasts; the females
left their pups amid the kelp while they dove for the big clams that
were their favorite food. A small sea-otter pup was not too difficult to
catch alive, and its squeals brought the distressed dam within easy killing distance. Informants say that whales seemed to spend more time on
the surface on fine summer days. Other things obtained along the out-

side shores of the island were: seabird eggs, giant mussels from whose shells the women's knives were made, giant kelp, the cured stems of which made fishlines and the hollow bulbs of which were used as whale-oil containers. And there was also dentalia fishery.

## Dentalia Fishing

Nootkan groups were the source of nearly all dentalia shells in the North Pacific area and beyond. The only non-Nootkan group known to take the shells were the neighboring Klaskino of lower Quatsino Sound, who were Southern Kwakiutl in speech but had intermarried so frequently with nearby Nootkans that many informants regarded them as much Nootkan as Kwakiutl.

The species of dentalium so valued by the Indians has a wide distribution along the North Pacific littoral. However, it is usually a relatively deepwater form which, perhaps because of special effects of ocean currents, grows in beds of moderate depth at only a few places on the seaward side of Vancouver Island. Shells of dead dentalia are reported to wash up on outside beaches in many parts of the Coast. As any shell collector knows, however, "dead shells" of any molluscs always lack the luster of those taken alive, and so the dull-surfaced drift shells never formed an important part of native commerce in dentalia.

The Nootkan fishing was the property of certain family lines, as were the grounds themselves, and certain parts of the procedure were carefully guarded family secrets. For example, as recently as a few years ago most well-informed elderly Nootkans knew the general locations of the dentalia beds, but not the exact locations. They knew also that the owners found the beds by doing what a mariner would call crossing two ranges, each range consisting of a distant and a nearer mountain peak or other prominent natural feature which were lined up by the observer offshore. When the bearings of the two ranges were separated by a moderately large angle, their point of crossing gave a very precise location. (This was the standard Nootkan technique for locating offshore points.) What informants did not know, unless they were of the proper family groups and sufficiently high in rank to have been entrusted with the secret, was just which natural features formed the ranges.

The ingenious dentalia-collecting gear consisted of a bunch of hardwood splints, elongated ovates in shape, tightly lashed at one end around the tip of a long slim pole so that their points diverged, thus suggesting in form our traditional Halloween witches' broom. Over the "broom" was fitted a board with a hole at the center of such a size that it passed freely over the bundle of splints at the point of attachment but was too small to be forced over the diverging points. Heavy stone sinkers were lashed one to each end of the board. A set of additional poles, or rods, with tough nettle-fiber cordage for lashing them end to end to the business end completed the device. Their exact lengths and number was another of the family-owned professional secrets.

The dentalia fisherman determined his position by using his ranges to place himself over the beds. There he might anchor, lowering away a conveniently shaped stone lashed to a long line of giant kelp stems, or he might drift for a time with the inshore current. He joined the rods, one by one, allowing the end piece with its broomlike attachment of splints and stone weights to sink the gear to a vertical position; the weights had to be nicely calibrated to give a very slight negative buoyancy to the apparatus. When the bunch of splints was a short distance from the bottom he jabbed downward hard. The resistance of the water retarded the descent of the flat board so that the bunch of splints, uncompressed and therefore flared apart, reached bottom first. The board with its stone sinkers slowly slid down over the splints, compressing them strongly. The fisherman hauled the apparatus surfacewards, unlashing the joints of the rods as he went. Were he lucky he might find a shell or two, or even several, pinched between the tips of the splints. Then he put the contraption back into the water to make another try. The device was apparently fairly efficient, the dentalia beds rich, and the Nootkan dentalia fishermen must have been industrious at their trade, for they obtained great quantities of the molluscs, which they carefully cleaned, sorted into three sizes (long, short, and in-between), and traded to neighbors packed in neat wallet-like cedarbark baskets or in fathom-long strings.

## Art

The Nootkans had a well-developed pattern of artistic expression, one they shared with their Kwakiutl relatives. Salish-speaking neighbors show similar skill that diminished with distance from the Wakashan source. This art style was executed in sculpture, as was the Northern style of the Tsimshian and their neighbors. The chief difference lies in the fact that Wakashan art was not an applied art like that of the northerners. Rather, it was intended to stand by itself as sculpture. There were decorated objects whose functional form modified the applied design, but they were in the minority. A Nootkan carved housepost was a statue with a beam resting on its head, not a post covered with a low-relief pattern. In Nootkan and Southern Kwakiutl decorated feast dishes, the dish itself was sometimes nearly lost in the intricacies of the carving. Arms, legs, wings, and other appendages were freely added with dowels. Hence the effect produced by Northern carvings of being enclosed within the housepost or spoon handle occurred but rarely. Instead, figures like soaring Thunderbirds with outspread wings expand exuberantly outward.

Another distinctive feature of Nootkan and Kwakiutl art was its suppression of unimportant detail; in terms of modern art, the treatment is "impressionistic." A figure holding an object might have the hand and arm depicted with skilled realism; if the limb was unimportant to the meaning of the carving, the arm might be a simple rodlike appendage, with a lump at the end to represent the hand. Coupled with this simplicity or impressionism, there was a tolerance of open space. It has been remarked that in the Northern style, especially among the Tsimshian, spaces were filled with small figures. Wakashan art was free from this tendency to clutter the design. Where there was no significance to filling an area with detail, it was left blank, and carvings are stark and bold. Houseposts, potlatch figures, and masks are perhaps best imagined as they were meant to be seen, by the light of the big central fireplace with flickering highlights and black shadows.

The Northern-type Raven or chief's rattle has been mentioned as an outstanding art product. Nootkans, too, had a wooden chief's rattle, carved in the form of a bird, also outstanding artistically, but completely different from the Northern specimens. The over-all form of a bird was shown in smooth sweeping curves. When shown, wings were barely indicated. The arch of the neck suggested a swimming duck, but no attempt was made to identify the species. The subtlety and restraint of these carvings gives them a different air at first glance from the large carvings such as houseposts, but the impressionistic style is fundamentally the same.

From the point of view of distributions of culture patterns, a good many, though not all, old Tlingit carvings depart from the rigid conventionalizations of the classic Northern style in the direction of Wakashan carving. Tlingit art in general was more realistic and vigorous than that of Haida and Tsimshian, and Tlingit artists used less inconsequential filler in their designs. It may well be that Wakashan and Tlingit art, as known in historic times, were close to the original art pattern of the area, and that Haida and Tsimshian work were specialized versions of the old style.

Late in the historic period, Wakashan art began to show a trend toward elaboration of detail, greater stress on symmetry, and less cursive treatment. The influence was clearly from Haida sources, and probably came about through close contact between Southern Kwakiutl and Haida in the late nineteenth century and early twentieth. This hybridization combines the serenity and symmetry of the Northern style with the vigor of the Wakashan art. Such work was produced in quantity for a brief period by the Southern Kwakiutl, and less abundantly by Nootkan artists, but some Nootkans produced excellent examples. While primitive-art purists scorn this blend of styles as bastard, from a purely artistic standpoint it represents some of the finest work of the coast.

A limited amount of geometric decoration, sometimes combined with very simple representative motifs, was applied to a few utilitarian objects by Nootkans. Such patterns may be seen on very old war clubs of whale's bone (not baleen), on the elk-horn barbs of whaling harpoons, and on other types of articles. Still simpler textural effects are the panels of narrow, very precisely spaced fluting on the fronts of storage boxes, which, with insets of sea-otter molars and sea-snail opercula in the lids, formed the only adornments. A Nootkan freight or "war" canoe was not properly finished unless it had four rows of shallow horizontal fluting around the inside of the gunwales, and sea-otter teeth or opercula insets around the outside.

## Religion

Nootkan religion was comprised of two distinct techniques for influencing or controlling supernatural forces. One was the spirit quest, culminating in the encounter with a supernatural being who bestowed talents or taught infallible methods of curing or performing a specialty. Not all people made a true spirit quest; those who deliberately sought such an experience were in the minority. The other method was the performance of ritual acts, publicly or privately, to attain one's end. Most ritual procedures were hereditary family secrets, in which practical and magical aspects were not differentiated. In dentalia fishery, the technique for locating the dentalia beds, the depth of the beds, which determined the number and length of pole segments necessary, and the special training required to produce good results were all equally parts of the hereditary secret of certain family lines. No distinction was made between skill in manipulation of the practical gear of dentalia fishing and skill in manipulation of supernatural power: all the ritual procedures were believed to be gifts of supernatural beings bestowed in ancient times on various ancestors.

Religion and society were integrated by the hereditary nature of the rituals. As heads of kin groups, chiefs were expected to be the recipients of the more important ritual secrets, particularly those of broadest interest to group welfare, for example, rites to ensure abundance of salmon, herring, and other staples. A chief was expected to spend a great deal of his time in ritual training—bathing, partial fasting, and continence for a certain phase of each moon. Proof that a chief complied with his obligation faithfully and competently was seen in bountiful runs of salmon, abundance of herring, and bumper crops of berries.

Despite the richness of natural resources, there was an apparent anxiety about food in Nootkan culture. It is difficult to account for such a pattern. True, there were occasions when rations were short, even in times of peace. Such unpleasant episodes can probably be attributed to overexuberant feasting on stored provisions followed by bad weather that prevented fishing and hunting. Yet in the very worst times something edible always could be collected or caught, even if it was only a batch of small mussels from a sheltered cove, or a brace of tough, rank-flavored seagulls. Periods of abject starvation, such as peoples of the arctic and subarctic regions chronically faced, were never experienced by the Nootkans, at least as far back as history or tradition can report. Nonetheless, these people did not place entire reliance on nature's bounty; they deemed it necessary to devote a great deal of time and effort to religious activities to keep natural food production at a high level.

### Whaling Rituals

A special variety of food-producing ritual, possessed by many groups, was performed by their chiefs to cause dead whales to drift ashore on one of their beaches. It was regarded not as a windfall, but as another form of whaling just as meritorious as hunting with the harpoon. Many family groups possessed both techniques, and their chiefs practiced both, although according to personal preference stressed one over the other. The scores of their successes were kept apart, harpooned whales in one count, dead whales brought ashore by ritual means in another. The ritual whaling technique revolved about a shrine constructed by the chief and his trusted aides in a secret spot in the woods. Human corpses or mannikins, carved of wood or formed of bundles of brush and surmounted by human skulls, were set up around the image of a whale, often arranged as though dragging the whale with a rope. The corpses and skulls were stolen by the chief and his helpers from burial places. Among many groups there was an unsubstantiated rumor that some chiefs occasionally stole commoner infants, killing them and using the tiny bodies in their gruesome rites. The essence of the rituals that caused dead whales to drift ashore in a group's territory consisted in rigorous ceremonial cleansing by the ritualist chief—the usual fasting, bathing, and continence—construction of the shrine and its tableau, and nightly attendance during the ritual period to pray and to chant supernaturally imbued songs. Because the Nootkans had a great fear of the dead, the handling of human corpses and skulls was not a casual matter, but they believed the dead had some mysterious power over whales. A chief would undertake this terrifying performance only when he felt sure of thorough protection by his ceremonial purification, and was letter-perfect in all details of the ritual procedure. The harpooners of whales also made use of the power of the dead over their intended quarry in their ritual preparations, but never in such an elaborate fashion.

The concept of supernatural power of the dead over whales was extended to other animals at times. A Nootka Sound local group, whose territory lay far up the Sound, had a secret ritual ensuring the arrival of salmon, herring, and sea mammals. To accomplish this, the chief, after preliminary training, swam by night from the entrance of the Sound to the river, towing a line of magically potent objects including human skulls. He did not accomplish this test of endurance in a single night. He swam with his cumbersome tow until exhausted by exertion and cold. The next night he swam another stage of the journey, beginning at the place previously reached. The group believed that as he towed the skulls, so would the dead tow the schools of salmon and herring from the open ocean to the river.

A few persons other than the ritualist had special powers to ensure abundance of food. Parents of twins, and the twins themselves, whose souls were thought to come from "Salmon's Home Beneath the Sea," had great influence over the salmon, and throughout their lives were expected to train to ensure bountiful runs.

The chief of each group also officiated in the welcoming ceremony honoring the first salmon and the first herring of each year's run. Details of these rites varied from group to group, but the basic pattern was common to all Nootkans, and the underlying concept was the classic one of the area: that these species were annually reincarnated for their voluntary sacrifice to man, and had to be treated in accordance with certain rules or else they would be angered and refuse to return.

During the critical phases of life according to the general North Pacific Coast pattern, the individual was restricted to avoid giving offense to Salmon spirits and spirits of other important animals. Parents of newborn infants, pubescent girls, women at menses, and mourners were subject to these restrictions as long as they were regarded as potentially dangerous to group welfare. The duration of these restrictions varied from a few days (in most cases four or ten, which were ritual numbers) to a year or longer. Parents of twins were restricted for four years. Because of their intimate relationship to the Salmon spirits, they dwelt in isolation in a little hut in the woods (they could be visited by their kin, but not visit them), lived on a monotonous diet of dried salmon, and could not fish, hunt, or gather any food, for a period of four years. A ritual bathing terminated all restrictions. Unlike their Northern neighbors, the Nootkans stuffed their dead into wooden boxes and hastened them to a burial place often distant from the village site.

Nootkan festivities and ceremonials were feasts, potlatches, and a form of the Dancing Society performances. Feasts were often jolly, and vast quantities of food were consumed. Potlatches were serious, highly formal, and with elaborate protocol. Competitive potlatches were never held; they were incompatible with the Nootkan attitude toward the institution. Among the groups of the central and southeastern parts of the Nootkan territory there was a pallid edition of the Guardian spirit-singing of Coast Salish neighbors.

### Dancing Society Performances

The main Nootkan ceremonial was that of the Dancing Society. It was referred to in English as the "Wolf Dance," because the principal spirits represented were those of wolves. In Nootkan, the name of the performance means "The Shamans." According to the origin-myth, an ancestor entered the House of the Wolves, where all the Wolf spirits dwelt. In their supernatural home, these beings had human form. To go abroad, they put on wolfskin robes, thereby assuming animal form. Instead of slaying the intruder, the Wolf spirits took pity on him. (This is one of the very few exceptions to the common areal concept that spirit-human relationships were compulsive, not compassionate.) They taught him songs, dances, and displays to take back to his home. After four days and nights of intensive tutelage, the Wolf spirits carried him back to his village, where he learned he had been away four mortal years. He instructed his people how to rescue him from the Wolf pack, then demonstrated the songs, dances, and displays that he had been taught. This legend was enacted in each ceremonial performance. The beginning of the rite was signalled by the sounding of large trumpetlike wooden instruments that represented the howling of the Wolf spirits in the woods behind the village, and by the mysterious hum of bull-roarers. The ceremonial began with simulated kidnapping of the novices, usually children and youths, by men wearing a conventionalized wolf disguise. Among certain groups other spirits also participated in the capture of the novices. The children were concealed behind a tremendous partition in the house in which the ceremonial was held for several days, during which they were taught their roles. Difficult dances and performances were usually performed by adults in their stead. During this period a constant round of feasts and festivities featured comic dances by villagers organized more or less by sex and age, such as boys, young men, old men, girls, young women, and old women. These aggregations have sometimes been compared to age-graded societies of other areas, but were so loosely organized and impermanent that it seems doubtful the similarity is significant enough for drawing close parallels. Frivolity and horseplay characterized the preliminaries. Parents of children carried off by the Wolf spirits might be upbraided for their "carelessness" and tossed bodily into the sea. People who were caught sleeping during festivities, which went on day and night, were doused with icy water. Words such as wolf were tabu during the ceremonial, on pain of being mauled, and pranksters went to great lengths to trap people into using a prohibited term.

Just before the day the children were to be returned, rafts were prepared by lashing planks across the gunwales of pairs of big canoes. At dawn on the appointed day, the Wolf pack, heralded by blasts on the wooden horns, appeared on a point across the cove with their "captives." The villagers embarked on the rafts and in canoes to rescue the Wolf spirits' prisoners. While this part of the ritual was serious, some comedy was permitted. Men might proclaim themselves expert wolf-catchers (using a circumlocution for wolf), and display a nonsensical device, such as an oversize bird snare or halibut hook, as the implement they intended to use. Tipping over a canoeload of such experts was good for laughs, and if the Wolves could catch a wolf-catcher and maul him, it added to the hilarity. As the flotilla beached, the Wolves retreated, taking the captive children with them, then charged the canoes. The stylized retreats and charges were repeated, until the fourth time, when the captives were left close to the shore. The rescuers hastily carried the captives and the symbols accompanying them to the rafts, and the Wolves simulated a final furious charge to the water's edge.

Each child's face was painted, and each wore a sort of cloak and kilt of hemlock branches. Each also had a symbol of the privilege the Wolf spirits had given him. Children of high rank might have a large representation of a crest, carried or worn by an attendant; those of low status usually wore a shredded cedar-bark headband that denoted the dance he or she was to perform. They were supposed to be "wild," that is, imbued with supernatural power, but the concept of spirit-possession was underplayed, and they performed few violent acts. They were "tamed" by ritual cleansing and parading daily through the houses of the village. During these processions novices occasionally became infuriated by breach of a tabu of the ritual, became possessed by their spirit power, and ran wildly through the village. They, or their attendants, tipped over food vessels, broke dishes and other objects, and bowled over spectators. Special acts were required to pacify them.

Finally the day came on which the novices demonstrated their supernatural gifts from the Wolf spirits. Each sang a hereditary spirit song, danced (or had a dancer perform in his stead), displayed a crest, or announced the hereditary name he had received. A potlatch ended the public performances, with more purifications of the children, minor restrictions on their activities, and the burning of their hemlock-branch apparel.

All children were "taken by the Wolves" at least once, usually just prior to adolescence. The youngster was then old enough to be able to learn and perform his spirit song and a simple dance routine. Some chiefs' scions, however, were carried through their first performances as infants in their mothers' arms, and nearly all persons of high rank repeated the ceremonial a number of times, each time receiving a different hereditary name and crest. The procedure was in no sense "tribal initiation." Rather, it was a method for defining each individual's place in the social order.

# CHAPTER 8

# Kwakiutl Dancing Societies

A BRIEF ACCOUNT OF the Dancing Societies of the Kwakiutl neighbors and relatives of the Nootkans is included, not only to round out the picture of regional specialization, but also to illustrate by a specific example of ceremonialism how areal patterns were elaborated and re-elaborated in the complex civilization of the North Pacific Coast.

In recent times there were three Dancing Societies among the various Kwakiutl-speaking divisions and some of their neighbors. All were related to the Nootkan Shamans' Society or Wolf Dance described in Chapter 7; they were not derived from it, but developed from some common older ceremonial pattern or at least a common interrelationship of religious and ceremonial concepts. The precise sequence of development of these rituals has never been worked out, but there is a substantial body of facts that suggests a specific history.

Best known from the early ethnographic literature is the Dancing Society that included a Cannibal Dancer among its performers. The native name for this complex does not refer to this personage, however, but translates "The Shamans," just as does the Nootkan term for their ceremonial. More restricted in distribution was a Dancing Society whose native title can be rendered "Those-who-descend-from-the-heavens." The third ceremonial—Nutlam, an untranslatable term—may derive from archaic Wakashan, but in colloquial English is often referred to as "The Dog Eaters" or "Dog Eater Society," after the characteristic behavior of its performers. These three cycles, like the Nootkan Wolf Dance, were dramatizations of ancestral supernatural experiences. The principal performers, usually referred to in the literature as "the novices," relived the ancestral experience and became inspired or possessed by the spirit who had been encountered by the ancestor. The gifts bestowed by the supernatural being thus became hereditary property. They consisted of songs, dances, names, masks, and the like, and the power to perform various magical acts. Use of these privileges was limited to performances of ceremonials; that is, they could not be used on secular occasions. In this regard, the Kwakiutl ceremonies differed from the Nootkan, in which certain, though not all, of the privileges were display crests that might be used apart from the Wolf Dance.

The Kwakiutl Shamans' Society emphasized encounters with monsters, who inspired their protégés to perform macabre or violent acts. Each local group, according to its traditional family history, had its own series of performers. A Cannibal Dancer headed each list, as the prerogative of the ranking chief or his heir; after him in order of precedence, which varied somewhat from group to group, came such personages as the Grizzly Bear, Warrior, and Warrior Fool, all of whom menaced the spectators and destroyed property, the Fire Thrower, self-mutilating spirits, and a host of minor representations of unspectacular nature enacted by persons of low rank. The plot of each performance called for the novices to go into hiding for some time prior to the public demonstrations. They were said to have been kidnapped by the spirits which were to inspire them. When they reappeared, they were possessed by their particular spirits, bereft of all human qualities. They had to be captured by combinations of force and magical procedures. Public and secret parts of the ceremonial exorcised the monstrous spirits possessing them: calm lucid behavior by the novices alternated with periods of possession during which they ran amuck, out of human control. When possessed, the Cannibal Dancer seized spectators and bit pieces of flesh from their arms. As a climax, he devoured flesh torn from dried human corpses. The public rites terminated with the "taming" of the novices and a potlatch, after which the novices underwent lengthy private purification rites.

The performers of these gory and horrible acts were not children, as in the Nootkan performances, but mostly able-bodied young men, and some young women. Theatrical illusion and trickery were involved in many of the performances: the climactic act of a beheaded female dancer involved use of a wooden head, carved in a faithful likeness of the performer's features, and blood that gushed and bespattered the scene came from codfish bladders filled with animal blood. Joined lengths of hollow kelp stems were buried beneath the floor, to make ghostly voices come from the fire and other unexpected places; dancers miraculously appeared and disappeared by using concealed pits covered with ingenious trap doors.

During the early phase of the ceremonial, there was much horse-play, and loosely organized age-grade groups staged special stunts, just as in the Nootkan Wolf Dance. There was also a long list of tabu words and acts; breach of these tabus roused partly pacified novices to frenzy and repossession by their spirits. The insignia of the Society, worn by dancers during their calm periods and throughout their final purifications, were, like those of the Wolf Dance, elaborately woven headbands, neck rings, and arm and leg ornaments of cedar bark dyed red.

The ceremonial, "Those-who-descend-from-the-heavens," had essentially the same plot as the Shamans' Society rites. Chief points of difference were that the supernatural beings inspiring the novices were not monsters, but Star, Cloud, Bird, and other beings associated with the skies, and spirits from the depths of the sea. They did not induce violent behavior. Only a War Spirit dancer destroyed property and performed violent acts. The rest danced quiet, stately dances, using elaborate masks and other paraphernalia. Some of the composite masks were articulated, and their forms could be changed by manipulating strings, thus representing magical powers. The novices were not physically captured, but were "called down" from the sky worlds to which they had been taken, by several nights of singing magical songs. As in the Shamans' Society, comic interludes contrasted with solemn parts of the ritual, and each group had its own spirit representatives, ranked in precedence; that is, each role was allotted to a member of the group according to his social status. The Society's insignia consisted of ornaments of bleached cedar bark.

The two societies were exclusive in the sense that an active performer in one was not permitted to enter the house in which the other was being staged, except as a spectator to occasions open to the general public. Also, the two ceremonials could not be put on at the same time. If by chance the two were performed the same year, the Shamans' Society rite had to be early in the winter season, the other late, just before departure for the spring herring- and olachen-fishing camps.

Less is known about the Nutlam Society than about the other two. It seems to have been declining in popularity during the period to which most ethnographic materials relate. There are suggestions that it was more limited in membership than the others, although this may have been a result of its declining popularity. Recent informants cannot define how its members were recruited. It appears that the individual performances were not ranked. One point is clear: the novices were inspired by Wolf Spirits, and this was the reason for their macabre act of killing dogs, tearing them apart, and devouring the raw flesh. (Wolves and dogs are mortal enemies.) All informants agree that active participants in this Society were barred from entry into houses where performances of the other Dancing Societies were being given.

The macabre and the violent were prominent themes in this ceremonial pattern. Even the comparatively gentle "Those-who-descend-from-the-heavens" included a dancer who became violent when inspired, and during the Nootkan Wolf Dance the novices were supposed to go berserk on certain occasions. The meaning of this motif is clear in analyzing the most extreme behavior, that of the Cannibal Dancer in the Kwakiutl Shamans' Society. The Kwakiutl, in ordinary life, had an exaggerated fear of the dead and of dead bodies, and the spectacle of the cannibal feast must have been shocking and horrible to them. Its performance was conclusive proof that the novice was for the time not a human being—he was the embodiment of a monstrous spirit and only therefore capable of horrendous deeds that no normal person would dare attempt.[1] The dog-eating stunt of the Nutlam Society was of the same order. It was without doubt an appalling sight to the Indian spectators. Universally on the coast, dog flesh was considered unfit for human consumption, even poisonous, and the idea of eating it was nauseating to normal persons. Even under hardship conditions such as those faced by traveling parties stormbound on barren islets or hungry groups under military seige, these Indians did not eat their dogs. The Nutlam dancers did so because they were temporarily inhuman. They acted compulsively to satisfy the appetites of the savage Wolf spirits who possessed them. All other forms of violent behavior in these ceremonials had the same purpose: to emphasize the basic premise about which these dramas revolved—that the novices were inhabited by supernatural beings.

In point of fact, there is considerable doubt that human corpses were actually consumed in the Cannibal Feast. Stern administrative and missionary sanctions on the ritual made the Indians aware of white disapproval, and the topic became difficult to discuss frankly with informants. Many other supposedly magical feats in the ceremonial were carried out by means of theatrical illusion—mechanical contrivances, sleight of hand, misdirection, and the rest—and these Indians were masters at stage trickery. It has been suggested that the corpses may have been stage properties, for example, bear carcasses, fitted with wooden heads skilfully carved to simulate features of dessicated human faces. Other informants insist that the corpses were real, but that the performers only pretended to devour them, disposing of the mouthfuls by sleight of hand. Illusion was certainly involved, for some performers purported to consume an entire corpse at a sitting, obviously an impossible feat.

Many violent acts—the smashing of canoes, wooden boxes and dishes, and other valuables—by dancers possessed by War spirits, Grizzly Bear spirits, and others, were carried out literally enough, but were not done at random. Prior arrangements were made with the

---

[1] The same attitude was manifested in a slightly different way in the Nootkan use of human corpses and bones in connection with whaling. These procedures, awesome and terrifying to the Nootkan mind, could be undertaken by the ritualist only because he was letter-perfect in the ritual, and perfection itself in his state of ritual cleanliness.

owner in secret. Afterward, at the potlatch, special gifts were distributed to the owners of damaged articles to pay for the destruction.

The Shamans' Society with the Cannibal Dancer was performed by all Kwakiutl-speaking groups, the Bella Coola, the southern Coast Tsimshian (Kitisu, Kitkahtla, and Kitqata), and in somewhat incomplete form by some Coast Tsimshian proper. Some Tlingit and Haida groups possessed masks and other regalia, along with songs and dances pertaining to the Cannibal and other dancers, but they used these privileges only as display crests without duplicating the entire ceremony. The same was true of certain Nootkan chiefs. All the non-Kwakiutl users of the rites, whether their use was complete or partial, used the Kwakiutl names of the personages and the rituals, and sang the associated songs in the same tongue. "Those-who-descend-from-the-heavens" was found in complete form among Heiltsuk- and Haisla-speaking groups, Bella Coola, and all Tsimshian-speaking divisions; and most of the associated nomenclature was in Heiltsuk. Southern Kwakiutl did not perform the ceremonial as such, but incorporated some spirit representations in their Shamans' Society, reporting a Heiltsuk source of these features.[2] The Nootkan Shamans' Society, or Wolf Dance, was restricted to speakers of that language with one exception, the Southern Kwakiutl-speaking groups of Quatsino Sound. The Nutlam Society had the widest distribution: among all Heiltsuk and Haisla, Bella Coola, and all Tsimshian groups, and among most if not all Coast Salish and Lower Chinook. Strangely, among the Salish and Chinook, the ceremonial was not called Nutlam as a rule, but by a garbled form of the Nootkan term for their Shamans' Society. Both Southern Kwakiutl and the Nootkan groups, who did not have this ceremonial in the period of ethnographic memory, at least, used its name for other performances. Among the Southern Kwakiutl, Nutlam was the designation for a dancer inspired by a War spirit; among the Nootka it referred to a dance performed by low-rank novices in the Wolf Dance. Three facts—distribution, the simpler form of the Nutlam, and the apparent trend toward its replacement by the more elaborate Dancing Society performances—suggests that Nutlam may have been closest to the original form from which the others were developed by the Wakashan-speaking divisions.

[2] In relatively late historic times a few Southern Kwakiutl chiefs have acquired rights to this dance cycle from Heiltsuk relatives.

As was suggested earlier, the pattern of all these rituals suggests strongly a derivation from the simpler, more widespread Guardian Spirit singings of the Salish, Coast and Interior, and the inland-dwelling neighbors of the latter. The Spirit singings were public displays of powers supposedly received through encounters with supernatural beings; the Dancing Society performances in essence were dramatizations of the whole episode of the encounter, plus the concept of hereditary right to such experiences.

# CHAPTER 9

# The Mercantile Chinook

THE CHINOOKAN-SPEAKING GROUPS held the valley of the mighty Columbia River, from its mouth to some distance above the boiling falls and rapids known as The Dalles. The great fame of the Chinook as traders or middlemen in the busy aboriginal commerce derived from their location. At the river mouth and on Shoalwater (Willapa) Bay they were in easy contact with Coast Salish neighbors to north and south, and through them with more distant peoples of the outer coast. From both Shoalwater (Willapa) Bay and the lower reaches of the Columbia there were routes of communication to upper Puget Sound, home of other Coast Salish-speaking neighbors. They had few contacts with the Calapuya of the Willamette Valley, perhaps because the backward Calapuya had little merchandise to barter. At the upper end of their territory the Chinook had frequent contacts with all the Sahaptin bands and many Interior Salish of the Southern Plateau, and even with Shoshonean-speaking groups of the northern Great Basin, because those peoples came regularly to the great aboriginal trade mart of The Dalles.

## The Dalles: Fishery and Marketplace

The Dalles is first a geologic phenomenon. The waters of the great river roared over the edge of a massive geologic structure and descended to a deep channel cut through softer formations. But the drop was not a vertical one, and the waters descended in a long steep slope, forming more rapids than falls. Salmon could traverse The Dalles and proceed to spawning grounds far upstream. Strong currents, however, forced the fish to seek eddies and sheltered pools along the banks to rest after fighting violent rapids. Hence, the enormous schools of salmon that annually ascended the Columbia were easy prey for the Chinook fishermen, who speared and dipnetted them from perilous scaffoldings over the edges of the river. Because the fishing was so good, interior groups who had no fishing grounds, or whose fishing grounds farther upstream were poor, flocked to The Dalles to trade for dried salmon. Others with adequate fishing grounds of their own came to trade for other products. They brought peltries lustrous from the bitter interior winters, jade celts from the middle Fraser, mountain-sheep horn, basketry, and woven rabbit-skin robes. The aggressive Klamath and Modoc of the Klamath Lake region brought captives snatched from unwarlike California neighbors, to sell as slaves. Besides salmon from The Dalles, dentalia from Nootkan waters formed the most important commodity of coast origin, but other articles as well were brought upstream by the Chinook for barter. The Tsimshian olachen-fishing center on the Nass has been mentioned as an important trade center, but the area from which it drew traders and goods was small compared with The Dalles. Trade connections with The Dalles ultimately stretched across the Rockies and into the Great Plains. Shoshoni-speaking groups of the interior were in contact with the Chinook of the lower Columbia, and for this reason, Lewis and Clark engaged "the Shoshoni woman" as official interpreter when they set out on their transcontinental march to verify reports of the great river that emptied into the Western Sea.

A tribute to the Chinook genius for commerce may be seen in the name of the trade language in wide use on the North Pacific Coast, the Chinook Jargon. The origins of this lingua franca are still a mystery. It is certain that its maximum elaboration and spread was not aboriginal: American and European traders on the coast used it and even disseminated it in early historic times. It is quite possible, however, that its bases were formulated in aboriginal times. While the Jargon includes words of many native languages of the coast, and in its final form a few of English and French origin, a sizable proportion are Nootkan. We can only speculate whether this indicates frequent Chinook-Nootkan contacts in past times. There are no historic or ethnographic records of common direct contacts between the two divisions, and presumably most of the trade between them passed through intermediate hands. However, there was a firm association of the Jargon with the Chinookan groups.

Chinook culture was disrupted long ago by the implacable advance of white civilization. The lower Columbia became the center of fur-trade operations, first of the Northwest Fur Company, then of Hudson's Bay Company. Still more devastating was the opening of the country to settlement in the Oregon Trail days, an episode culminating in 1855 in the treaty-making and removal of the Chinook to reservations. The removal brought an end to the Indian way of life in all but the eastern desert regions, the Plateau and Great Basin portions of Oregon and Washington. When serious ethnographic studies were begun, only fragmentary memories of Chinook culture could be rescued from oblivion. However, there is a rich record of observations by early explorers and traders that makes it possible to reconstruct a picture of the aboriginal civilization. The appearance, dress, and weapons of the Indians are recounted in several traders' journals. Lewis and Clark recorded a still fuller picture of Chinook life, particularly of material culture. And later the traders stationed at the forts on the Columbia added to the documentary record.

Ships engaged in the Northwest Coast fur trade began to call at the mouth of the river from the time of its discovery in 1792 by the ship *Columbia*. The traders learned that the beautifully tanned elk hides offered them in trade by the Lower Chinook were in great demand farther north. And probably more than a few hapless California Indian slaves, sold into bondage at The Dalles, were taken aboard and exchanged for sea-otter robes up the coast. In return the mariners gave guns, powder and shot, steel knives and axes, and other goods that the Chinook received avidly and traded inland at fabulous profit to groups who had no direct contacts with white traders.

Dialects of the Chinookan-speaking people were regional, beginning with the Clatsop at the river mouth, and ending with the Wishram at The Dalles. There were also a few groups on Shoalwater (Willapa) Bay in southwestern Washington, probably much intermingled with Coast Salish. Estimates in historic documents on the size of the Chinook population are probably not very accurate, but it seems that the linguistic unit was not a numerous one. Each of the subdivisions probably had one or more principal villages, like the winter villages farther up the coast, from which the people moved seasonally to temporary camps. The differences in dialect among the Chinook were minor, and cultural differences were also slight. The latter were most marked in aspects of economy that reflected environmental differences. At the river mouth and on Shoalwater (Willapa) Bay, shellfish, particularly clams and mussels, were collected; the Wishram, it is reported, occasionally staged antelope hunts on the arid plains above their section of the river, as did their Sahaptin neighbors. But to Chinook, as to all North Pacific Coast peoples, salmon fishing was the basis of economic activity.

The Chinook version of the rectangular plank house was a gable-roofed structure with vertical plank siding. Its distinctive feature was its placement in a deep pit. Only the roof was above ground level, and the side walls were not visible from outside. The entryway was a round hole cut through a wide plank a little above ground level in one of the gable ends. Inside, a notched log ladder reached from entry to the floor. Shelflike platforms about three feet above the floor ran along the side and back walls and served for sleeping and storage. These structures were large enough to house a number of biologic families. Although there is not adequate information on the makeup of Chinook house-groups, it seems reasonable to assume that they were constituted of small lineages or parts of lineages, as elsewhere on the North Pacific Coast.

Wooden ladles, trays, and dishes, hollowed out of single blocks of wood, were used for culinary purposes and for serving food. Kerfed and bent wooden boxes were in common use, but were apparently trade articles from the Coast Salish of northwestern Washington and from the Nookta. A Chinook specialty was the bowl of mountain-sheep horn, molded into shape after steaming or boiling, and carved with a combination of geometric and rude representative patterns. The

material was obtained through trade with neighbors of the interior;
the bighorn did not occur in the lower Columbia valley.

The Chinook had a variety of canoe types, few of which they constructed themselves. One of the most popular was the Nootka canoe,
in such common use that early settlers on the Columbia and the Oregon
coast referred to it as a Chinook model. However, the craft were not
only Nootkan in type but obtained originally from Vancouver Island
or Cape Flattery. A few were made by Quileute, Hoh, and Coast
Salish-speaking Quinault of the Washington coast, whose master canoemakers' work could scarcely be distinguished from that of the Nootka
from whom they had learned. The numbers of these canoes on the
lower river attested not to the industry of the Chinook but to their
trading abilities. Lewis and Clark observed a number of other canoe
types as well, one of which with huge wood figures mounted over the
prow may have been a vessel of the Northern type. The Strait of
Georgia-Puget Sound modification of the Northern canoe type—low
prow and stern adapted to sheltered inland waters—was also known
to the Chinook through their contacts with Puget Sound Salish, and
they apparently had a few of them in Lewis and Clark's day. A small
blunt-ended craft, suitable for use in swift water and known on Puget
Sound as the "shovelnose" canoe, was used by the Wishram and other
Chinook.

Early travelers devoted lengthy paragraphs in their journals to descriptions of Chinook head flattening and the way it was produced.
A padded board was bound against the forehead of an infant in his
wooden cradle so as to produce the desired shape with the forehead
sloped back from the eyebrows to a wedge-shaped crest above the
occiput. The heads of small babies are fairly plastic and can be manipulated with no demonstrable undesirable effects on mental processes.
There was no particular rationale for this disfigurement, although
presumably it satisfied an aesthetic need on the part of those who
practiced it. Head flattening is an example of the many cultural practices that yield to no logical explication. It has been in use at various
times in various parts of the world, and the custom was in vogue with
local variations beyond the Chinook area, from the central Oregon
coast northward throughout western Washington and the Strait of
Georgia, as well as among the Nootkans and their Kwakiutl relatives.

Chinook dress conformed to general areal patterns, that is, in fine weather men went naked except for ornaments, and women wore apronlike skirts. The Wishram were an exception to the standard mode: among them men often wore buckskin breechclouts. In inclement weather, robes of furs were used, or dog- and goat-wool robes from Coast Salish looms, or rabbit-skin robes from Plateau and Great Basin trade. Tule-mat rain capes, also used by Puget Sound Salish, were in common use. Lewis and Clark saw a number of men wearing what were clearly Nootkan "chiefs' hats"—finely twined basketry rain hats of conical form surmounted by a spiked knob, with whaling scenes woven around the brim—another demonstration of the ramifications of Chinook commerce.

## Society

The structure of Chinookan society is least clearly depicted in historical sources. There is frequent mention in the early accounts of a chief on the lower part of the river whose name, or title, is usually given as "Concomly." The accounts endow him with enormous and regal authority, but it must be remembered that the white explorers and traders expected to find native kings and princes. Concomly was obviously an acute individual, who saw advantage in becoming a middleman in the traders' dealings with other Indians, thereby gaining prestige and material profit. He became friendly with the traders, doing them favors, some of which would put him in jail as a panderer under modern Oregon law. In return for his favors, the traders treated him as though he were chief of all the Chinook, which he certainly was not. By ethnographic interpolation one may assume that Concomly was, like other North Pacific Coast chiefs, head of a kin group whose authority derived from his genealogical seniority and the strength of the kinship bond that gave him the solid support of his so-called subjects. Probably a truer picture of Chinook chieftains in general is found in Lewis and Clark's description of the limited authority of a Wishram chief who could not prevent his unruly young men from molesting the expedition.

Despite the tales about Concomly, there is little reason to doubt that Chinookan society and polity differed in any important respect from that of their Coast Salish neighbors. Among the latter, the basic social unit was the local group, consisting of an extended family with stress on kinship ties in the paternal line, but without any formal unilateral ("clan") organization. The head of such a group was its senior member on the basis of primogeniture, and he and his close relatives were regarded as nobility. It is repeatedly reported for Coast Salish groups that a weak incompetent chief might be replaced by a better qualified junior, which makes clear the absence of absolute authority of the hereditary chiefs. Real authority was vested in the kin group itself, which could thus select its head. I have been unable to find record of a specific instance in which a chief was deposed in this fashion, but the fact that informants considered such action possible indicates that the Coast Salish concept of hereditary rank was less rigid than the Nootkan or Tsimshian, for example, who insist such deviation from the hereditary principle could never happen. It seems reasonable to assume a similar pattern for Chinookan society, since these people conform to areal and subareal patterns of social and political organization in all other aspects of culture on which there are fuller data.

## Religion and Ritual

Chinook religion was focused on two themes: the First Salmon rite and the individual spirit quest. Each group conducted its own ritual to welcome the annual run of salmon to its territory. The spirit quest was an ordeal undertaken by all males during adolescence, and some women, as among the Coast Salish. Curing power was greatly desired, but other powers might be acquired, hunting, for example. There were guardian spirits that brought good luck in general, and some simply gave songs and dances for the winter sessions of spirit singing. Spirit singing was the major ceremonial among the Chinook, as it was among most of their Salish-speaking neighbors. Although not entirely clear, data from certain Coast Salish groups indicate that guardian spirits bestowed special powers for curing, hunting, gambling, canoemaking, etc., and songs used in connection with these pursuits. Separate from these, the guardian spirits bestowed songs with dances and other performances, which were intended for "secular" use at the spirit singings. At these public demonstrations of guardian-spirit power, one person, then another, displayed his dance and often some magical performance involving sleight of hand, while he sang the songs his supernatural mentor had given him. His fellows sang in accompaniment, keeping time with a Chinookan musical instrument—long poles with bunches of deer hooves—that gave zest to the chants. The ends of the poles were bumped against the roof planks and combined drumming and rattling. The dramatized voyages of the Spirit Canoe, as performed by Puget Sound Salish, seem not to have been made by the Chinook.

Some years ago, when it seemed likely that no new data would be recovered on the Chinook, an ethnographer encountered an aged Lower Chinook from whom he collected a great deal of information.[1] Unquestionably some of the data relate to the post-1855 period, when, uprooted from their ancestral homes and ethnically intermingled on reservations, the Indians were still trying to carry on something of the old way of life. Other incidents recounted by the informant must have been secondhand reports of ancient customs as heard from elderly relatives. The account as a whole is both internally consistent and consistent with data from historic sources. Among hitherto unreported features of Lower Chinook culture, the informant said that the potlatch was a well-established institution among his people, and that they had a modified version of one of the more northerly Dancing Societies. Although neither of these complexes had been reported previously among the Chinook, neither is incompatible with what was known about them. The potlatch was firmly integrated in the cultures of the central Washington coast, such as the Quileute and Quinault, and the Salish groups of Puget Sound. It was precisely with these groups that the Chinook had many close trade relationships. In addition, the Chinook as prosperous traders could accumulate plentiful wealth goods for these festivals.

The Dancing Society performance was known in historic times in western Washington as the "Black Tamanawus" ("tamanawus" is Jargon for supernatural being, especially guardian spirit). This performance was a marginal form of the Nutlam ritual of groups north of Vancouver Island, the distinctive feature of which was the dog-eating by the possessed performers. The Black Tamanawus from lower Puget Sound and the central Washington coast is usually described as though it were a sort of native Mafia. It is difficult to judge from the fragmentary accounts available whether the ritual actually acquired this nature, or whether in the epoch of acculturation in which the accounts were written, this interpretation was fostered by missionaries who opposed the performances as pagan.

[1] Ray, 1938.

# CHAPTER 10

# The Thrifty Yurok

THE LOWER VALLEYS OF the Klamath River and its chief affluents in northwestern California, together with the rugged seacoast north and south of the mouth of the Klamath, formed the habitat of three tiny linguistic enclaves—Yurok, Karok, and Hupa—who formed the southern focus of North Pacific Coast culture. This sketch is concerned with the Yurok, but there was a high degree of cultural uniformity among the three groups: neighbors on the same river highway, they visited each other's performances of the same festivals, intermarried, and feuded over the same issues. One wonders how they preserved their linguistic differentiation. The tongue spoken by the Yurok is ultimately related to Algonkin. The Karok language seems to have no close relatives, although some linguists include it in a superstock called Hokan. Hupa is an Athabascan language. The civilization shared by the three represented a peak in complexity and intensity of the southern subarea.

Flanking the Yurok on the south were their linguistic relatives, the

Wiyot, southernmost of the groups properly classifiable as North Pacific Coast culture, and clearly marginal in areal terms. Farther south and inland, ringing the three components of the cultural focus, were simple patterns of Central Californian genre. North of the Yurok along the coast were the Athabascan Tolowa-Tututni and Oregon coast groups as far north as the Coos of Coos Bay who, like the Wiyot, had North Pacific Coast cultures of diminished intensity in comparison with Yurok-Karok-Hupa.

## Dentalia "Money"

The whys and wherefores of this northwestern Californian culture focus, from the standpoint of areal culture history, remain to be discovered. Many distinctive features of areal culture were lacking, such as the potlatch, masked dances, representative art, and the like. But the local pattern cannot be regarded as a marginal watered-down manifestation in the process of diffussion from a higher center far to the north. Elaboration of many complexes went far beyond that practiced in the north. The handling of dentalia is a case in point. The Yurok (and the Karok and Hupa), like all peoples of the area and most interior neighbors, cherished the glossy tusk-shaped shells that came to them through intergroup trade. They engraved simple, neat little geometric designs on the shells, and glued brightly colored tufts of down to the bases and tips, where their neighbors were content with unadorned dentalia. The Nootkans who "fished" the shells, like other northerners, rather casually sorted the shells into large, medium, and small sizes, and strung them by an imprecise fathom. Yurok, on the other hand, graded their shell treasures like jewelers sorting fine gems, and devised a standard of measurement. Yurok strings were all of the same length. The unit of highest denomination was a string filled from end to end by ten shells of nearly equal length.

If without detectable flaws of cracks or chips, one ten-shell string was equivalent in worth to any other. Thus, Yurok use of dentalia was more nearly like modern currency than most "money" of primitive peoples. The next lower denomination was a fathom string of eleven shells, and of slight value were strings containing twelve. Every adult male had a mark tattooed on his upper arm by which he could check the accuracy of the length of a string of dentalia held between thumb and forefinger. A few shells, giants by lower Klamath River standards, surpassed the limits of ten-to-the-string size and had no standardized evaluation, being of the nature of treasures. Trimmed bits of broken shells and shells too small for the standard length strings served for women's necklaces and similar adornments. In short, Yurok handling of dentalia was a specialization of the areal pattern, more elaborate than was common among their neighbors to the north, rather than less so as would be expected among a group distant from the high centers of culture development. The same phenomenon may be noted in numerous aspects of the culture of these people.

## Villages and Houses

Yurok villages were small. Unlike villages of coastal neighbors to the north where houses facing on the beach gave an effect of orderliness, there was no discernible planned layout. Dwellings were rectangular structures of planks riven from giant coast redwood. A central pit formed the main living space in the house. Low plank walls were set two to three feet back from the edges of this pit, leaving a bench used chiefly for storage, a form reminiscent of the house type of the Northern subarea. There were, however, differences. At the doorway end of the house there were two walls—the outside wall and one at the edge of the pit a few feet away—so that between them they formed a narrow anteroom whose long dimension was the width of the house. This chamber suggests a survival from a long-forgotten structure of different type, and it had no particular purpose among the Yurok of ethnographic times except to serve as a catchall for miscellaneous gear. The principal doorway was near one corner of the outer wall. It consisted of a round hole cut through a wide plank, and was closed by a sliding-plank door.

In roof form, another lower Klamath specialization may be noted. Although a few men, poor in worldly goods and lacking in ambition, might cover their houses with a simple gable roof, a properly built house had a three-pitch roof. No functional purpose has been ascertained for the feature; it was just another local elaboration. A small terraced platform of flat river cobbles, pleasant for lounging and for doing sedentary tasks on sunny days, was commonly laid along the house front.

The houses, at least those of men of standing, like those to the north, were named. Since the Yurok did not have crests, house names usually had geographical reference, such as "By-the-Trail House" or "Upstream House." In a sense, the house site, rather than the structure of timbers and planking, bore the name. A house rebuilt over an old house-pit bore the same name as its predecessor. The house names, in turn, provided casual names for the people: "Downstream House Old Man," "Widow in Across-the-Creek House," and the like, for the people were very secretive about their true names.

### Sweathouses

Functionally, the dwellings just described served only individual biologic families, who used them for the storage, preparation, and service of food; for the storage of individual possessions; and as sleeping quarters for women and children. Houses were small, in contrast to other house types of the area, and did not directly reflect the kinship group basis of social organization. This aspect of Yurok culture appeared in the sweathouse rather than in the family dwelling, for the sweathouse served as the dormitory for the men and older boys of a kinship unit.

The head of each group of relatives, reckoned in the paternal line, was referred to by a title literally translated as "rich man." With the aid of his kinsmen, he constructed or maintained a sweathouse for use by himself and his male relatives—the basic social unit. In small communities, there might be but one sweathouse; in a few larger places situated at major fish-weir sites on the river, there were several. These villages were occupied by two or more kinship units.

The Yurok sweathouse was a rectangular structure of planks, but there its similarity to the dwelling ended. The walls lined the sides of a deep pit. These structures had no anteroom, no surrounding platform, nor were they ever covered with the three-pitch roof. A large fire pit in the floor provided direct heat, not steam, for sweating. Men entered through the usual round doorway, but left the sweathouse through a sort of flue that terminated in a channel across the floor to the fireplace.

Ethnographers and others who observed the Indians still using their typical structures were impressed by the neatness of the sweathouses, especially when contrasted to the dwellings. The latter were cluttered with baskets of provisions, bales of dried fish on overhead scaffolds, storage boxes, and a profusion of materials, utensils, and the like. Sweathouses rarely contained more than neat wooden stools and well-polished wooden headrests, which were individual property of each occupant, and perhaps a load of wood stacked beside the fireplace. Men carved their own stools from blocks of redwood. Gathering sweathouse wood was an especially meritorious form of ritual training. Men often brought small chores to do in the sweathouse—a salmon harpoon head in the making, nettle fiber to be spun into cord, and similar portable tasks—but when finished, the tools and materials were taken back to the dwelling. An ample platform of flat cobbles fronted the sweathouse and was used as a resting place on fine days.

The sweat bath was an important part of ritual purification for good fortune. The men usually assembled in late afternoon for the sweat bath; when they left the sweathouse by the flue-exit, they plunged into the chill river water, then spent several hours alternately immersing and scrubbing with aromatic herbs, while reciting formulaic prayers for good fortune. They returned to converse awhile, then slept. The floor was divided into named sections, although without visible lines, and places considered most desirable were reserved for men of highest rank. Each occupant was assigned a certain section according to his social standing. At night they stretched out in their places, many with tubular tobacco pipes (of Central Californian type) that were most comfortably smoked while lying flat on the back. Informants say that a few whiffs of the strong tobacco were enough to overcome any tendency to insomnia.

## Canoes

Like all North Pacific Coast watercraft, the main portion of the Yurok canoe was hollowed from a single timber. The turbulent waters of the Klamath demanded maneuverability, even at the expense of stability. The Yurok and their cultural congeners constructed dugouts of redwood with hulls that were round in cross section and rounded at both ends. The shape eliminated flat vertical surfaces at bow and stern that would impede turning or offer resistance to cross currents.

A steersman's seat at the stern and two knobs for footrests were carved from the same piece as the hull. The steersman used seat and footrests when bracing himself for a thrust with his combination pole and paddle. The upturned bow and stern were finished off in high points, formed by concave curves rising from either side. At the bow a separately carved yokelike piece was painstakingly fitted over the double curve. This appendage was nonfunctional, but in Yurok eyes, essential to a properly constructed canoe. One can only speculate whether it is a survival of a fitted prowpiece similar to the Northern and Nootkan types, or of a harpoon rest, or whether it was never anything but an ornamental appendage. On the river these canoes in skilled Yurok hands performed well. At sea they were hazardous, in constant peril of being capsized by any wave of moderate size. Yurok of the village of Rekwoi at the mouth of the river, and of the few nearby small coastal villages, occasionally ventured short distances offshore during fine weather, to club and harpoon sea lions, but this feat was not for the timid.

## Food

Yurok subsistence economy revolved about the salmon, like that of all North Pacific groups, and about the acorn, a product not available to most other peoples of the area, except a few neighbors of southwestern Oregon. The use of the acorn illustrates not only exploitation of an environmental opportunity but cultural influence from Central California where the acorn was a universal staple. The importance of the salmon was reflected in various ways in Yurok life. The villages were situated at major fishing places, for example, where long weirs were constructed annually by combined effort of several family groups, each of which owned a segment of the structure and the right to use it for netting or harpooning. From pole scaffolds over the weir, the netting was done with long conical bags of webbing affixed to frames shaped like the letter "A." The harpoons were of standard areal design, each with a pair of composite barbed points mounted on diverging foreshafts lashed to the shaft. Another important fishing device, used independently of the weir, was the gill net, set between stakes in eddies where schools of salmon played during their upstream migration. The efficacy of this device depends on tying mesh of a size that permits entry of only the head of the fish, the strands ensnaring the creature by the gills as it tries to back away. Such nets are useful for fish of nearly uniform size. They appear to represent a special development of the lower Klamath region and were not known aboriginally in other parts of the area.

With their stores of dried salmon and acorns the Yurok were ensured of a goodly amount of leisure during the mild, rainy winters of their homeland. They did not subsist entirely on these two foods, however. There were other fish—trout, steelhead, sturgeon, and lamprey eels in the river—and in the woods, an abundance of game, particularly deer and elk—all of which they exploited. The divisions living near the seacoast also took smelt when they came to spawn on sandy beaches and shellfish when the tide ebbed low, and they had infrequent but spectacular sea-lion hunts. When a dead whale drifted onto a Yurok beach, it was not allowed to go to waste, but was partitioned according to a complex system of salvage rights. Vegetable foods other than the acorn were not abundant, but seeds, fruits, and roots gave variety to the diet.

### Woodworking and Carving

Some of their leisure time the Yurok devoted to manufactures which, as has been remarked, were not elaborate but consistently neat and well finished. This emphasis on good workmanship signalized the great cultural difference between groups of the lower Klamath River and their Central Californian neighbors. Such features as the sliding-plank door of the dwelling, the stools and headrests in the sweathouse, the dugout canoe with its seat and footrests and peculiar yoke fitted over the bow, the treasure chests made, not by kerfing and bending a board as in the north, but by hollowing out a block of redwood and fitting it with a cover—all represent local specializations of the woodworking typical of the North Pacific Coast area. Small manufactures of materials such as elkhorn spoons with handles carved into geometric patterns, dentalia "purses" of hollowed-out sections of elkhorn, tubular wooden tobacco pipes with fitted steatite bowls, similarly demonstrate the competence of Yurok carvers.

## Wealth

Another use to which these people put their leisure was in thinking about wealth. There was an extraordinary preoccupation with wealth in Yurok culture, despite the fact that in comparison with Tsimshian or Nootka their stores of riches were not great. In part, this preoccupation was deliberate. An often-expressed Yurok ideal of behavior to ensure success was that a man should devote his thoughts to the subject of wealth. He should spend as much time as possible in the ritual training routine of sweat bathing and cold-water bathing, partial fasting, observing strict continence, gathering sweathouse wood, and praying for riches. It would seem that this ideal was not entirely in vain, for among the principal kinds of Yurok treasures there were some that with good luck a man dedicated to the wealth quest might acquire.

The chief valuables on the lower Klamath River were dentalia, huge obsidian blades, scalps of a giant pileated woodpecker, and the skins of albino deer. The first two classes were imported. Strangely, almost nothing is known about the trade through which the Yurok got their beloved dentalia shells, and what they exchanged for them. Presumably some were bartered from group to group down the coast; others may have been traded down the Klamath River after the Kalmath acquired them in their slave-trading expeditions to The Dalles. Probably the Yurok and their neighbors were end-of-the-line for the glossy little shells as far as intertribal trade went. They hoarded the dentalia they received, and apparently made no effort to barter the shells to alien groups for other goods. After all, what did Central Californians have more precious to the Yurok than dentalia?

Origin of the obsidian blades is also enveloped in mystery. It has been speculated that the material of which they were made probably came from deposits in the volcanic area in Klamath and Modoc territory in northeastern California and southeastern Oregon, but whether the blades were traded already finished, or whether the predecessors of the recent Yurok did the exquisite Solutrean-like flaking that characterizes the pieces, is unknown. The woodpecker scalps are a different story. The birds from which they were taken are at home in the redwood forest, and although not an abundant form, a man with perseverence and luck might collect enough to improve his status slightly. Scalps were in demand to make mosaics on the wide buckskin headdresses worn in the "Jumping Dance," and as appliqué ornaments on other regalia. The scalps were, however, in the small-change category of native wealth. A man would have had to kill great numbers of woodpeckers to alter his economic status markedly. The real stroke of fortune, which could make a poor man rich at the twang of a bowstring, was to kill an albino deer, for the skin was immensely valuable. This was the prize of prizes, such as might fall to one who dedicated all his thoughts and prayers to getting rich.

### Feuds, Law, and Society

Yurok leisure was also used in incessant feuds and suits at law to settle those feuds. Like most North Pacific Coast peoples, the Yurok employed the principal of wergild as a device for resolving conflicts between social units, but as with so many other areal patterns, they added their distinctive touch to the basic concept. With the same kind of precision shown in their refinement of the dentalia-grading system, they worked out an elaborate scale of seriousness of offenses against the person, from a murder to an insult. Their legal philosophy achieved the neat equation that the value of a man's life was equal to the bride price paid for his mother, thus giving an exact measure to the general areal principle that the value of a man's life, in demands for wergild, depended on his social status.

This systematic approach gave an orderliness to Yurok law that was lacking in the wergild settlements of groups far to the north, where grandiose demands for blood money were just as grandiosely rejected. Yet despite the nominal precision of the code, there was still room for haggling, and the constant threat of violence was a potent factor in the settlements, just as to the north. After hearing a fair number of case histories of conflicts and their resolutions among the Yurok, I have the impression that there was a peculiarly combined set of motivational factors: first, the Yurok had a more mercenary approach to exacting wergild than the northern groups; and second, the Yurok enjoyed the tensions, suspense, and thrill of danger that accompanied these conflicts. It seems that there was always trouble of some sort brewing somewhere along the lower Klamath in olden days. Many conflicts were over minor issues—a casual or even accidental trespass on property rights, a careless insult—but such matters were never passed off lightly. The conflicting groups immediately became the center of attention of the whole region, the rest of the people watching the maneuvers and probing for weakness with rapt attention. Gossips busily carried news of the latest development from village to village. A constant menace in the minor cases was that rash youths might take it on themselves to settle the conflict, thereby compounding the original minor offense with mayhem or a slaying, setting the stage for reprisals. The go-betweens, who were men of standing, hurried back and forth with demands and counteroffers until an accord was reached, payment made, and tranquility restored.

Yurok society was made up of small groups of patrilineally related males, clustered around the genealogical senior of the unit, the "rich man." Nominal owner of the sweathouse and of the group's wealth, he directed activities at group-owned economic tracts, such as a section of a salmon weir or the acorn grounds. However, as among other Coast Indians, wealth was really group, not individual, property. The rich man drew on it to assist in paying the bride price when a member of the group married, or the blood money exacted when a member of the group committed an offense. And he, not the principal in the case, directed the negotiations of the go-betweens during the long-drawn-out settlement of one of these matters.

Marriage among the Yurok was accompanied by lengthy haggling over the bride price, and legalized by payment of the agreed amount. This bride price was important, for, as already indicated, it established the base for reckoning the wergild value of the children of the union. Residence was strictly patrilocal, the wife going to live at the husband's village, or section of a large village. An exception to patrilocal residence committed the husband to live with his wife's group: if a rich man had no sons, but only daughters, he, thus, brought a young man into his household. Such an arrangement is referred to in English by the Indians as "half marriage" because only about half the normal bride price was exacted. Under the circumstances, it was usually a young man of inferior social status who would be willing to meet these conditions. Half marriages were sometimes arranged to patch up an illicit affair in which the man involved was of low rank. Seduction and adultery were very serious offenses in the Yurok code, being crimes against property. They were also frequent causes of conflict, for not all Yurok achieved the ideal of devoting their thoughts solely to wealth and their spare time to ritual training.

## Religion and Ritual

In broad outline, Yurok religious patterns conformed to those of the area, consisting in the individual quest for supernatural aid, and, quite apart, priest-conducted rituals for public welfare. A local specialization, however, gave a distinctive lower Klamath flavor to the individual rites: the guardian-spirit concept, common to the rest of the groups of the North Pacific Coast and to all native western North America, was submerged. The Yurok engaged in training procedures did not expect to encounter a supernatural being. Rather, he expected that because of his ritual cleanliness "dentalia would like him" and would be easy for him to acquire. But these were real dentalia shells he was thinking of, not spirits. If his rites were for good luck in hunting, he expected his state of purification to be pleasing to the deer, who would then stand before his bow without flinching, or would willingly put their heads into his snares. These were real deer, incarnations of the Deer Spirits of the forests, like the immortal Salmon Spirits that voluntarily made their nourishing flesh available to man.

Even for Yurok shamans (they were women) the guardian spirit was of limited importance. When her arduous training ritual was rewarded with success, the shaman acquired control over what informants call "pains," tiny animate but nonpersonified objects that flew about invisibly and lodged in human bodies, thus causing disease. As a climax of the power quest, a guardian spirit in some vague way assisted the shaman to acquire her first pair of "pains." She could see these mysterious objects and catch them in mid-flight; she could make them visible to secular eyes, swallow, then vomit them forth, and send them away. This power, acquired after long vigils in lonesome places in the hills and forests, she displayed in her novitiate dance performance in the sweathouse of her male relatives, the only time a woman was permitted to enter those exclusive premises. Thereafter she might administer to the sick, for a fee, utilizing her power for controlling the "pains" by sucking them from the patient's body, spewing them up, and sending them away. This ability to control the malevolent little objects was her principal power; after the first encounter, she had little contact with her guardian spirit.

A Yurok minor festival was the "Brush Dance," so called in local English because it was staged not in a house but in an unroofed brush enclosure. The nominal purpose of this performance was to celebrate a girl's puberty, but actually the principal motive was diversion. Regalia was not elaborate, but singing and lively dancing were featured.

The major ceremonials performed at the more important Yurok villages were those of the World Renewal cycle—an elaboration of the First Salmon ritual, with priests rather than supernatural beings and their protégés as the key figures. The plot was a repetition of the procedures established by a mysterious prehuman race who set the world in order and defined the way in which mankind was to live. The priest of each local group, after lengthy preparations of fasting and bathing, followed the route of the ancient beings from one spot to another to kill the First Salmon at the spot that was to become the major fishing site. As he moved, the priest uttered the lengthy formulaic prayer describing the acts of the prehuman race. When the season's First Salmon was taken by one of the priest's assistants, it was given the same ceremonious treatment as had been accorded the first fish ever to be caught there, back when the world began. Not only the First Salmon, but other natural resources, such as the locally important First Acorns, were formally treated.

The underlying belief was that the procedures of the prehuman race of beings had caused the salmon to come in vast numbers and the oaks to bear bountifully. By repeating these acts in the proper ritual way, abundant salmon, acorns, and other foods, as well as riches and general well-being, were assured for the whole world (the Yurok's whole world—the lower Klamath region). Hence the designation "World Renewal" has been applied to this cycle of ceremonies. Following several days of esoteric rites by the priest, a public festival was held, featuring one of the two major dance displays of the region. In the "White Deerskin Dance," performers carried the decorated light-colored deerskins that were the major treasures in that area. Others danced displaying tremendous obsidian blades. In the "Jumping Dance," the performers marched to sacred spots where they gave great leaps, and the distinctive appurtenances were wide, semirigid headbands of buckskin adorned with scarlet scalps of the pileated woodpecker.

Each local group participating in the ceremony equipped performers with valuables from their store, held by the "rich man." However, these riches were not distributed afterward, as in the potlatch of more northerly divisions, but were thriftily stored away by the owners and displayed again another year. Spectacular and impressive as these shows of local wealth may have been, the display dances were mere appendages to the important part of the ceremonial—the quietly serious procedure by the priest who renewed the original bounty of the world.

As was indicated, each local group centering in a major fishing ground staged its version of the World Renewal ritual. As the salmon progressed up the Klamath River, the performances were given in succession from the mouth of the river to the upper portions, and there is evidence that the Indians regarded the individual rites not as isolated, but as integral parts of an observance essential to the well-being of their world.

# CHAPTER 11

# Becoming Modern

IN THIS BOOK FREQUENT mention has been made of "aboriginal times" and "the historic period," pointing out differences of native custom between the two. The inference, where not explicitly stated, was that the change was due to influences deriving from Western, chiefly British and American, civilization, which suddenly came into contact with the native cultures. These cultural changes were not the result of isolated incidents of contact, but were part of a sweeping and drastic change in the native way of life which began with the first contacts with white explorers and continues to the present day. The Tsimshian, Nootka, Yurok, and their neighbors of a century ago differed culturally from their forebears of prehistoric times. Those of sixty years ago had modes of life that involved greater changes, and their present-day descendants—still Tsimshian, Nootka, Yurok, and the rest—live after a fashion that would be unintelligible in many respects to their ancestors. This final chapter offers a brief survey of acculturation on the

North Pacific Coast, that is, of the major changes resulting from the impact of white culture on the native civilizations.

Acculturation has attracted increasing interest in recent decades, as anthropologists have come to recognize the significance of changes that have taken place in native cultures in a relatively brief time span. Changes from shredded cedar-bark robes to dungarees and seaboots, from red-cedar dugouts to diesel-powered seine boats, involve much more than discarding ancient culture elements and adding modern ones. They involve changes of concept and of culture values, and ramify into other elements of the changing culture. A man's wife could weave him a shredded-bark robe, the dungarees he must buy with money, for example; buying with money requires involvement in economic activities of Western civilization. And the wearing of trousers, whether of dungaree or other material, is related on the North Pacific Coast to Christianity, for the early missionaries devoted considerable effort toward getting their converts to cover their nakedness. They introduced new concepts of "decent" apparel, morality, and shame. And so it goes.

It is not the mere listing of culture items added or subtracted that is significant, but the culture processes and the psychological factors involved. Since these changes have occurred relatively recently, many relevant data are available to the student who wishes to analyze their cultural significance. The innovation of the shredded cedar-bark robe among Tsimshian and Nootka occurred so long ago that its precedent factors and accompanying effects can only be guessed. However, there are good pictures of the details of Tsimshian and Nootkan cultures at the time of the introduction of trousers for daily wear. Accounts even distinguish between this event and the prior introduction by explorers and traders that was accepted only as a novelty. There is information on the missionaries who introduced the new garb, on their techniques of applied anthropology, and on many of the early converts. The conditions of the change, like the conditions of a laboratory experiment, are thus available to the student. Thorough analysis of acculturative change on the North Pacific Coast remains to be made, but broad outlines of the changes can be summarized.[1]

[1] Only two individual groups of the area have been studied from the point of view of acculturation: the Quileute (Pettitt, 1950), and the neighboring Makah (Colson, 1953).

The acculturation of the North Pacific Coast natives may be roughly divided into three successive phases, according to the nature of predominant white contacts: the exploration and fur-trade period, the epoch of establishment of administrative and religious controls, and the period of industrialization and white colonization of the area. This breakdown is for convenience in discussion, not a listing of a sequence of exclusive types of incidents. That is, the fur trading as a background for Indian-white contacts did not cease abruptly with the inception of white administrative controls; it simply ceased to be the principal manner in which representatives of the two civilizations met. In fact, in many parts of the coast commercial taking of peltries, and their sale, remains an important economic activity for the Indians. There was considerable chronological variation in these phases in different localities: Puget Sound and lower Vancouver Island were densely settled by whites when not far away in miles, other regions like the Washington coast and the West Coast of Vancouver Island were still wilderness.

## THE EARLY INFLUENCES

White discovery and exploration of the area began in the early half of the eighteenth century with the discovery of the Dane Vitus Bering of the strait that bears his name. Sorties were made by his second in command, Chirikoff, during which he made landfall at two points in southeast Alaska in Tlingit territory. This expedition laid the basis for the subsequent establishment of the Russian outpost at Kodiak, and later probes along the shores of the Gulf of Alaska. Of more importance was the third expedition of exploration by Captain Cook, during which Nootka Sound was discovered and trade relations were first made with the natives. (A few years earlier, a Spanish vessel of exploration had hove to, apparently off the mouth of Nootka Sound but without noting the Sound, and had been boarded by a small party of Indians, but the effects of this contact were ephemeral.) Cook sailed from Nootka around the tip of Vancouver Island, and then across the Gulf to southwest Alaska. The importance of the Cook expedition to North Pacific Coast history derived from the sea-otter pelts bartered at Nootka Sound, which were greatly desired by the Chinese merchants at Canton. The luxurious furs were known to the Chinese from the few they received through trade with natives of the western shores of the Pacific. However, the Asiatic source of supply, whether because of difficulties of communication or because of long-continued intensive hunting, could not meet the demand. Hence, the Chinese offered the English "fabulous" prices for the furs.

European exploration and interest in the Pacific in that day was motivated to a great extent by political considerations, the hope of dominating trade routes to the Orient, and to some extent by search for lands suitable for colonization. But the tradition of treasure trove lingered on. The immensely valuable fur was the nearest thing to treasure that had been found in many years. Consequently, not long after the Cook expedition returned to England, plans began to be laid to exploit this new El Dorado. The Hanna, Meares, Dixon, and Portlock expeditions were fitted out and sailed to the new adventure. Their pioneer successes resulted in a new trade, in which more vessels participated each year. British and American, chiefly Boston, ships dominated the trade, rounding Cape Horn to sail north, often via the Hawaiian Islands to the Northwest Coast, where they cruised trading for sea-otter hides, thence to Canton, to sell the furs and buy a cargo of tea, silk, and other luxuries of the Orient to take back home. The voyages took two or three years, perils were numerous, and hardships constant. But the rewards were enormous.

Spain, worried over her tenuous grip on California, and the Russian traders on Bering Strait made efforts to strengthen their claims to Northwest America, but they could not halt the busy British and American traffic. The seafaring traders combed the coast as they wished in their quest for the rich peltries. Almost from the first, the trade assumed a distinctive pattern. One of its characteristics was an atmosphere of semihostility: Indians took several ships, among them the *Tonquin*, the *Atahualpa*, and the *Boston*. They would have taken more had it not been for the superior arms of the whites, the use of boarding nets, the traders' custom of permitting only a few Indians to board at one time and of demanding noble children as hostages. The traders, too, committed depredations. A captain who expected to spend several months on the coast tried not to offend the natives, but he had less scruples when ready to set sail for Whampoa Roads. Good furs, with which an Indian refused to part if he did not like the trade goods offered, might be taken by force. There are reports of ships firing on parties of Indians who came without pelts to offer in trade, apparently to cadge drinks of rum that normally opened negotiations. Revenge, if taken by the Indians, would fall on the heads of other "King Georges" or "Bostons," as the British and Americans were termed in Chinook Jargon.

Another characteristic of the trade was the free choice exhibited by the Indians in their selection of trade goods, that is, the elements of white culture they acquired. Captain Cook noted that the natives at Nootka Sound had a considerable number of iron-tipped weapons, and were anxious to acquire more iron. The first traders consequently loaded their vessels with iron "toes," malleable blanks suitable for chisel and adz blades, knives, and so on. Finally they glutted their market. An era of fads and novelties followed, during which the traders racked their brains to find ways of tempting the Indian fancy. One captain had his ship's armorer make up quantities of iron bracelets and neck rings, which for a time delighted the Indians. As supercargo on a previous voyage, another had learned of the great store the natives set on ermine skins. (They were traded in scant numbers from interior Indians for use as trailers on the Northern type forehead maskette headdresses.) He gambled on a large quantity of cheap ermine skins, purchased at Leipzig, which he traded for sea-otter hides at a spectacular profit. Another established a short-lived fad for European clothes by presenting chiefs with full-dress uniforms. He traded all the spare clothes aboard for sea-otter pelts, and even had his sailmaker make shirts and trousers of the ship's spare canvas and summer sails. When he found Indians who showed an interest in crockery cups and bowls, he traded off most of the ship's mess gear. When he finally sailed for Canton with a fairly good cargo of furs, he still had barrels of useless "toes" and glass beads in the bilges, but he had averted financial disaster.

Sale of firearms and ammunition to Indians was generally regarded in that day as unwise because the musket or pistol one trader bartered sooner or later would kill some other white man. But few of the seafarers let this principle stand in the way of closing a good trade, and before long the Indians had a sizable arsenal. Novelty foods became a popular trade item, especially sugar, flour, and molasses. West Indies rum lubricated the wheels of this commerce, and was in great demand. "Indian sugar," that is, sugar brought not as ship's stores but for trade, was half bran, according to frank chroniclers of the era. "Indian rum" was rum cut with an equal amount of water. A few traders experimented with articles of native commerce—tanned elk hides from the Columbia, Nootkan dentalia, and slaves bartered from the Kwakiutl. These frenzied efforts of traders to satisfy the capricious Indian fads are recorded in ships' journals.

The effect of this seaborne trade on the Indian cultures is not easy to gauge. The natives received large quantities of material goods from the new source. Some of these, such as the iron for tools and weapons, and some ready-made tools and weapons (knives, cutlasses, and the like) which might have been expected to have far-reaching cultural effect, probably produced little change. The Indians were already familiar with iron; they used it for tipping arrows and spears, and for cutting tools. Their eagerness for the metal indicates that it was in scarce supply. Satisfaction of this need may have resulted in an increase of woodworking and carving, an increase in production but with little change in types of the manufactures. While early historical records do not give complete inventories of material culture, they show that the carver's art was firmly defined, even to subareal distinctions in art styles.

Introduction of firearms likewise resulted in intensification of an existing pattern: warfare. It was some time before sufficient skill was acquired with these weapons, and ammunition became plentiful enough so that a hunter would prefer a musket to his reliable yew-wood bow. But the advantages of firearms in warfare were immediately perceived, because they fitted existing tactical patterns. While there may be a question whether a musket in unskilled hands produced more slaughter than aboriginal arms, it is certain that the roar of gunfire in the standard night attack within the house of the foe added to the panic of the victims and ensured victory to the attackers.

Another addition to areal culture dating from this era is the use of sail in native canoes. In the historic record are specific statements by several observers that sail was not originally in use, statements consistent with the fact that all canoe types were without true keels and ill-adapted to sailing. There are also records of captains who, usually to ingratiate themselves with a chief, ordered their sailmakers to cut and rig suits of sails for the chief's canoe. Within a few decades the big canoes everywhere but in the southern extreme were made with a socketlike projection on the floor of the hull for stepping the mast, and carried a small mast, spars, and sail, either squaresail or lateen rigged. Unlike the deep-keeled outriggers of Polynesia and Micronesia which can tack and beat, these craft could only run before the wind when the sails were set, but even that was an obvious advantage.

The ornaments, articles of dress, and the like, which the Indians chose on one occasion and rejected the next, to the traders' anguish, had meaning in terms of native culture and could be absorbed without producing major dislocations. Some of the ornaments served for daily use, but most were utilized in costuming ceremonial performers. An early observer who witnessed a portion of a Heiltsuk Dancing Society performance described a procession of dancers, each carrying a red silk parasol. Extravagant costumes and regalia were characteristic of the age-grade group displays of the Dancing Societies, and for special performances at interludes in the Northern-province potlatches.

It is apparent that much more time was devoted to sea-otter hunting in the period of the fur trade than in aboriginal days, for in the course of a few years the herds that had abounded on the coast were nearly exterminated. However, sea-otter pelts had always been prized by the natives, and they obviously had more skins than they used for robes when the very first traders were able to obtain considerable quantities of the furs. As far as is known, there was no change in the hunting technique, except for the development of a surround hunt as the animals became scarce. In short, there is no evidence of major change resulting from the intensified hunting of sea otter.

The sea otter began to dwindle early in the nineteenth century. In the decade 1810–1820, it became very difficult for a trading vessel to assemble a worthwhile cargo of the pelts and consequently fewer ships made the hazardous voyage. Those who did bought land furs as well—land otter, beaver, marten, and mink—but these were much less profitable than sea otter. In the following decade trading ships were few. But a new form of trading developed. After merger with the Northwest Fur Company, Hudson's Bay Company began establishment of permanent posts on the coast. In the late 1820's and early 1830's, in rapid succession Forts Langley, Rupert, McLoughlin, Nass, and Simpson were built (Fort Simpson replaced Fort Nass). The Russians had already established posts in Tlingit territory—at New Archangel, near modern Sitka, and another at Yakutat Bay—both of which were captured and burned by the Tlingit. Fort New Archangel was re-established and remained the only Russian post in the area until purchase of Alaska by the United States. Its influence was limited, for the Sitka groups jealously maintained their position as middlemen in trade, and a new generation of seafaring traders cruised the coasts in search of whatever furs they could find. They offered better trade goods and alcoholic beverages than the Russians, as well as firearms and ammunition, commodities the Russians preferred to keep out of native hands after their bitter experiences. Consequently in 1839 the Russians leased the entire mainland coast of southeast Alaska to Hudson's Bay Company.

There were important differences in the trade at permanent posts. The very fact of permanence was significant, for the trader who intended to deal with the same group over a long period sought a different sort of relationship than one who expected never to return. There were differences as well in the types of trade goods. Hudson's Bay Company, with its long experience in the Indian trade, was not stampeded into purveying novelties of brief vogue. Rather, it attempted to supply merchandise for which there was a lasting demand. It has not been made clear when and how the blanket came to be almost a monetary standard on the coast, but once accepted by the natives, the trade blanket continued to be made available to them for many years. As a matter of policy the Company intervened very little in Indian culture, apart from economic matters. It offered them the trade goods they steadily demanded in return for their furs, and made little attempt to modify their culture in other respects.

The entire trade period of culture contact may be summarized as one in which the Indians exercised considerable choice of the items of white civilization they adopted. They consistently selected things that fit readily into existing culture patterns without strain or dislocation. "Meaning" [2] was the paramount factor in this intercultural transfer, since it guided the Indians in their selectivity. They chose articles that had immediate and obvious meaning, and which therefore slipped neatly into place in the cultural pattern. The iron "toes" were made into adz and chisel blades, as always. They were not made into axes and hatchets, whose use requires learning a different set of motor

[2] Barnett, 1953.

habits and coordinations. Firearms were used for warfare. Only gradually, as increased familiarity and skill in their handling developed, did these weapons come to replace the bow in hunting. Sails did not replace paddles in the canoes, but merely supplemented them, since, so long as the form of the canoe hull was unchanged, they could serve only with a fair breeze. Beads, brass buttons, and pocket mirrors did not replace dentalia as valuables or ornaments, but merely supplemented the shells for adornment. The Hudson's Bay blanket did not replace the shredded cedar-bark robe for a long time. Its eventual use in potlatches was an obvious equation with the sea-otter or marmot-fur robe and the robe woven of mountain-goat wool.

The over-all picture of the effects of the trade period in North Pacific Coast culture is one of acquisition of great amounts of foreign goods accompanied by very little significant change in the general patterns. In modern economic terms, there was a great increase in consumer goods and in luxury goods, resulting in general prosperity and improved standard of living. Far-reaching culture change may originate in such eras of prosperity, but it is likely to be a gradual development, deriving from elaboration of existing culture patterns and hence in accord with their fundamental principles, with the pre-existing ideals and culturally approved attitude patterns. An example may be seen in the increase in frequency and exuberance of the potlatching complex, which dates from this epoch.

One force toward change of this period, which has been mentioned in other connections, was the concentration of groups about the sites of trading posts—Fort Rupert, Fort McLoughlin, and Fort Simpson. Even there, however, the problems and conflicts were solved according to traditional concepts: the various groups of each new agglomeration were assigned relative rank; the basic social units retained their fundamental sociopolitical autonomy, and so on. The rivalry potlatch was the only observable new development, and the rivalry had meaning only in terms of the concepts of the traditional noncompetitive potlatch.

One accompaniment of Indian-white contact had more far-reaching results than any instance of cultural diffusion: the introduction of various diseases. There are a number of reports of prevalence of venereal disease among the Indians at early dates, and there appear to have been some localized smallpox epidemics, but the first devastating smallpox epidemic probably occurred in the middle 1830's. Several others in later years cut back the native population drastically. The full cultural implications of these disasters has not been analyzed in detail, but there is no question that they have been far-reaching.

Deliberate acculturation began with the appearance on the scene of the administrator and the missionary. In the area south of the Canadian border, this event was telescoped with the rapid white settlement of Oregon and Washington territories, the treaty-making of 1855,

William Duncan.

and the removal of Indians to reservations with consequent violent disruption of native cultures. The Indians of western Oregon were rounded up and put on Siletz and Grande Ronde reservations, far from their fishing grounds. In western Washington and northwestern California the Indians fared better, for most of the reservations were established on parts of the river valleys in which the people had formerly lived. The northwest Californians, and those of the Washington coast from the Quinault north had the added good fortune to live in areas that did not attract white settlement for a good many years, and disorganization of their culture was slower in coming about.

## MISSIONARY WILLIAM DUNCAN

The history of acculturation and its effects in coastal British Columbia and southeast Alaska is lengthy and complex. A brief summary might begin with an incident that occurred far from the coast during the mid nineteenth century. A short, slight young man in England volunteered for a post, offered by the Church Missionary Society, to Christianize the savage Indians at a little-known place in British North America. The young man was William Duncan, and the place was Fort Simpson, among the Tsimshian. In his missionary career, Duncan developed a highly successful technique for acculturation, one imitated but never applied with equal success by other missionaries in the area. He came to be regarded as the great authority on "civilizing" the Indians, and was consulted on Indian problems by officials. His was a complicated personality. He was brilliant and perceptive, and about some matters, singularly obtuse. He was a gentle shepherd to his flock, and a despot. He preached and lived humility and discipline, and rebelled against the orders of his own superiors. And he left a deeper mark than any other single person on North Pacific Coast Indian history.

When Duncan arrived at Fort Simpson, the Tsimshian were at the zenith of their splendor and opulence. They exploited the fur resources of their own territory, and acted as middlemen in the fur trade between the Company and surrounding groups—their Niska and Gitksan relatives, the Tahltan, Southern Tlingit, and Haida. During the winter when the tribes assembled at the village next to the fort, feasts and potlatches were celebrated nightly. To add to the wildness of the scene,

Tsimshian frequently made voyages down the coast to Victoria, returning with the big canoes loaded to the gunwales with cheap liquor. The "rum feasts" and "whisky feasts" given on these occasions turned into wild debauches, often ending in bloodshed. The Tsimshian seemed uncontrollable. The Hudson's Bay Post was called a "fort," and was one in fact. It was like a military post, palisaded, with loaded cannon mounted at strategic points, and armed sentries standing a constant round of watches.

When Duncan arrived, he took up residence at the Post, where the Company provided his board and lodging. His first years he spent in a fashion any modern ethnographer would approve of: he learned the Tsimshian language. Company personnel dealt with the Indians in Chinook Jargon, which they had learned on the Columbia, but Duncan was not satisfied with this clumsy means of communication. When he finally preached his first sermon to the Indians, it was in fluent Tsimshian, and before long he began to make converts.

Duncan soon had a sizable following and established a school where he, or later his assistants, taught English, the three R's, and gave religious instruction. The converts were undergoing rapid culture change —Duncan called it becoming civilized. He associated religious conversion and complete adoption of white culture. In his concept, for the former to be significant and lasting, it had to go hand in hand with the latter, which suggests considerable anthropological insight on Duncan's part. However, his view was related to a widespread theory that guided Indian policy in Canada and the U.S. for many decades: that the way to solve the "Indian problem" was to get the Indian out of the forest onto a small reservation where he was easy to watch, take off his feather bonnet, stuff him into overalls, and put him behind a plow. To make a farmer of the Indian meant making him over culturally into a complete imitation of a white farmer. Duncan realized that farming was not the solution for these coast people, for the land was unsuitable for agriculture. Otherwise his thinking was in line with his times. He admonished his new converts that faithful attendance at religious service was not enough; they must also sever themselves completely from all heathen rituals, which he considered to be religious observances—feasts and potlatches as well as shamanistic séances. He perceived that he could not get his entire plan in operation until he had converted all the Tsimshian. And this he could not do. There remained a large group of Indians who persisted in their feasting and potlatching, who turned a deaf ear to Duncan's pleas, arguments, and threats of everlasting damnation if they did not mend their ways. And worst of all, they mocked and badgered the faithful for abandonment of their duties at feasts and potlatches and abandonment of the ways of their maternal ancestors since days immemorial.

Duncan's flock included a number of chiefs of high rank, whose absence from the festivals appalled the conservatives. Participants in movements of major cultural change are not necessarily all recruited from the poor and lowborn who have nothing to lose. For the change to achieve significance, it seems essential for some persons of high status to be included. Successful missionaries have always directed a large measure of their salesmanship toward the chiefs. And the prestige of Duncan's chiefs aided him in controlling converts of low rank at the same time he was actually taking prestige and noble status from the chiefs.

After several years, Duncan reached the point of diminishing returns at Fort Simpson. A very large group of Tsimshian were impervious to his techniques of persuasion, and this culturally conservative group resentfully attacked the converts. Perhaps at the suggestion of the converts, Duncan and his entire flock left Fort Simpson in a fleet of big canoes, taking with them tools, clothing of European type, utensils, and provisions. They left behind, literally and figuratively, masks and headdresses, chiefs' dance rattles, mountain-goat-wool blankets, and other ceremonial regalia. From Simpson they proceeded to the head of Metlakatla Pass, near the old winter-village sites, where they camped while cutting and sawing lumber to build a church and a new village, which he named Metlakatla.

The energetic missionary was now in the situation he had idealized. His converts were grouped closely about him, and far from all pernicious influences. Metlakatla was too far from Fort Simpson for casual encounters with scoffing pagans. He was in absolute control. He set up a model village of individual family houses, built according to the plan he designed—small cubicles with sleeping quarters "decently" partitioned off, and with windows. In teaching "Cleanliness is next to godliness," he showed the women how to wash the new European-type garments, and to make this possible, he built a small soap works. He built a brick kiln, set up a small sawmill for local needs, and a salmon saltery. Salted salmon, in barrels, the precursor of the canned article, had some market value, and Duncan was looking for sources of cash income for his flock. He is reported to have tried to establish a small textile industry, teaching the women to weave, but it came to naught. The labor for all these and other projects was provided by the Metlakatlans; proceeds of sales, if any, went into community funds, administered by Duncan. The Indians did his bidding to the letter. He planned a village government, with an elective council, and other officers, who then drew up a set of ordinances. He controlled not only his own congregation, but as the representative of law and order could also control other Indians and white men who came into the vicinity. Sir James Douglas, then Governor of the new Crown Colony of British Columbia, gave Duncan a Magistrate's commission to aid him in his battle against unscrupulous white bootleggers, and with the power of the law in his hands, the missionary was the uncrowned king of the northern coasts.

The model village prospered. Duncan had excellent commercial sense, and under his administration the village became self-sustaining. It began to attract attention as a model of what civilized Indians could do under proper guidance. The Metlakatlans were devout Christians, industrious, and without vices. They were acquiring fluency in English. They fished, hunted, and cultivated extensive gardens on the nearby shell middens, worked on Duncan's various projects for community benefit and eventually for wages as well. Their houses were like those of whites, as was their dress. They had no shamans, gave no potlatches or feasts. They were said to have completely abandoned all concepts of hereditary social rank, living in complete democratic equality. They had also given up their matrilineal system of inheritance. Small wonder that British Columbian authorities invited Duncan to advise them on the knotty Indian problem, or that Duncan was able to obtain for the Tsimshian the largest reserve on the coast at a time when the trend was to allocate only small tracts to Indian groups.

Other coast Indians observed the Metlakatlans with interest. The fur trade, which had brought a wave of prosperity to the Indians, was dwindling as fur-bearing animals decreased with heavy trapping. The canned-salmon industry was still to develop, and there was no visible substitute for the former bonanza of furs. The Metlakatlans were better off than other Indians: they were treated differently by the whites because they spoke English and were reliable workers. Whites sought them out for such remunerative work as there was—cutting cordwood for steamers and for the Army post at Wrangell, acting as guides, paddlers, or packers for surveyors and prospectors, in short, for any gainful occupation. This employment altered the pagan Indians' attitude toward missionaries completely, and before long missionaries were winning converts right and left. One went to Fort Simpson and was received with enthusiasm by the very conservatives who had rejected Duncan; two or three went to the Nass; another to the Bella Bella; and another to the Haida. In Alaska the Tlingit were requesting missionaries to be sent to them.

Duncan's model Indian community continued to prosper for a number of years. Finally the Church Missionary Society recognized Metlakatla as an important enough operation, and sufficiently in the public eye, to elevate it in status, and hence assigned a bishop to the post. Duncan was a lay minister, unordained, which had no bearing on his talents but defined his ecclesiastic rank. The assignment of a bishop was a terrible blow to Duncan. Metlakatla was his lifework. Further, there were reports that Bishop Ridley intended to make drastic policy changes in the operation of the community, changes that Duncan thought would be disastrous. At all events the two men were in immediate conflict. Duncan refused to turn over the Mission to his superior until Ridley produced documents authorizing him to receive Church Missionary Society property. Duncan had no recourse but to accede, for the buildings had been reported as Society property, including the prosperous Mission store, its stock of merchandise, and various funds. But he presented Indian witnesses to prove that the community had never ceded to the Society the two-acre plot on which the building stood, and the conflict came to revolve about the two-acre plot. It became a highly publicized issue, widely reported in the press. The Bishop through legal means obtained confirmation of his claim to the land for the Society. There was nothing left for Duncan to do but to leave. But when he went, he took most of his congregation with him.

On a visit to Washington, D.C., where he had many admirers, Duncan was offered aid if he wished to move his colony to Alaska to settle as "squatters." He made a reconnaissance with Metlakatlans familiar with the region, and on their advice found an ideal location

on Annette Island. The island was part of the territory of a southern
Tlingit group, the Tantakwan (or Tongass). So once again Duncan
and his followers loaded their tools and other belongings into the big
canoes and set out to hew a new home out of the forests. It is significant that some of the flock deserted Duncan at this time, a clear
indication of conflict. But this dissident group was small; the majority
of the Metlakatlans, nearly 800, went with Duncan to Annette Island,
to build the village he named New Metlakatla in 1887.

The community prospered again in the new location, after the hardships of getting settled were over. They built not only their church,
mission facilities, and homes, but a salmon cannery, a sawmill, and a
trade school. In 1891 special legislation was enacted setting off Annette
Island and its surrounding waters as a reservation for the Metlakatlans,
thus ensuring their right to stay in Alaska.

Early in the present century another factional split occurred. William Duncan was an old man, and he could no longer control the
people. At his death, the schism widened. The Christian Mission
Church, as Duncan had called it since his split with the Anglicans, continued, but another Protestant church was established in the village by
the opposition faction. The split soon assumed such proportions that
community projects—the cannery, the sawmill, the fish traps—could
no longer be operated efficiently, a state of affairs that has continued
until very recently. Such factionalism, accompanied by personal
antagonisms and bitterness to the point of restricting group effort, is
a common phenomenon on many Indian reservations. It means that the
Indians are not able to cope with the conflicts and stresses of the ac-
culturational situation. There is no evidence that such impasses occurred
in aboriginal times. It seems fairly obvious that the rapid but thorough
acculturation of the Metlakatla Tsimshian was the direct result of
Duncan's personal control of their destinies. Without his dynamic
guidance they could not have made the complete cultural change that
they did.

It must be emphasized that this is only a sketch, and the complete
Duncan story is still to be analyzed by a culture historian. Voluminous
correspondence and journals are said to be preserved, and conditions
at both modern villages called Metlakatla would provide further data
for study.

## CULTURE CHANGE IN ALASKA

If this survey of acculturation followed a strictly chronological order, the Russian establishment at Sitka would have been discussed before Duncan and Metlakatla. As remarked, this post was first built in 1799, captured and destroyed by the Sitka groups two years later, and rebuilt in 1804, from which date it was maintained by the Russians until the transfer of Alaska to the United States in 1867. New Archangel was intended to be the administrative center and base for fur-trade operations for a great area of the coast. However, the Russians were never able to establish effective control over the Sitka people, much less over the rest of the belligerent Tlingit. Russian accounts report that the Tlingit openly remarked that they tolerated the Russians for the convenience of having a constant supply of trade goods. Hence, Russian cultural influence was roughly comparable to that of the trading ships, in which the diffusion of culture, mainly in the acquisition of trade goods, was dictated by native choice. A feature of the Russian trade was the large amount of alcoholic beverages they purveyed to the natives, in an effort to compete with the trading vessels and with the Hudson's Bay posts when these were established farther south. One point of difference from the maritime traders was the Russian missionary effort, as a direct result of which there are two small congregations of the Greek Orthodox Catholic faith in modern Tlingit communities. However, the group of faithful is not large and never was. The Russian priests made many converts, incredibly many to judge by their own reports, particularly after they began giving attractive gifts to Indian converts, but such conversions had little permanence, and negligible cultural effect.

In brief, at the time of transfer of Alaska to the United States, that is, after sixty-odd years of Russian contacts, the Sitkakwan, next-door neighbors to the Russian center, showed few signs of culture change. A very few people spoke Russian—presumably members of the Greek Orthodox Church. There was considerable familiarity with alcohol and a good deal of prostitution, but these vices were not Russian monopolies—the Boston and British seafaring traders were also expert instructors. The record shows little else. The Sitka people lived in

Tlingit deserted village.

typical Tlingit dwellings, traveled about in Northern-type canoes, and carried on the same economic activities as their linguistic congeners. The occasional article of dress of cloth, that is, a trade item, may have been seen a little more often at Sitka than in other Tlingit villages, but social organization was unaltered. Shamanism, an inevitable target of missionaries and often of administrators as well, was in full swing. In short, in terms of acculturative effects, Russian contacts produced little.

With the coming of American rule to Alaska, a new set of accultura-tive forces came into play. But they were slower in developing, and some were more devious in their effect than might be expected. Change was retarded because of the lack of adequate legislation for Alaska for many years. History records that "Seward's Ice-Box" transaction was unpopular with the American public, and Alaska was the unloved stepchild of the U.S. Congress, which consistently refused to enact laws providing for civil government and administration of the ter-ritory. Any legislation would involve expenditure, which was regarded as throwing good money after bad. Consequently Alaska was administered by departments of the Executive branch of the government, establishing a pattern that had a far-reaching effect even after Alaska finally became an organized territory, and continued until Alaska belatedly won its long battle for statehood.

In 1867, Alaska was believed to be a place full of Eskimos and Indians, and since the War Department had most to do with Indians in those days, administration was turned over to that department. Accordingly, an artillery regiment from the Presidio in San Francisco was assigned to take charge of the new possession. This organization garrisoned Sitka after the formal ceremony of transfer, and subsequently established posts at Wrangell and Tongass. The only law for Alaska was the orders issued to the Commanding General, in which he was authorized to protect and encourage the former Russian subjects who elected to remain in Alaska and also the citizens of the United States who should extend their enterprises into Alaska. He was also directed to "impress upon the Indians and especially upon their chiefs, that our government will regard them as subject to its laws and entitled to its protection; that while they are protected by our government they will be required to respect the rights of all citizens of the republic; and that if any member of a tribe maltreat a citizen of the United States, the whole tribe and especially its chief, will be held responsible for the offense or crime committed by one of its members, unless they expel such criminal or deliver him to us for punishment." General Jeff C. Davis, the Commanding General, visited the Tlingit and Haida villages, holding "talks" with the Indians and warning them against molesting white men. The meetings with General Davis gave them their first specific knowledge that the United States intended to regulate their behavior. The Indians had been aware of the sale of Alaska by the Russians; in fact there are reports of intertribal meetings of chiefs at which the Indians objected to the deal on the grounds that the Russians had no right to sell Tlingit land.

The landbound Army was nearly impotent in its attempt to control the Indians. However, early in 1869 an incident occurred that shed new light on U.S.-Indian relations. Members of the Kuiu tribe, which was out of reach of the troops, killed two American prospectors. On the General's request, a U.S. naval vessel was assigned to carry out the punishment, or revenge. The Indians had not understood sea power before. In the brushes their forefathers had with seagoing traders, they had been fired on with cannon, with some casualities, but they had never imagined destruction of the villages. The trader could not shoot up a village effectively; he needed the space in his holds for trade goods, not powder and shot. So the Indians believed that by fleeing into the woods when the ship came in view, they would escape punishment, but they were in error. The ship deliberately allowed them to flee, and when the village was abandoned, opened fire, completely destroying the houses. Landing parties, under arms, systematically smashed and burned the canoes on the beach, and whatever had survived the gunfire. The ship methodically sought out and destroyed the eight Kuiu villages (winter villages and fishing stations). The deed was done without loss of life, but when the Kuiu took stock of their situation, and finally realized what had happened to them, they were aghast. They were completely pauperized. They drifted about for a few years, demoralized, eking out a miserable hand-to-mouth existence and trying to patch up their lives, but in vain. They could not build canoes and houses because they had no stores of dried salmon to live on while so doing. They could not accumulate a surplus of dried fish because without canoes, they could not exploit their fishing grounds, and without houses, they could neither smoke nor store the staple in adequate amounts. Eventually they scattered, going to live with kinsmen in other tribes.

This demonstration resolved any doubts the Tlingit and Haida might have had about the efficacy of U.S. military might. They had feared neither the traders nor the Russians, in fact, had boasted that they could drive the Russians out any time they wished. Even though Baranof claimed a great victory on his return to Sitka in 1804 when he took a Tlingit fort under his guns and forced out its defenders, the Tlingit did not consider this a serious defeat. The Kuiu episode was different. The Indians realized for the first time how vulnerable their villages were to naval attack, Threats by U.S. military commanders were not idle boasts. A completely new set of forces had become operative in native life.

One of the few early legislative enactments for Alaska directly concerned the Indians. It was an act extending certain provisions of the Indian Trade and Intercourse Act of June 30, 1834, to Alaska. These provisions specifically prohibited the sale of firearms and intoxicating liquors to the Indians. This law had various effects, not all of which were what Congress intended. The provision about firearms was almost meaningless, for the Tlingit and Haida were already armed to the teeth with muskets and pistols of Russian, British, and American manufacture. The measure was locally interpreted to mean breech-loading weapons. The problems created for the Indians by the pro-hibition on sale of alcoholic liquors were soon remedied by two deserters from Fort Wrangell, who taught them how to distill "rum" from a mash based on molasses (molasses was brought out in large quantities for the Indian trade). The product was called "hootchenoo" (hence the term "hootch" of the later Prohibition era). No one knows the origin of the term. Tlingit consider it a garbled form of an expres-sion in their tongue containing the element "huts," meaning "Alaskan brown bear," but can carry their etymology no further. Making hoot-chenoo, reportedly foul in odor and vile in taste but highly intoxicating, became prevalent among the Indians. It was used in the traditional manner of any prized foodstuff, that is, it was served at feasts, which usually terminated as drunken orgies and frequently in bloodshed, leading to bloody feuds between clans. Native cultural patterns con-trolled the working out of the problems created by the chosen innovation. Later, under a subsequent authority, the hootchenoo brought upon the natives a new cultural concept, when their houses were raided by police authority, liquor and stills confiscated and de-stroyed, and the owners tried, fined, or jailed. This acculturative force made the Indians still more aware of the administrative controls over their behavior, and was one of the early influences in the formation of a new attitude pattern.

A far-reaching effect of the legislation was a legalistic one. Corre-spondence in the archives shows that Secretary of State Seward be-lieved the Act of June 30, 1834, should be extended to Alaska in toto. This was a very complete and specific law. It defined as "Indian coun-try" the area to which it was to apply, and spelled out in precise terms the status before U.S. law of the Indian tribes therein residing. There was a belief in some quarters that the Act automatically applied to Alaska, and when legal analysis showed this was not so, the need for special legislation was obvious. Russia had made no treaties with Tlingit and Haida, and had made no definition of their status (certain natives of southwest Alaska and creoles were by law Russian subjects). British policy in colonial days, and U.S. policy since the founding of the republic, had been to make formal treaties with Indian tribes. The treaties normally involved stipulations for extinguishment of Indian title to all or part of their lands, defining the areas reserved to the Indians for their use, and specifying the natives' legal status. However, the United States diverged from its long established policy, and no treaty was ever made with the Tlingit and Haida. Congress did not extend the Act of June 30, 1834, to Alaska, but simply extended the firearms and liquor prohibitions to the Indians of the Territory, acting under its authority to regulate commerce with Indians. The status of Alaskan Indians was not defined for fifty-seven years, when Federal legislation in 1924 provided for citizenship of all Indians of continental United States and Alaska. This long delay created problems that affected acculturation for all those years.

The Army unit was pulled out of Alaska in 1877: the ineffectiveness of land troops in southeast Alaska was recognized, and redispositions of troops were made necessary by the Nez Percé wars. A Special Treasury Agent became the ranking U.S. official in Alaska. A revenue cutter was to call at the territory to patrol the Indian villages on occasion. Non-Indian residents of Alaska at this time numbered about 300 Americans and Europeans, a few at Wrangell, but most of whom were located at or near Sitka, as were about 250 Russian creoles. The Sitka white and creole population, numbering slightly less than 500, soon found themselves in serious difficulties. Tensions and antagonisms between them and the Indians of the nearby village had been growing. These unhappy relations came to a climax when word was received that a Sitka Indian arrested for the murder of a white man and sent to Portland for trial (U.S. Federal Courts in Oregon had jurisdiction over Alaska) had been summarily tried and hanged. Clansmen demanded revenge and talked in terms of exterminating the colony at Sitka. They enlisted the active support of other Sitka clans by giving hootchenoo feasts at which they combined inflammatory speeches with inflammatory liquor to inspire their fellow Sitkans. They played cat-and-mouse with the alarmed whites, who were advised of the progress made in the meetings. The Army had been gone two years and had not returned; the Tlingit sneered at the revenue cutter and its one-pounder. When they reported that the clans had agreed to cooperate, and were assembling ammunition, the whites became frantic. Their pleas for protection, sent to Washington via the monthly mail steamer out of San Francisco, disappeared into the void of Washington's indifference to Alaska. When in desperation they sent a letter requesting emergency aid of the British naval authorities at Esquimault, those good neighbors responded promptly. H.M.S. *Osprey* stood into Sitka Harbor, mooring so as to bring her main batteries to bear on the native village. Her commander announced to whites and Indians that his orders were to remain on that station as long as the American citizens requested his presence, or until relieved by an American vessel. The Indians recognized the military capabilities of the smart, well-armed warship; their interest in mass murder dissolved.

When news of the dramatic rescue by the British of the American pioneers at Sitka reached Washington, via both official dispatch and newspapers, there was embarrassment in certain official circles. As a result, telegraphic orders were sent Commander L. A. Beardslee, USN, to ready the U.S.S. *Jamestown* for sea "earliest possible," to sail and proceed to Sitka, Territory of Alaska, to maintain peace and protect American lives and property. In due course the *Jamestown* anchored off the Sitka Indian village; Beardslee relieved the British commander and began the five years of naval rule of Alaska.

Beardslee and his immediate relief, Commander Henry Glass, USN, were men of great capability. One of the first things Beardslee did was to hold a series of sessions with various Tlingit and interpreters to get a working picture of Tlingit culture (apparently none of the Army people had thought of doing so). Before long, as his monthly reports show, he had a good understanding of Tlingit clan and tribal organization, the functions and authority of the chiefs, native law and feuds, and various other matters. These data he utilized in his dealings with the Indians, which he regarded as his primary function under the broad discretionary authority of his orders.

The naval commanders intervened a great deal more, and more directly, in Indian life than the Army had done. They made clear that wars and feuds were to be stopped by bringing the participants together to make settlement on neutral ground, and by personally checking on the completeness of wergild payments. They conducted numerous raids on hootchenoo distillers and white bootleggers. They took steps to aid the establishment of schools for Indian children by the Presbyterian Board of Home Missions (the first school, one for Indian girls, had been established in 1877 at Wrangell). They per-

suaded groups, such as the Aukkwan, and the Chilkatkwan, to permit
entry of parties of white prospectors and miners into their territories.
They hired Indians to work on projects, such as the beacon and range
system for Sitka Harbor, and at Sitka, where they had the most effective
contacts, gave special assistance to men who wished to build individual
family dwellings, abandoning the old clan houses. Glass, particularly,
conducted a vigorous campaign against shamans at Sitka, and made
school attendance compulsory for Sitka children. All measures, even
those in which Indian participation was more or less voluntary, they
fostered from the aegis of their potent authority as commanders of the
*Jamestown,* the symbol of U.S. naval power (later in Glass' tour of
duty the *Jamestown* was relieved by the U.S.S. *Wachusett,* of which
he took command). In other words, even their suggestions and recom-
mendations to the Indians were in the voice of authority.

The naval-rule period thus saw the beginnings of effective administrative controls to which the Indians submitted, and the beginning
of a combined program of education and missionary activity, in the
Presbyterian mission schools. In addition, there was a small but significant increase in industrialization of the area: the exploitation of
mineral and fishery resources. During the Army administration there
had been pioneer efforts in this direction. Salmon salteries were operated at Klawock and Kasaan, chiefly with Indian labor. During the
Cassiar gold rush of 1874, many miners went in via the Stikine River,
rather than the dangerous Skeena or the arduous Nass River routes.
Wrangell, briefly a ghost town, took a new lease on life. The Stikine,
whose principal villages were close by, were not only ringside observers
of the activity at the jumping-off place for the gold fields, but participated in it by freighting up the Stikine River. In 1879, when Commander Beardslee arrived at Sitka, there were two salmon canneries in
Alaska, one at Klawock and one near Sitka, both employing Indians as
fishermen and "inside workers," and a mine some miles from Sitka that
also used Indian labor. During the Beardslee-Glass era, three more canneries began operating, two in Pyramid Harbor and one at Cape Fox, a
herring and fertilizer plant was set up at Kilisnoo, gold was discovered
at what is now Juneau, and the first large prospecting party had gone
through Chilkat country, over the pass to the interior. There were also
a great many minor enterprises: prospectors hired Indians as guides,
packers, or laborers for a few days or weeks.

All this activity meant more intensive forces of acculturation affecting the Indian. Future industrialization presaged in these few enterprises was to affect the Tlingit and Haida in several ways. Industry offered opportunities for gainful occupations. Although the aboriginal Indian concept of wealth was not identical to that of Western civilization, because the two systems had points of similarity, acculturation in this area was not difficult. North Pacific Coast Indians in general were much more willing and quicker to work for wages, submitting to the discipline of labor, day after day, than Indians of many other culture areas. The motivations that led them to work for wages were not the same as those of white laborers, but were adequate to make of the Indians satisfactory workers.

Once the Indian began to work for wages, even seasonally, several things happened to him. He had put himself in closer contact with white men and, therefore, had the opportunity to learn more of white culture—the English language and customs in addition to new skills connected with his work. His incentives were to learn, to keep his job, or to get another one. It has been said that earlier the Stikine and other southern Tlingit observed with envy the ease with which English-speaking Tsimshian from Fort Simpson and Metlakatla got well-paid jobs at the Army post. However, not every Indian who worked availed himself of these opportunities. There are elderly Indians today who have fished commercially every season throughout their adult lives who cannot speak English. But they are acculturated in other ways.

Still little-felt at that time was the reduction of lands and economic tracts available to the Indians. The existence of five small canneries and the herring-reduction plant prior to 1884 did not make a perceptible dent in Alaskan fisheries. But as the canneries increased in number, each not only taking fish but restricting streams from Indian use, economic pressure began to develop. The increase in the number of mining developments had the same effect. The Juneau case affected the winter-village site of Aukkwan. Although it was not a major economic area, some salmon used to be taken in a stream running through the site. The removal of the village was arranged peacefully, through negotiations between Glass and the Auk chiefs. However, as a safeguard against difficulties with the Indians as well as to maintain order, Glass stationed a shore party of armed sailors in the new mining camp, a gesture not lost on the Indians. The withdrawal of lands and fishing areas from Indian use along with decline in fish populations, the imposition of hunting and trapping regulations, and the like—all tended to force the Indian into commercial fishing and other wage work.

The first Organic Act for Alaska (May 17, 1884) provided executive and judicial branches of civil government for the territory and extended the mining laws of the United States to Alaska. This last meant the beginning of withdrawal of large areas of land from native use, for Indian right was restricted to areas "in actual use and occupance"—home sites and gardens, as the law was usually interpreted. Whites wanting to secure a mining claim, for example, staked off, posted, and recorded a tract of land to establish "squatter's claims." Home and business sites, and commercial tracts, were thus claimed. Legally squatter's claims had no validity, for they could not lead to title to the land, but since only the Government could dispute such a claim before the courts, they were treated as though they created real property. Most if not all the salmon canneries built after the Organic Acts and prior to March 3, 1891, utilized the squatter's-claim technique to obtain exclusive use of a salmon stream (modern regulations prohibit commercial fishing of salmon in fresh water, or even close to a river mouth, but in that day fishing was done within the mouth of the river). A prospective cannery operator would stake off and post his 160 acres, the maximum permitted under mining laws, 80 on either side of the river mouth, and record this claim in the land office. And on that basis, he prohibited as trespass entry of any other person who wanted to fish the stream. Then he built his cannery and went into production. When his cannery floor was full of fish, if he wished to allow some Indians to fish the stream, he might do so; if not, he drove them off.

Many canneries were built immediately following the effective date of the Organic Act. By 1890 it is reported that there was a plant on every river in southeast Alaska that supported a major salmon run. The Tlingit and Haida were forced to get the winter's supply of their basic food from the smaller streams with inferior runs or to ask permission of the cannery manager to fish the best streams when he had all the fish he could handle. As a result, purchased foodstuffs that had been luxuries became necessities to supplement the reduced supply of fish. To purchase food, the Indian needed money. Thus the squatter's-claim concept put the Indian to work for wages.

Hunting and trapping activities, both economically important to the Indians, likewise were curtailed by the rapid and extensive spread of squatter's claims. Even berry picking was affected. The only solution was to become more and more involved in the new industrial economy.

A solution that might occur to the reader as a logical and easy way out of the Indians' economic predicament—that the Indians themselves take up squatters' claims on their economic tracts—was specifically prohibited to them. No Indian was permitted to file a claim for a legitimate mineral development, or a squatter's claim for other purposes. This refusal derived from the assumption by white Alaskans that these Indians were not *citizens* of the United States. The legal status of Alaskan natives had never been defined, and they were assumed to be like the treaty (and some nontreaty) Indians on reservations "down below" in the States, *wards* of the Government and hence legally incompetent to perform the duties or enjoy the rights of bona fide citizens. Since the U.S. mining laws prevented "stateside" Indians from filing mineral claims, Alaskan officials consistently abided by the letter of that law, thus effectively barring the Tlingit and Haida from this solution to their economic problem.

In a sense, the development of Alaska and its resources was paced by Congressional enactments, which, piece by piece, remedied deficiencies in the Organic Act of May 17, 1884. A number of these measures referred to land, and were included in the Act of March 3, 1891, which extended the general land laws of the United States to Alaska. Setting off of townsites, provisions for acquiring industrial sites, and certain provisions regarding timber lands were specifically provided for. Later, in 1898, a bill on homesteading for U.S. citizens was enacted into law. These measures continued the trend established by the extension of mining laws to Alaska, in still further reducing the areas available to Indians for fishing, hunting, and gathering.

During this same period, and continuing into the early decades of the twentieth century, the Tlingit and Haida were subjected to increasing restrictive pressures. Their legal status was still unsettled. Although they learned to protest, they were regarded and treated as wards of the Government, but afforded none of the dubious rewards of that status—they had no reservations set aside for them, no Government ration issues were ever made them, and they had no Indian Agents to look out for them. (United States Commissioners were eventually designated to perform certain legal functions for them, and to maintain law and order.) The only Government agency with direct concern for them was the Bureau of Education, not of Indian Affairs, and the Bureau of Education for a good many years limited its activities in Alaska to allocating funds for education in the Territory as subsidies to mission schools. In general, they were subject to the same laws as white citizens. A drunken Indian in Juneau or Wrangell or any other white settlement was arrested, jailed, and fined as quickly as a drunken white, or maybe a little quicker. Their only friends during this period were the missionary and the cannery operator.

In 1877 a Christian Tsimshian, while working for the Army post at Fort Wrangell, began to preach to the local Indians, and to teach them as well. The post commander gave him a room to use, and aided him in getting schoolbooks. His efforts created great interest among the southern Tlingit, who were well acquainted with the Coast Tsimshian and envious of their advantages. His crusade might have had important results, had not the Army pulled out of Alaska when it did, but the interest he created stimulated the founding of a mission school for girls at Wrangell.

Organized missionary activity in southeast Alaska began, as stated, during the period of naval administration of the Territory, with the establishment of seven schools by the Presbyterian Board of Home Missions. The schools were primarily for children, but at Sitka a fair number of adults voluntarily attended regularly. This program was inaugurated chiefly through the efforts of Dr. Sheldon Jackson, who was associated for many years with missionary work in the region. The naval commanders gave him considerable cooperation in putting his projects into effect.

When Dr. Jackson was appointed General Agent for Education in Alaska in 1885, the mission school system was making great progress. Since the number of white children in Alaska was still small, appropriations voted annually by Congress for the education of Alaskan children were limited. However, appropriations were made "without reference to race," and Jackson was influential in allocating a considerable share of the limited funds to the mission school system to supplement monies granted by the Board of Home Missions. Within a few years there was a mission school operating in every Indian community in southeast Alaska. (The Friends, the Salvation Army, and the Methodist Episcopal Church carried on some mission work in southeast Alaska, but on a less intensive scale than the Presbyterian Church Board of Home Missions.)

Dr. Jackson dedicated his efforts to Indian education because he understood that education of the young combined with religious instruction laid the groundwork for the surest and firmest type of conversion to Christianity. Communication between teacher and pupil was of good quality: religious tenets and other educational materials were accepted totally and unquestioningly. In addition, the pupil-teacher attitude pattern provided a model for the relationship between the member of the congregation and his missionary minister later on. There is no evidence that Jackson formulated his views in these terms, but he believed in the efficacy of education in a successful missionizing program. In the missionary thinking of the day, "Education," that is, facility in English and the three R's, was *the* solution to the Indian problem, a crucial phase of the program aimed at detribalizing the Indian and changing him into a sober, peaceful copy of a white man. Just where he would fit into white society was not clearly expressed.

Thus the missionaries taught their converts that acceptance of Christian doctrines was not enough. They must abandon all pagan customs, including their native language, and must learn and practice the virtuous ways of the white man, but not his vices. It was to this end that the missionaries taught white techniques of organization and government and thus set the stage for village self-government. Clubs were organized for church work. The members were taught to elect their officers, conduct meetings according to parliamentary procedure, appoint committees for various tasks, and so on. Approved amusements —basket socials and box suppers, held on mission premises—replaced pagan feasts and potlatches. The potlatch particularly came in for censure by the missionaries because of its association with mortuary rites and its frequent references to clan ancestors, which were denounced as heathen "ancestor worship." Shamanism, too, was vigorously attacked by the missionaries. In the realm of daily life, the individual family house, use and care of white man's furnishings, acceptable methods of cookery, and at least the fundamentals of kitchen and personal hygiene were taught. The resident missionary's wife, in a Tlingit or Haida village, was a combination social worker and domestic-science teacher. The missionaries and their spouses labored hard and contributed effectively to many aspects of Tlingit-Haida acculturation.

There were areas of culture to which the missionaries gave little or no attention. One was the economic plight of their charges, the disappearance of the Indian economy with the withdrawal of lands for fishing and trapping. Probably none of them made the attempt that Duncan had made (and was still making) with his Metlakatlans, because they considered it unnecessary. Missionary progress in southeast Alaska was roughly contemporary with the development and expansion of the canned-salmon industry, which became a significant source of cash income to the Indians.

Among the aboriginal usages not attacked was the system of rank. The clan chiefs typically were among the stalwart supporters of the missionaries and their "Progress." This activity was consistent with the concept of the chief's duty to look after the welfare of his people. When the Indians realized their old way of life had gone and they were unable to cope with the complex and restrictive Western civilization that had suddenly enveloped them, they looked to their chiefs for leadership; and the chiefs accepted the missionaries' statements that *they* offered the solution to the Indians' problem. As a result, the chiefs used their influence in favor of the missionary movement.

The clan and moiety social structure of the Tlingit and Haida did not come under fire, probably because the missionaries failed to understand the intimate functional connection between these institutions and the potlatch, which they did attack. Consequently, clans and moieties still exist, regulating Indian life and behavior in various ways; and potlatching, although dropped for a time, had a vigorous revival. Some portions of the mortuary potlatch were never suspended but continued with approval of the missionaries who did not perceive their significance. Elaborate marble tombstones, ordered in the States, were substituted for the totem poles previously set up in connection with the mortuary potlatch.

It remains to be considered why the Indians accepted the missionaries and their teachings, which from the very first demanded extensive changes in native life. An answer has been suggested in discussing why many chiefs took the lead in supporting the missionaries. The Indians of southeast Alaska, even during the Army and Navy administrations, were beginning to feel the pinch as the fur trade dwindled. At first the pinch was in the luxury economy to which they had recently become accustomed. Immediately on passage of the Organic Act, their basic economy began to be affected. They realized they were in trouble, but could find no solutions. Pleas and protests got them nowhere. Delegations of chiefs met with each of the early Territorial Governors (beginning in 1884) to protest the loss of fishing streams and hunting and trapping grounds, demonstrating that the white pressure on Indian life increased very rapidly. But the only person interested in the Indians was the missionary. He offered them a specific recipe for their troubles: "Become Christians," he said. "Abandon the old customs, learn English, learn to read and write, learn to live like white men, and your problem will be solved." The Indians had no recourse but to accept.

Eventually, change occurred in the educational situation. The groundwork for a Territorial school system for white children was laid by legislation passed in 1900, and appropriations for Indian education were made specifically for that purpose. The schools had become a heavy burden on the missionary organization, and it was with relief that they were handed over to the Bureau of Education for direct administration. The missionaries could then occupy themselves solely with their mission activities. The early generations of mission-school trainees, and of Sitka Industrial School (later the Sheldon Jackson School, and now Sheldon Jackson Junior College), were taking their places as leaders in their communities, and there was a great surge of interest in the mission churches, Christianity, and church activities. The missionary and his teachings had been a potent force in guiding Tlingit and Haida acculturation, and in the first two decades of this century controlled Indian destiny almost as closely as Duncan had done that of his flock.

There were other forces, however. As the direct administrative interest of the Bureau of Education increased, it attempted to bring about changes by administrative pressures. Perhaps the outstanding change thus produced was the consolidation of nearly all the Alaskan Haida into a single village, the modern community of Hydaburg. In their Queen Charlotte Islands home the Haida had no federations of lineage-local "clans" as did the Tlingit. Each unit had its own village and was quite separate from all others. How the Haida invaders organized themselves when they crossed Dixon Entrance is not known.

It seems reasonable to suppose that they made some sort of alliances among themselves to present a solid front to the Tlingit. But after settling on Prince of Wales Island, they resumed their separatist habits, so that in early historic times there were a great many small Haida villages. Even though population decline and similar historic factors resulted in some consolidation of groups, in the first decade of the twentieth century the Haida still occupied a number of small villages. For establishment and operation of schools and other community facilities, this situation created very difficult problems, and an administrative decision was made to consolidate the villages. Assembling these people into a single community was accomplished by persuasion, not compulsion, according to reports of the Bureau of Education official who accomplished the feat. It remains open to question whether or not he could have done so as a private citizen, without the weight of his position as representative of the administering agency of the U.S. Government.

The industrialization of the Tlingit and Haida has been affected by various factors. Southeast Alaska's principal natural resources are the fisheries, the mineral wealth (chiefly gold), the timber, and water power. The Indians never became miners to any extent, perhaps because the skills involved were very different from any the natives already possessed, and mining reached a peak before the majority of the Indians had acquired enough English to be able to learn such a complex activity. The timber industry was harassed for many years by restrictive legislation and consequently did not develop enough to require a large labor force. Development of water power and the new industries it may bring still lies in Alaska's future.

As noted, early-day salteries and the first fish canneries in the Territory utilized chiefly Indian labor. There was no other large local labor force, and the Indians were skilled fishermen already, with a great deal of knowledge about salmon. It is apparent why the canners hired Indians and why the Indians turned readily to commercial fishing. Although the fishing techniques used were not Tlingit-Haida ones, they were not particularly complex operations: beach-seines were commonly used at and within the river mouths as terrain permitted. Improvements and complexities in gear for commercial salmon fishing came gradually, and Indian fishermen learned to handle them. The transition from beach-seining, and a little later gill-netting from skiffs, to modern purse-seining from a large diesel-powered seine boat was very great, but the transition took fifty or sixty years.

A pattern developed for Indians to go en masse to the canneries nearest their villages, just as they used to go to their clan fishing stations in the fall. Most of the men fished, and the women became "inside workers," cutting and cleaning the fish and packing them into tins. As time went by, Orientals were brought to Alaska as inside workers, and white fishermen increasingly engaged in the salmon industry, but the Indians retained their place. Indian labor involved no transportation costs to the companies, whereas both white and Oriental labor had to be brought in and returned. Thus the Indians were assured of remunerative work every fall for the major cash income they needed. After the peak of the season, when the run was insufficient for canning operations, the natives fished for their winter supply. Those who had fished through the canning season were most likely to be permitted to fish the cannery stream. To hold the good fishermen, canneries constructed shacks for the Indians during the salmon season, and often operated the cannery store the year around, supplying provisions on credit, thereby obligating the Indian debtors to fish the following season.

Other work in which the Indians engaged was seasonal, or of brief duration. During the Klondike gold rush, many Tlingit engaged in the backbreaking but relatively well-paid task of packing miners' supplies over the passes. Trapping remained a winter activity, which at times supplemented other earned income substantially, the rise in value of furs partly offsetting their scarcity. Manufacture of novelties for the tourist trade has also provided a limited source of income for many years. But the commercial salmon fishery became the economic mainstay of the Indians. Its chief disadvantage was in the shortness of the season and the scant income it produced.

By the end of the first decade of this century, the Tlingit and Haida villages consisted chiefly of individual family houses of sawed lumber. They centered about the mission church, in interest if not physically. The old clan houses were for the most part in disuse; many were already in disrepair. The totem poles along the village beach were weathered to the soft grays and browns that old cedar assumes on lengthy exposure. There were no new ones with bright red and black painting. There were still some red-cedar dugouts on the beach, but alongside them were skiffs and clinker-built boats. Even more important than these changes in the village scene were the changes in the villagers themselves.

Although Tlingit or Haida was still their basic language, many of the younger people were at ease in English, and were literate as well. Nearly all were devout Christians. Most of the active men were commercial fishermen for a couple of months each year; during this short period they, and their womenfolk who worked in the canneries, had to make enough money to provide for their many wants—factory-made clothing and footgear, tools, steel traps, provisions such as flour and sugar, soap, kerosene, and other items needed to live in a fashion similar to that of white Americans. These articles have never been cheap in Alaska. The Indians regarded their economic problem as their major one, but the question of their civil status was related, for it was their alleged wardship status that kept them in poverty in the midst of Alaska's vast wealth of gold and salmon. It seems that they did not understand the legal aspects of their ambiguous position. As they saw it, they were deprived of the right to file mineral claims, or to establish ownership of industrial sites, or to take up homesteads, because they were said to be "wards of the Government." The Indians insisted, although to deaf ears, that they were *not* wards of the Government because they did not live on reservations, which was not a valid argument.

The Organized Village Act of 1910, by which a community might receive a charter with the authority to set up a limited form of municipal self-government, was received by the Indians as an opportunity in their program of imitating the white man. The formerly conservative village of Kake was the first to obtain a charter under this Act. Other Tlingit communities followed suit in the course of the next few years.

### The Alaska Native Brotherhood

In 1912, a group of Indians in Sitka formed an organization to further "Progress" (acculturation) among the Indians. These ten men—nine Tlingit and a New Metlakatla Tsimshian who had lived many years at Sitka—were well educated by Indian standards of the day: most were graduates of the Sheldon Jackson School. They were active in church work, and hence generally respected among the Indians. The organization was the Alaska Native Brotherhood, which became a real force in southeast Alaska, and continues to be of significance.

The Alaska Native Brotherhood had no roots in aboriginal culture. Its avowed goal was acculturation, and it was patterned after white men's clubs and societies. It had a constitution and bylaws, elective officers, and provisions for chartering local chapters in the villages. As models the founders had the various church societies established in the villages by the missionaries. They also had the example, among others, of the Arctic Brotherhood, originally a fraternal organization of Klondikers that became active in the struggle of white Alaskans for a measure of self-government. The Organic Act of 1884 that gave civil government to the territory gave no self-government. All officials were Executive appointees. Finally in 1906 provision was made for the election of a Delegate to Congress. And in 1912, the year of the founding of the Indian organization, an elective legislature was provided for —an act regarded as a great victory, not only for Alaska, but also for the Arctic Brotherhood. The fact that local chapters of the Alaska Native Brotherhoood are called "Camps," like those of the Arctic Brotherhood, is not coincidental.

The early policies of the Alaska Native Brotherhood included three specific goals: recognition of the citizenship rights of the Indians of southeast Alaska, education for Indians, and abolition of "aboriginal customs." The first of these was based on the assumption, legally unproven, that the Indians were in fact U.S. citizens; the other two were but repetitions of missionary teaching. No very clear ideas were expressed about how these goals were to be attained. Nonetheless, the Tlingit and Haida demonstrated their approval of the goals by joining the organization almost to a man, and the auxiliary, the Alaska Native Sisterhood, almost to a woman.

Over the years the specific goals were changed, although the generalized one, pro-acculturation, was retained. Indian rights became a theme. The Alaska Native Brotherhood at times involved itself in labor relations on behalf of the Indian fisherman, in territorial politics, in economic developments under the Indian Reorganization Act, and in the legal test of aboriginal right in land in Alaska. It was not always effective. Personal interests and factional splits at times threatened to disrupt it. Bad fishing years and other economic pressures kept the

Brotherhood's treasury bare, making accomplishment of some projects impossible. But all this while the real strength of the Alaska Native Brotherhood—its strong and effective organization at the grass-roots level—has kept it alive, and functioning. By uniting and giving expression to Indian opinion in southeast Alaska, the organization contributes to the cultural adjustment of the Indians in the modern milieu.

## CULTURE CHANGE IN BRITISH COLUMBIA

In British Columbia the acculturative situation of the Indians paralleled that in southeast Alaska in some ways and differed in others. In British Columbia, British officials departed from their long-established practice of making treaties with the Indians. The legal status of the Indians was nonetheless defined: on confederation of the Crown Colony of British Columbia with the Dominion of Canada in 1871, Canadian Federal law, including the Indian Act, went into effect. From that moment, Indians of the new Province were Candania nationals, subject to the special provisions of the Indian Act, but not Canadian citizens. Indian title to the land was not extinguished, and this fact created problems for years.

In the Colony of Lower Vancouver Island, occupied principally by Coast Salish groups, settlers swarmed to the fertile prairies of temperate climate that flanked the Gulf of Georgia. Sir James Douglas, the first Governor, attempted to obtain funds to extinguish Indian title to these lands. He placed the Indians on small reservations with the understanding that they would be compensated for the surrendered areas. The money was never obtained, and the Indians complained bitterly for many years. Failure to obtain the needed funds apparently led Douglas, after merger of the Island and Mainland Colonies to form the Crown Colony of British Columbia, to order some very large "reserves" (reservations) laid off in the Fraser Valley, although he had been, hitherto, an advocate of small reserves for the Indians.

After confederation of the colony with Canada, the Dominion Government assumed responsibility for administration of the Indians and undertook to provide them with adequate reserves. Since such lands had to be taken from the Provincial domain and became Federal property, Provincial agreement was essential. Provincial authorities balked at turning over any substantial areas. They held that all the

Indians needed were the lands in "actual use," which on the coast they defined as village sites, fishing stations, cemeteries, and the like, in opposition to the Dominion concept of a subsistence tract of 80 to 100 acres per family. Provinicial-Dominion relations were difficult anyhow, and some of the ill-feeling had nothing to do with the Indians: failure of the Dominion Government to build a railway connecting British Columbia with the East created great resentment in the province. In this atmosphere, no progress could be made on the question of Indian lands, although the issue was widely discussed.

The issue might have passed unnoticed by the Indians themselves in remote sections of the coast. However, the Duncan-Ridley feud over title to the two-acre plot on which the Mission buildings stood was well known to the Indians. Also, after Duncan's success with his Indian settlement, other missionaries followed his example and established new communities. As their work of conversion to Christianity advanced rapidly, these missionaries taught their Indians to set up village governments, with elective officers, village ordinances, constables, and so on. The custom of issuing Magistrates' Commissions to missionaries, begun with Duncan, had continued, and gave the missionary absolute control over his congregation. The backslider who fell from grace, missed Sunday service, and brought home a jug of rum could be not only publicly admonished in next Sunday's sermon, he could be tried. The missionary put on his Magistrate's hat instead of his ecclesiastic one, charged the Indian with infraction of a village ordinance on Sunday activities and for possession of alcoholic beverages, found him guilty of both charges, and sentenced him to so many days labor on public-works projects, such as repair of the village street. (Neither the ordinances nor the village governments themselves were legally constituted under Canadian law.) This sort of control led the missionaries to insist that their charges lead well-ordered, civilized lives, and hence needed no Dominion interference, that is, legal and secular control by Indian Agents. Therefore, the missionaries did not want reserves of any size for their congregations. They wanted their charges to be given title in fee simple to plots comparable to those given white settlers, so that they, the missionaries, could continue unmolested to guide their Indians to complete Christian civilization. It must be recognized that the missionaries believed they were acting in the best interests of their native charges. They did not regard themselves as rebels against con-

stituted authority but believed sincerely that no one else could guide
the Indians along the path of righteousness as well as they could. There
is direct evidence, not only from Indian informants of recent times but
from sources of that day, including a Provincial Commission of Enquiry, that certain missionaries openly advised their congregations to
demand the return of the lands that had been taken from them. In 1887,
the first of many delegations, consisting of a group of Niska and Fort
Simpson chiefs, went to Victoria "to petition for the return of their
lands," and to demand a formal treaty guaranteeing their rights to those
lands "forever." The idea of the treaty, to repair the omission of such
agreement in the past and to define Indian rights in perpetuity, obviously did not originate with the Indians, who knew nothing of Indian
treaties made elsewhere. The delegation accomplished nothing, but the
Indians were not discouraged. Their attention had been directed to the
land question, just as that of Tlingit and Alaskan Haida was directed
toward the question of citizenship, as the solution of their problems,
and this issue was their battlefield for many years.

Roman Catholic missionaries were most active among the Coast
Salish and the Nootkans. Their policies differed in many respects from
the Duncan model of most Protestant missionaries. In the early days of
their work, they insisted on white man's clothing, at least for church
attendance, and made vigorous attacks on shamanism, but they did not
attempt immediate drastic change in native life outside the area of
religious belief. They avoided entering the field of administration.
Rather, they pursued a long-range program, relying on education of
the children. As remarked, this was also an aspect of Protestant mis-
sionization, but the Catholic program revolved about the boarding
school, where the children could be taught hygiene and table manners,
be accustomed to white man's foods and how to prepare them, as well
as learn the textbook lessons. This system is slow, and it remains to be
seen if it produces an easier and better adjustment to the new culture.

Meanwhile, administrative authority was being established, albeit on
a limited scale. Respect for the Crown had been imposed for years by
warships on station at Esquimault. These vessels periodically showed
the flag along the coasts, warning the natives against molesting white
men or fighting among themselves. They fired on a few villages, but
there were no major disturbances. This Pax Britannica was not without
its cultural effects, although most of them were acculturative in a very

special way. The dictum against intergroup warfare created a new era of intergroup contacts and diffusion of native culture elements. There had been peaceful contacts between distant groups, even across linguistic boundaries in ancient times, particularly for trade and intermarriage, but long-range contacts were always adventures that might end in a treacherous surprise attack or ambuscade. Once the new extracultural force stopped native warfare, such contacts became common. Distant groups were invited to feasts and potlatches. Interchange of material articles was greatly accelerated. Haida-carved wooden boxes were acquired by Southern Kwakiutl. Southern Kwakiutl masks reached Tlingit hands. Nootkans came to possess Chilkat woven robes. Carved gold and silver bracelets made by a few Haida and Tlingit craftsmen were seen along the coast as far south as the Strait of Georgia. However, there is no evidence that major complexes and concepts were transmitted far beyond the limits of their aboriginal distributions. Probably the period of intensive intertribal contacts was too brief, and followed too closely by other factors for change to produce significant effects.

In the early 1880's Indian Agents were assigned to various sections of the coast. At first their influence was negligible. An important part of their function was preservation of law and order. They were empowered to try and punish Indians committing minor offenses. For more serious infractions they were supposed to be able to call on the Provincial law-enforcement system—constabulary, courts, and jails. During the era of strained relations between the Province and the Dominion, however, they could get no cooperation from constabulary or courts. Hence for this law-enforcement phase of their duties they were rendered impotent. Nonetheless, the Provincial Commission of Enquiry (into Indian affairs) of 1887 recommended assignment of more Indian Agents to the coastal groups. To avoid indicating approval of Dominion handling of Indian affairs, the Commission specified that not only "more" Agents, but "better-qualified" ones were needed. However, early Indian Agents were able to effect very little change in historic native culture patterns.

Following the brief and useless fad of the delegations demanding return of Indian lands, the land issue was dropped, and for a number of years only Coast Salish, chiefly those of lower Vancouver Island and the Fraser River valley, were concerned about the land issue. About the turn of the century they sent two delegations to England to present their grievances directly to the Crown, thus attempting to bypass Canadian authorities. Other coast groups evinced no interest during this period. A system of reserves, consisting for the most part of small tracts, had been surveyed and formally transferred to the Dominion Government. However, the fact that the reserves constituted the totality of Indian lands had little immediate effect on the Indians. They were not subjected to the same pressures as the Indians of Alaska. Canneries were not able to acquire exclusive rights to salmon streams. No major gold strikes brought hordes of miners to tantalize the Indians with fabulous riches just out of their reach. And, except in the limited sections of the coast, there was no influx of white settlers. Lower Vancouver Island and the lower Fraser River Valley were densely settled long before this time, but they were exceptions to the general rule. Logging was a growing industry in the lower Strait of Georgia area. Elsewhere, with minor exceptions, the fact that his land had been taken from him did not yet affect the Indian much.

Of all the non-Salish groups, only the Niska on the remote Nass River did not forget the land problem. They formed a Land Committee consisting of the clan chiefs, who continued to ponder the question while other groups forgot it. In 1912 they retained an attorney who drafted a document known as the "Nishga Petition," in which requests for 160-acre allotments per family head and remuneration for remaining lands taken were made. The document was sent to Ottawa with the request that it be transmitted to the Judiciary Committee of the Imperial Privy Council in England, which the Indians had been advised was the court of final appeal in the Empire. They were advised on this occasion, and many times subsequently, that they could not submit their petition directly to the Privy Council. The proper procedure was to try their case before a Canadian court and then, if they were not satisfied with the decision, to appeal, with the consent of the Dominion Government, to the Privy Council. This advice they disregarded, and for years stubbornly continued to try to submit their case directly to the Privy Council. This vain effort to bypass Canadian courts cost them much time and money, and cast doubt on the quality of their legal advice.

This same year a Royal Commission was appointed to restudy the Indian land question in British Columbia. In the course of three years this commission accomplished the enormous task of visiting every Indian village or community in the Province, appraising its reserve or reserves, and recommending continuance, additions to, or deductions from the reserves of each group. The findings were eventually accepted by both Provincial and Dominion Governments, and form the basis of the Indian reserve system. Before adoption of these findings, however, a number of years passed, during which the Indians formed an organization called the "Allied Tribes of British Columbia," dedicated at first to support of the "Nishga Petition," and eventually drafting petitions of its own in which, as a refinement, the basis of the Indian claim was derived from "aboriginal right."

This organization was taken over by two men of Indian descent, both well educated by white standards, who made it their career for several years. They traveled up and down the coast, arousing interest in and raising funds for the Indian land case. All the coastal groups, and a number of interior ones as well, became members of the Allied Tribes. A feature of the organization's strategy was the continuance of the Niska's impossible demand for an initial hearing before the Imperial Privy Council. When finally forced to a hearing before a Parliamentary committee in 1926, the end came quickly. The legal case for aboriginal right in the land, as presented by the Allied Tribes' attorney, was singularly weak and faulty. The committee found the claim of aboriginal right to have no basis in fact, and so rejected it. In addition, a special fund to supplement appropriations for Indian education and welfare in British Columbia, in lieu of the "treaty money" paid other Indians in Canada, was recommended. Further legislation was recommended to prevent solicitation of funds among the Indians to continue presentation of claims now "decisively disallowed." With this blow, the Allied Tribes organization collapsed.

The story of the land claims by the Indians is an important part of their recent history. Its significance in regard to acculturation remains to be considered. One fact shows through very clearly: the inspiration throughout was non-Indian, or by sophisticated Indians long removed from the native way of life and thought. The techniques used were non-Indian—petitions drafted by attorneys, attempts to utilize British legal procedure, fund-raising campaigns to implement the legal contest, and the like. The obvious conclusion is that Indian interest in land, outside the few heavily settled areas, was largely artificial. Although the land was technically no longer the Indian's, as long as it was not settled or logged off, he had use of most of it, and hence did not feel that his economic plight resulted from loss of it.

Another significant point is that the Indians knew enough about white Canadian culture to appraise realistically their own situation in relation to it. They did not let themselves be carried away into nativistic movements, although about the time the Niska were forming their Land Committee, the 1890 Ghost Dance excitement was sweeping the Plains in the United States. The missionary influence would have combated such a pattern, but there is no suggestion that one ever appeared.

The salmon canneries affected the British Columbia coast Indian about the same way that those in Alaska did the Alaskans. They gave him at least a partial solution to his economic problem, although the economic problem on the Canadian side of the line arose less from deprivation of subsistence resources than from acquiescence to missionary insistence on adoption of the paraphernalia of white culture—clothes, utensils, and furniture—which had to be purchased with Canadian dollars. As in Alaska, the British Columbia Indian grew with the industry. He began commercial fishing with the rather simple gear used in early days, learning to operate more complex equipment as it was adapted to salmon fishery. In so doing, he learned many other things about Western civilization. I recall an elderly Southern Kwakiutl informant who wandered from the theme we were discussing—the function of the potlatch, about which he knew a great deal—into a long discourse on marine insurance, about which he also knew a great deal. The old gentleman owned a seine boat worth some forty thousand dollars, and, sensibly, kept it insured from keel to masthead light. Other facets of white culture Indians have learned through participation in the fishing industry include trade unionism, the strike, wage and price negotiations.

The British Columbia Native Brotherhood was modeled on the Alaskan organization, and the man who founded it was a Haida who attended two annual conventions of the Alaska Native Brotherhood while visiting relatives in Hydaburg. He was supported in his endeavor by Coast Tsimshian leaders, and the movement developed until it now includes most of the coast Indians, except Coast Salish and Nootkans, from whom it gets little support. In function the Brotherhood has come to differ from its model. It is weakly organized in the villages, where the local chapters must compete with numerous social clubs. Its strength from the point of view of the rank and file derives from the fact that it acts as a bargaining agent for the Indian fishermen, negotiating fish prices with the canned-salmon industry. In other fields, it attempts to represent the Indians in dealing with the Office of Indian Affairs and other Government agencies, usually in a cooperative role in matters concerning its membership. It is less aggressive in policy and operation, and less effective than its Alaskan model.

Many of the issues in which the Native Brotherhood claimed interest—better education, public health services, welfare services, and the like, for Indians—have been achieved in recent years, but they have been brought about by Canada's modern liberal Indian policy, not by the British Columbia Indian organization. The implementation of these new policies is achieving, through administrative methods, what the Indians could not achieve for themselves, successful adaptation to and integration into modern Western civilization.

# Bibliography

THE BIBLIOGRAPHY OF THE Indian cultures of the area, including both ethnographic and historical materials, is very long. Therefore, only the fullest and most accessible descriptions of the various Indian groups are listed here, along with works specifically cited in the text. The interested student will obtain from any of these references further bibliographic guides.

BARNETT, HOMER G.
1938    The nature of the potlatch. *American Anthropologist*, n.s., vol. 40, pp. 349–358.
1953    *Innovation: The Basis for Cultural Change.* New York, McGraw-Hill.
1955    *The Coast Salish of British Columbia.* Eugene, University of Oregon Press. (University of Oregon monographs. Studies in Anthropology, no. 4.)

BENEDICT, RUTH
1932    Configurations of culture in North America. *American Anthropologist*, n.s., vol. 34, pp. 1–27.
1934    *Patterns of Culture.* Boston, Houghton Mifflin.

233

BOAS, FRANZ

1897 The social organization and the secret societies of the Kwakiutl Indians. *U.S. National Museum. Report*, for the year ending June 30, 1895, pp. 311–738. Washington D. C., Government Printing Office.

1909 The Kwakiutl of Vancouver Island. *American Museum of Natural History. Memoirs*, vol. 8, pt. 2, pp. 301–522.

1916 Tsimshian mythology, based on texts recorded by Henry W. Tate. *Bureau of American Ethnology. Annual Report*, 31st, 1909/1910, pp. 29–1037. Washington, D. C., Government Printing Office.

COLSON, ELIZABETH

1953 *The Makah Indians: A Study of an Indian Tribe in Modern American Society*. Minneapolis, University of Minnesota Press.

COOK, JAMES

1785 *A Voyage to the Pacific Ocean*. 3rd ed. 3 vol. London, G. Nicol & T. Cadell.

CURTIS, EDWARD S.

*The North American Indian*. 20 vol. Cambridge, Mass., The University Press.

1913 Vol. 9: Salishan tribes of the Coast. The Chimakum and the Quiliute. The Willapa.

1915 Vol. 10: The Kwakiutl.

1916 Vol. 11: The Nootka. The Haida.

DRUCKER, PHILIP

1936 A Karuk world-renewal ceremony at Panaminik. *University of California Publications in American Archaeology and Ethnology*, vol. 35, no. 3, pp. 23–28. Berkeley, University of California Press.

1937 The Tolowa and their southwest Oregon kin. *University of California Publications in American Archaeology and Ethnology*, vol. 36, no. 4, pp. 221–300. Berkeley, University of California Press.

1939 Rank, wealth, and kinship in Northwest Coast society. *American Anthropologist*, n.s., vol. 41, pp. 55–65.

1940 Kwakiutl dancing societies. *University of California Anthropological Records*, vol. 2, no. 6, pp. 201–230. Berkeley, University of California Press.

1943 Archeological survey on the Northern Northwest Coast. *Bureau of American Ethnology*. Bulletin, no. 133, pp. 17–154. Washington, D. C., Government Printing Office. (Anthropological papers, no. 20.)

1948 The antiquity of the Northwest Coast totem pole. *Washington Academy of Sciences*. Journal, vol. 38, pp. 389–397. Washington, D. C., Washington Academy of Sciences.

1950 Culture element distributions: Northwest Coast. *University of California Anthropological Records*, vol. 9, no. 3, pp. 157–294. Berkeley, University of California Press. (Culture element distributions, 26.)

1951 The Northern and Central Nootkan tribes. *Bureau of American Ethnology*. Bulletin, no. 144. Washington, D. C., Government Printing Office.

1955a Sources of Northwest Coast culture. *New Interpretations of Aboriginal American Culture History; 75th anniversary volume of the Anthropological Society of Washington*, pp. 59–81. Washington, D. C., Anthropological Society of Washington.

1955b *Indians of the Northwest Coast.* New York, American Museum of Natural History. Reissued 1963. Garden City, New York, The Natural History Press.

1958 The native brotherhoods: modern intertribal organizations on the Northwest Coast. *Bureau of American Ethnology*. Bulletin, no. 168. Washington, D. C., Government Printing Office.

n.d. Unpublished field notes on Coos, Alsea, Tillamook, Chinook, and Southern Kwakiutl.

EMMONS, GEORGE T.

1907 The Chilkat blanket. *American Museum of Natural History. Memoirs*, vol. 3, pt. 4, pp. 329–404. New York. (Anthropology, vol. 2, pt. 4.)

1916 The whale house of the Chilkat. *American Museum of Natural History. Authropological Papers*, vol. 19, pt. 1, pp. 1–33. New York.

GARFIELD, VIOLA E.

1939 Tsimshian clan and society. *University of Washington Publications in Anthropology*, vol. 7, no. 3, pp. 169–339. Seattle, University of Washington Press.

GUNTHER, ERNA

1927 Klallam ethnography. *University of Washington Publications in Anthropology*, vol. 1, no. 5, pp. 171–314. Seattle, University of Washington Press.

KRAUSE, AUREL

1885 *Die Tlinkit-Indianer.* Jena, H. Costenoble. Published in English as: *The Tlingit Indians*, translated by Erna Gunther. Seattle, University of Washington Press, 1956.

KROEBER, ALFRED L.

1925 Handbook of the Indians of California. *Bureau of American Ethnology. Bulletin*, no. 78. Washington, D. C., Government Printing Office. Reissued, Berkeley, California Book Co., 1953.

McILWRAITH, THOMAS F.
   1948   *The Bella Coola Indians.* 2 vol. Toronto, University of Toronto Press.

NIBLACK, ALBERT P.
   1890   The Coast Indians of Southern Alaska and Northern British Columbia. *U.S. National Museum. Report,* for the year ending June 30, 1888, pp. 225–386. Washington, D. C., Government Printing Office.

OLSON, RONALD L.
   1936   The Quinault Indians. *University of Washington Publications in Anthropology,* vol. 6, no. 1, pp. 1–194. Seattle, University of Washington Press.
   1940   The social organization of the Haisla of British Columbia. *University of California Anthropological Records,* vol. 2, no. 5, pp. 169–200. Berkeley, University of California Press.

PETTITT, GEORGE A.
   1950   The Quileute of La Push, 1775–1945. *University of California Anthropological Records,* vol. 14, no. 1, pp. 1–120. Berkeley, University of California Press.

RAY, VERNE F.
   1938   Lower Chinook enthnographic notes. *University of Washington Publications in Anthropology,* vol. 7, no. 2, pp. 29–165. Seattle, University of Washington Press.

SMITH, MARIAN W.
   1940   *The Puyallup-Nisqually.* New York, Columbia University Press. (Columbia University contributions to anthropology, vol. 32.)

SUTTLES, WAYNE
   1960   Affinal ties, subsistence, and prestige among the Coast Salish. *American Anthropologist,* n.s., vol. 62, pp. 296–305.
   1960   Variation in habitat and culture on the northwest coast. *34th International Congress of Americanists Transactions,* Vienna, pp. 522–537.

SUTTLES, WAYNE, AND WILLIAM W. ELMENDORF
   1963   Linguistic evidence for Salish prehistory. *Proceedings of the 1962 Annual Spring Meeting of the American Ethnological Society,* pp. 41–51.

SWANTON, JOHN R.
   1909   Contributions to the ethnology of the Haida. *American Museum of Natural History. Memoirs,* vol. 8, pt. 1, pp. 1–300. New York.

WELLCOME, SIR HENRY S.
   1887   *The Story of Metlakahtla.* London & New York, Saxon & Co.

# Index

(See color illustration section for entries identified by *color*. Page numbers in *italic* indicate illustrations.)

237